China's 'Everything Online' Company

AF215868

How did Tencent become one of the world's most innovative tech giants? This book offers a rare, in-depth look at Tencent's rise through the lens of innovation management. From early products such as QQ to the creation of WeChat and its expansive digital ecosystem, the book explores how Tencent drives continuous and breakthrough innovation across technology, management, platforms, and social value. It introduces Tencent's unique sequoia-like innovations (deep, directed, invisible, and compound), market-type organisation, and OCEAN ecosystem, which promotes openness (O), coopetition (C), empowerment (E), autonomy (A), and attentiveness to stakeholders' needs (N). Readers will discover how Tencent leverages corporate values, internal coopetition, digital human resource management, internal talent mobility, platform ecosystems, and social value creation to remain innovative, competitive, and forward-looking. Accessible and insightful, this book is essential reading for students, academics, business leaders, and policymakers interested in innovation management, technology development, digital platforms, and China's evolving technology landscape.

XIAOLAN FU is Professor and Founding Director of the Technology and Management Centre for Development at the University of Oxford, a fellow of the Academy of Social Sciences, and Founder of OxValue.AI. She is a winner of the 2021 Falling Walls Scientific Breakthrough Award and author of *Innovation under the Radar* (Cambridge University Press, 2020) and *China's Path to Innovation* (Cambridge University Press, 2015).

GEORGE YIP is an emeritus professor of marketing and strategy at Imperial College London and a distinguished visiting professor at Northeastern University, Boston. He is the author of the highly acclaimed *Total Global Strategy* (1992) and co-author of *China's Next Strategic Advantage* (2016) and *Pioneers, Hidden Champions, Changemakers, and Underdogs: Lessons from China's Innovators* (2019).

XUECHEN DING is Assistant Professor in Business Administration at the Beijing Technology and Business University, a postdoctoral researcher at the University of Oxford, and Consultant at OxValue.AI. Her research interests are innovation strategies, digital innovation, and national innovation systems. Her recent publications appear in *Management and Organization Review* and *Industry and Innovation*.

WEI WEI is Assistant Professor in Management and Associate Fellow at the Digital Futures at Work Research Centre at the University of Sussex. Her research focuses on platform work, digital human resource management, and innovation management. Her recent publications appear in *New Technology, Work and Employment* and the *Review of International Political Economy*.

China's 'Everything Online' Company

The Unique Innovation Model of Tencent

XIAOLAN FU
University of Oxford

GEORGE YIP
Imperial College London and Northeastern University

XUECHEN DING
Beijing Technology and Business University

WEI WEI
University of Sussex

CAMBRIDGE
UNIVERSITY PRESS

CAMBRIDGE
UNIVERSITY PRESS

Shaftesbury Road, Cambridge CB2 8EA, United Kingdom

One Liberty Plaza, 20th Floor, New York, NY 10006, USA

477 Williamstown Road, Port Melbourne, VIC 3207, Australia

314–321, 3rd Floor, Plot 3, Splendor Forum, Jasola District Centre,
New Delhi – 110025, India

Cambridge University Press is part of Cambridge University Press & Assessment,
a department of the University of Cambridge.

We share the University's mission to contribute to society through the pursuit of
education, learning and research at the highest international levels of excellence.

www.cambridge.org
Information on this title: www.cambridge.org/9781009738972
DOI: 10.1017/9781009738996

© Xiaolan Fu, George Yip, Xuechen Ding and Wei Wei 2026

When citing this work, please include a reference to the
DOI 10.1017/9781009738996

First published 2026

A catalogue record for this publication is available from the British Library

*A Cataloging-in-Publication data record for this book is available from the
Library of Congress*

ISBN 978-1-009-73895-8 Hardback
ISBN 978-1-009-73897-2 Paperback

Contents

Figures

Tables

Preface

In today's interconnected world, emerging digital technologies – from artificial intelligence (AI) to smart infrastructure and financial technology (fintech) – have become pivotal drivers of economic growth. Yet for decades the global digital economy has been shaped by a handful of dominant players, such as Google, Microsoft, and Meta, headquartered in developed economies. Our research began with a simple question: How do companies in emerging economies rapidly catch up in digital innovation? This book is the outcome of a four-year, in-depth study of innovation at Tencent, one of China's most influential technology giants. China's rise as a global leader in transformative innovation offers compelling answers. From AI's seamless integration into daily life to breakthroughs in generative AI, Chinese companies are redefining technological frontiers. A striking example came in early 2025, when DeepSeek, a Chinese AI start-up, stunned the world with a generative AI breakthrough rivalling OpenAI's capabilities. This example further proves the importance and necessity of delving into how Chinese-born digital companies have risen to the global frontier in the digital era.

While academic literature has extensively analysed innovation by US tech titans, the innovation of Chinese tech companies remains underexplored – and the stories behind this innovation and success, underappreciated. Tencent, a global powerhouse responsible for ground-breaking products and services, epitomises this gap. Despite its dominance across sectors from social media to fintech, its innovation model has rarely been systematically examined. To address this, we launched the Innovation and Catch-up in the Platform Economy project, aiming to examine the key drivers of technological innovation and catch-up among world-leading technology companies from developing countries in the digital era. Professor Xiaolan Fu leads the project as the Principal Investigator. Professor Fu is supported by two postdoctoral research officers and several senior research advisors, including Professors George Yip, Eric Thun, Henry Chesbrough, and Hengyuan Zhu. Over four years, we employed mixed methodologies, including a large-scale survey and over 100 interviews, to unravel Tencent's unique path.

China's 'Everything Online' Company: The Unique Innovation Model of Tencent delivers the first systematic, comprehensive, and pioneering analysis of the various forms and mechanisms of innovation at Tencent in the digital era. Each chapter explores a distinct facet of its innovation model, such as coopetition, digital human resource management, and ecosystem orchestration, while collectively weaving a cohesive narrative. We hope that the insights gained from this study will enrich global discourse on innovation management, while offering actionable insights for businesses and policymakers navigating the challenges and opportunities of digital transformation.

Many acknowledgements and thanks are due. We appreciate the support of Tencent, which granted us access for fieldwork. Special thanks to Yu Zhao, Yuling Zhang, Miao Yue, Ke Xu, Jun Zhang, Sheng Meng, Ling Ge, Hao Xu, Ming Li, Shengyu Zhang, Juhong Wang, Yan Ge, Doudou Ye, Siling Li, Cong Zhou, Daoyuan Yang, Chang Su, Shunyu Yao, and Xike Yi for their assistance with research access as well as their valuable suggestions. We also appreciate the time and effort of all survey and interview participants in this project.

Among the numerous colleagues and friends we wish to thank for helpful and constructive comments and discussions are Richard Nelson, Bengt-Åke Lundvall, David Gann, Wim Vanhaverbeke, Christopher Adam, Diego Sanchez-Ancocher, Jocelyn Alexander, Marc Ventresca, Daniel Armanios, Paavo Ritala, Xielin Liu, Jizhen Li, Hui Liao, Sonia Bashir Kabir, Taidong Zhou, Nobuya Haraguchi, Hua Cheng, Kevin Collins, Kevin Shimota, Laura McCracken, Rui Ma, Yifan Li, and Qinlin Lu.

Prototypes of various chapters have been presented in past years at various conferences and seminars at many universities, all of which we cannot acknowledge here in detail. A few examples include the South-South Cooperation in Science, Technology, and Innovation online forum in 2022, the Oxford Technology and Management for Development Centre (TMCD) and the Saïd Business School (SBS) joint workshops in 2022, the R&D Management Conference 2022, the British Academy of Management Conference 2022, the Global South in the Age of Digital Revolution: Innovation and

Capabilities Development international workshop in 2023, the Academy of Management Conference 2023, the European Academy of Management Conference 2023, the Strategy Innovation and Entrepreneurship and International Business Conference 2023, the British Academy of Management Conference 2023, the 'Can the All-in-One App Be Replicated?' online workshop in 2023, the ninth e-HRM International Conference 2024, the R&D Management Workshop China 2024, the European Academy of Management Conference 2025, and the Academy of Management Conference 2025. We are grateful to the organisers and participants for the opportunity to receive valuable feedback from experts and practitioners and to share our research findings with the wider digital technology and innovation management community.

We are grateful to the Department of International Development at Oxford University for hosting our research. We also thank colleagues and students of the Technology and Management Centre for Development, Oxford University, for stimulating discussions and help. We thank Kristen Weber and Louise Chapman for their work in copyediting the manuscript, as well as the D'Amore-McKim School of Business, Northeastern University for its financial support of most of the copyediting.

We also would like to thank the editors of Cambridge University Press, Valerie Appleby and Carrie Parkinson, as well as three anonymous reviewers of the book proposal.

Finally, we extend our heartfelt gratitude to our families for their unwavering support of our research.

1 Introduction

We are living in an age of rapid technological change. Technological breakthroughs occur regularly, and we see major advances more frequently. Driven by progress in artificial intelligence (AI), robotics, the Internet of Things, and biotechnology, the Fourth Industrial Revolution has transformed industries and created new paradigms in manufacturing, healthcare, and communication. Marking a significant shift in technological applications, this revolution is characterised by a fusion of the physical, digital, and biological worlds that has led to unprecedented changes in the way we live and work.

At the same time, the generative artificial intelligence (GenAI) models that appeared in the early 2020s (such as OpenAI's GPT series) were the outcome of rapid evolution beginning when GenAI emerged as a significant field in the early 2010s. Within a ten-year period, GenAI had become accessible and visible in real-world applications ranging from creative industries to text-based customer support systems. This has brought profound opportunities and challenges both to the field and to society.

In today's interconnected world, these emerging digital technologies and the overall technology revolution play a pivotal role in driving economic growth and development. By facilitating faster and more efficient communication, digital technologies break down geographical barriers and enable businesses to reach global markets. Customers, too, can now access a wider range of products and services. The digital economy enhances productivity through automation and data analytics, allowing companies to streamline operations, reduce costs, and innovate rapidly. Digital platforms foster entrepreneurship by lowering entry barriers for start-ups and small enterprises. They create social and economic value by bridging gaps, creating connectivity, and facilitating engagement between two or more individuals or economic agents. They foster business activities alongside income, as well as create more inclusive jobs. As digital infrastructure expands, digital platforms also promote financial inclusion and access to education and healthcare. Overall, such contributions are leading to more equitable and sustainable economic development.

As a result, American internet companies and platform-based enterprises have dominated global market capitalisation rankings in recent years. Giants such as Apple, Amazon, Alphabet (Google's parent company), and Microsoft consistently occupy the top positions in market capitalisation, reflecting their massive influence and financial power. According to Forbes's (2019) top 100 digital companies list, ten of the world's top fifteen digital companies were founded in the United States, the world leader in innovation and the first mover in digital technology. These companies are at the forefront of technological innovation, leveraging their substantial market capitalisation, extensive user bases, and cutting-edge research to maintain their leadership positions.

In the meantime, the rise of internet companies in emerging economies, particularly in China, signifies a transformative shift in the global digital economy. Three of the remaining top digital companies are from China: China Mobile, Alibaba, and Tencent (Forbes, 2019). The other two are from South Korea (Samsung) and Japan (Softbank). On the Boston Consulting Group's (BCG) 2021 most innovative companies list, Huawei, Alibaba, Tencent, Lenovo, and Xiaomi are among the top fifty (BCG Global, 2021). Several digital companies from China have also rapidly gained global recognition in recent years, transforming industries and reshaping global markets through innovative business models and advanced technologies. Companies in sectors ranging from e-commerce and social media to transport, such as Pinduoduo, Shein, TikTok, Xiaohongshu, and Didi, have positioned themselves at the forefront of global trends to become influential players in the digital economy. Many observers might be curious to know how China's internet giants became the leaders at the frontiers of innovation. Are there any differences in the Chinese approach?

Among such companies, Tencent (one of China's largest and the most influential technology companies in the world) has consistently maintained a market capitalisation of more than USD 400 billion.[1]

---

[1] The Chinese name for Tencent is 腾讯 (téng xùn), a combination of the character 'teng' (腾), which is part of founder Pony Ma's Chinese name, Ma Huateng, and also signifies 'soaring' or 'developing', and 'xun' (讯), meaning information. The name was chosen to represent the company's aim of providing fast and developing information services.

This makes it not only one of the most valuable companies in Asia, but also the world's fifteenth most valuable company by market capitalisation as of October 2024 (CompaniesMarketCap, 2024a). The three giants of China's internet industry were once known as BAT, which stood for Baidu, Alibaba, and Tencent. However, Tencent has grown and is now in a class of its own as the most valuable publicly listed internet company in China. Tencent's market capitalisation surpasses the combined valuations of Pinduoduo (in second place) and Alibaba (in third). With over 1.3 billion users, its flagship social media platform WeChat seamlessly integrates messaging, payments, e-commerce, and entertainment into daily life. Tencent has thus become a dominant force in digital communication.

This dominance extends to other areas as well. As the world's largest video game company by revenue, Tencent owns or holds stakes in iconic gaming companies such as Riot Games (which produces *League of Legends*) and Epic Games (*Fortnite*), both of which have millions of daily active players worldwide and have captured 13.2 per cent of the market share across the world's gaming market (Elad, 2023). Its extensive investment in digital content, social networking, and gaming has positioned Tencent as a central hub in the daily lives of billions of users. The company's ecosystem includes globally recognised products such as QQ, Tencent Games, and Tencent Cloud, along with a vast presence in sectors ranging from gaming and social media to financial technology (fintech) and AI. It consistently delivers impressive financial results, generating profits of over RMB 150 billion (around USD 20 billion) in 2023 (Tencent, 2024). This impressive outcome is driven by its diversified revenue streams from social networking, digital content, fintech, and enterprise services. Tencent's ability to innovate and integrate various digital services into a seamless user experience has made it a formidable force and cornerstone of the digital economy – not just in China but also globally.

Founded in November of 1998 in Shenzhen, China, as a mobile messaging service provider, Tencent has developed rapidly over the past two decades. Although Tencent enjoys a large domestic market, it is the company's capacity for innovation that has driven its rise in the digital world. In 2018, Tencent was ranked fourth in the world and first in China on the list of the World's Most Innovative Companies for 'honouring content as king' (Fast Company, 2018), showing its mastery of creating and distributing high-quality digital content across platforms. In 2022, *Forbes* magazine listed Tencent among the world's top five technology companies (Ponciano, 2022). Currently, Tencent ranks first in patent applications among all Chinese information technology (IT) companies – far ahead of peer competitors in the domestic internet field, such as Alibaba, Baidu, and Qihoo 360.[2] Globally, the number of patent applications Tencent has filed is second only to Google's.

Tencent uses first-class technologies to support its provision of stable, high-quality IT services. Since 2018, Tencent's total investment in research and development (R&D) has exceeded RMB 300 billion (about USD 43 billion). In 2023, Tencent was the second-highest investor in R&D among all private Chinese enterprises. The company's R&D investment totalled RMB 64.078 billion, with only Huawei spending more on R&D.[3] By the end of 2024, Tencent had filed for over 85,000 patents globally and received over 45,000 patents.[4] Of those granted patents, inventions accounted for 90 per cent. Tencent has about 104,500 employees, of whom 74 per cent are R&D personnel.[5] Tencent invests significantly in R&D with a focus on cutting-edge technologies, such as AI, blockchain, and quantum computing, ensuring that its technologies remain capable and can adapt to changing market demands.

So far, Tencent has become a leading internet company by providing numerous innovative products and services that prioritise user experience and security. These include communication and social media, high-quality digital content, and cloud services geared towards improving quality of life and supporting the growth and digital transformation of businesses throughout the world. The company has unquestionably set benchmarks for technological growth and

[2] Tencent internal document calculated by IP department using patent applications worldwide: www.rmzxb.com.cn/c/2024-09-23/3609218.shtml

[3] '2024 Top 500 Chinese Private Enterprises' list and the '2024 Research and Analysis Report on the Top 500 Chinese Private Enterprises' released by All-China Federation of Industry and Commerce: https://baijiahao.baidu.com/s?id= 1812715715992184470&wfr=spider&for=pc

[4] Top 100 Global Innovators 2025 released by Clarivate: https://clarivate.com/top-100-innovators/

[5] Tencent 2022 Annual R&D Big Data Report released by Tencent in 2023: www.szdaily.com/content/2023-03/22/content_30132027 .htm#:~:text=CHINESE%20internet%20giant%20Tencent%20has,Big%20 Data%20Report%20released%20Monday

business success. As a world-leading, internet-based platform company, how did Tencent achieve innovation in the digital era? What can companies in other countries, whether developed or developing, learn from the Tencent model?

In this book, we provide an in-depth and pioneering analysis of the innovation story of Tencent, which we call 'China's everything online company'. Tencent's approach to innovation combines technology, product, process, organisational, and social innovation, which is unusual. However, this multiplicative method of innovation is conducted at scale in a company that had over 100,000 employees at the end of 2023 – comparable in size to the largest internet companies in Western countries – and with a scope that combines many of the activities of Amazon, Alphabet (Google), Meta (Facebook), eBay, PayPal, and YouTube. All of this converges to establish Tencent as an all-encompassing, 'everything online' company. We are especially interested in how WeChat developed into a super app that provides a wide range of functions and services in various scenarios while also connecting and supporting partners (including users, businesses, and third-party service providers) in its ecosystem.

We are also interested in exploring how Tencent's internal organisational management has contributed to the company's success in the digital economy, as this is not yet clear. For example, Tencent's mix of internal 'coopetition', small team autonomy, and internal mobility has yielded organisational agility and stimulated creativity and breakthroughs. For this reason, we focus on discovering how Tencent developed into a digital giant by exploring the innovative mechanisms and models that have propelled its growth.

1.1 The Literature and Our Approach

Digital platforms and companies at the forefront of innovation have been the subject of wide-ranging interest amongst scholars of organisation management, strategy, and innovation for decades. As Western companies pioneered the digital and innovation sectors, setting global standards with ground-breaking technologies, much academic attention has been devoted to the success stories and innovations of top IT companies in the United States. These include Google (Schmidt and Rosenberg, 2014; Vise and Malseed, 2008), Amazon (Stone, 2013), Apple (Isaacson, 2014), Microsoft (Stross, 1996), and Facebook

(Kirkpatrick, 2011). In contrast, very little attention has been paid to the paths that Chinese IT companies have forged towards innovation.

The story of the rise and innovation of Chinese IT companies remains under-researched, even though China's IT companies have emerged on the world frontier in the digital era and despite the increasing importance of innovation in China (Fu, 2015; Fu et al., 2021; Greeven et al., 2019; Yip and McKern, 2016). Several English-language books have introduced emerging and world-leading companies from China, such as Tencent (Chen, 2022; Tang, 2019) and Alibaba (Clark, 2016) in the IT sector, Huawei (Fu, 2015; Tian et al., 2018; Tian and Wu, 2015; Wu et al., 2020) in the information and communication technologies (ICT) sector, and Haier in the manufacturing sector (Fischer et al., 2013; Yi and Ye, 2003). However, the scope of these books is relatively limited as they mainly focus on corporate development without paying particular attention to the innovation model.

When considering the development of China's internet and digital economy, Tencent is an essential part of the discussion. The rise and innovation of Tencent have changed the internet landscape in the digital era, creating multipolarity in platform businesses throughout the world. As a representative internet company from China, Tencent has developed many innovative products and services – some of which have been investigated by scholars in recent years (Birkinshaw et al., 2019; Luo et al., 2015; Yang et al., 2016). While several books have been published on Tencent in particular, these books mainly focus on perspectives of political economy (Tang, 2019), leadership (Hu, 2017), or business development (Chen, 2022; Wu, 2016). They do not analyse the company's internal micro-mechanisms for innovation, relevant management practices, and innovative achievements. Existing research publications that mention Tencent are also largely qualitative case studies based on secondary data or indirect interview material (Casanova et al., 2018; Chen, 2022; Tang, 2019).

In response to this void, we offer an in-depth and pioneering analysis of the innovation story behind Tencent. This book aims to fill a gap in the literature by examining the forms and mechanisms for innovation at Tencent in terms of technologies, products, management, ecosystem development, and social value – all of which have gone unexplored or under-examined in existing studies. The findings of the book are based on a four-year, in-depth case study undertaken from a mixed-methods approach that integrates qualitative

Table 1.1 *Data sources*

Data sources	Department/people involved	Numbers (participants)	Main topics
Interviews	HR department	16	Digital HRM
	Business departments	14	
	Business departments	14	Coopetition
	WeChat group	8	WeChat innovation and ecosystem
	Tencent Docs team	3	Product development and innovation
	QQ team	2	Product development and innovation
	Open-Source Office, Quantum Laboratory, Intellectual Property department	5	Technological innovation
	Sustainable social value department	3	Social innovation and social value creation
	Tencent Ads team, Tencent meeting team	8	Product innovation
	Corporate development group, Chief European Representative	2	R&D management, innovation model
	Academics	12	WeChat innovation, platform ecosystem, innovation model of Tencent, digital HRM
	Industry leaders	7	WeChat innovation, platform ecosystem, innovation model of Tencent
	Other stakeholders (users, businesses, other players in its ecosystem)	16	Platform ecosystem

Table 1.1 (*cont.*)

Data sources	Department/people involved	Numbers (participants)	Main topics
Focus groups	Tencent social research centre in Beijing	6	Innovation model
	Tencent London office	12	Innovation model
	Tencent social research centre in Shenzhen	8	Organisational culture, technological innovation, business operations, international strategy
Network video interviews	Chief executive officer Senior vice presidents Chief operating officer Head of WeChat group	18	Corporate strategy and development, product launch, R&D, technological development
Questionnaires survey	Employees in Technology, Product, and Design Groups	1970	Innovative product, internal mobility, organisational culture, individual performance, etc.

Secondary data	Types	Numbers	Main topics
Documents	Company reports	32	Corporate strategy and development, product launch, R&D, technological development
	News articles and webpages	64	

and quantitative methods with multi-source combined data. In addition to a comprehensive review of a large volume of public information, internal documents, reports, news articles, and literature about the company, we conducted a large-scale survey within Tencent. The survey was sent out to a total of 30,000 employees in the technology, design, and product groups, who are more likely to participate in innovation activities in relevant areas. We collected and comprehensively analysed 1,970 valid responses. Moreover, we conducted in-depth interviews with over 100 stakeholders from both Tencent's internal departments and external organisations. Within Tencent, our interviewees included senior executives, such as vice presidents and the general manager of corporate marketing and public relations, as well as scientists, product managers, R&D managers, marketing managers, software engineers, and human resources (HR) staff. These participants represented a variety of business units and groups, such as the Intellectual Property Department, the WeChat Group, and the Sustainable Social Value Department. Beyond Tencent, we also interviewed academics, industry leaders, customers, and partner companies. The interviews addressed a broad range of topics, including digital human resource management (HRM), coopetition, product development, technological innovation, and social innovation. Table 1.1 presents the data sources for our research.

1.2 Highlights of the Book

Our in-depth analysis revealed that Tencent's approach to innovation is building a market-type organisation with an ecosystem, characterised by openness, coopetition, empowerment, autonomy, and needs (or, briefly, OCEAN). As the semi-legendary ancient Chinese philosopher Lao Tzu once wrote in *Tao Te Ching*, 'The supreme good is like water, which benefits all of creation without trying to compete with it' (in Chinese:上善若水，利万物而不争). Like the ocean, Tencent supports and nourishes its members to create value for everyone without seeking to dominate. This reflects a powerful yet gentle strength as the organisation embraces inclusivity and freedom, flows around challenges with ease, and gracefully adapts to change. Through this harmony and humility, Tencent unites individuals and the players in its ecosystem into a collective force, achieving meaningful impact and competitiveness with quiet resilience. With this approach, Tencent has achieved a distinctive type of sequoia-like innovation, characterised by deep, directed, invisible, and compound (or, briefly, DDIC) innovation, making it a leading internet-based platform company – despite fierce competition – with the ability to adapt to the complex demands of today's dynamic markets.

1.2.1 Chapter 2: 'Tencent: A Rising Technology Giant in China'

Chapter 2 describes the history of Tencent's development, the transformation of its corporate strategies, its core business distribution, the adjustments made to its organisational structure, and its innovations in both product offerings and underlying technology. These details are provided within the larger context of the development of the internet industry in China. The chapter summarises innovation milestones for Tencent products and services, and then shows how the company developed its businesses through the use of major strategic investment and venture capital in several fields. It also describes Tencent's R&D endeavours in an attempt to provide a detailed picture of its technological innovation over the past two decades. The chapter ends with a comparison between Tencent's patent applications and those of other foreign and domestic companies, revealing Tencent's leading position in this category both globally and domestically.

1.2.2 Chapter 3: 'Competition and Cooperation: Using Organisational Resilience to Foster Innovation'

Chapter 3 illustrates how a combination of cooperation and competition – or what we call 'coopetition' – has driven innovation processes at Tencent. The outcome was the creation of a variety of excellent products for the market, including a national-level product (WeChat) and the online game *Honor of Kings*. Coopetition led to innovation not only by sparking creativity and driving significant efforts on the part of employees and teams but also by fostering the recombination of diverse yet complementary areas of knowledge. This knowledge recombination occurred between similar and competitive teams, as well as teams from different functional departments.

The chapter also highlights how Tencent's recent reform of strategy changed the role of competition and cooperation in organisational development. One of our surprising findings was that this reform was not designed by executives through a top-down mechanism but rather occurred naturally as a result of the autonomy the company provides its employees, along with its tolerance of risk. Rich interview material provided more evidence of how coopetition promotes the individual growth of employees and the development of work teams, leading to innovation within the company.

1.2.3 Chapter 4: 'Serving Talents through Digital Human Resource Management: Motivating Great Creativity'

Chapter 4 sheds light on how Tencent leveraged digitalised HRM practices to enhance employee creativity and drive organisational innovation. Recognising that organisational innovation depends on employees' skills, motivation, and engagement, Tencent has taken a leading role in applying digital technologies and products to HRM practices. Given the company's drive to produce leading internet-based platforms and its 'born digital' nature, one of Tencent's greatest goals is to provide a superior user value through its products and services. Such a user-oriented corporate principle also affects its digitalisation of HRM. Emphasising providing service to employees, Tencent adopted a 'productisation' approach, treating employees as internal users and focusing on their needs and experiences. As a result, HR teams design and provide various products that go beyond administrative functions to serve, support, and empower staff. These digital HR products are designed not only to enhance service quality but also to foster motivation and creativity, aligning HRM innovation with the company's broader goal of value creation through digital transformation.

1.2.4 Chapter 5: 'Flowing Water for Dynamism: Internal Mobility to Boost Innovation'

In 2012, Tencent established an internal mobility programme called Flowing Water (活水 *huoshui*). The programme was recognised as a representative managerial strategy for fostering employee innovation and enhancing organisational agility. Chapter 5 illustrates how

Tencent carried out its internal mobility policies and how the Flowing Water programme promoted dynamic minds, stimulated employee self-motivation, sustained organisational agility, and drove the company's innovation. Tencent not only fostered an open 'flowing water' culture but also developed an employee-friendly digital product to improve internal mobility policies. The company enabled information sharing and transparency in the process, engaging more employees with the programme.

The successful operation of the programme not only supported employee skills and career development but also offered employees autonomy as they were able to take an active role in shaping their own professional journeys even amid organisational changes. Flowing Water provided a continuous and dynamic supply of talent to the organisation; it also retained that talent despite a fiercely competitive environment. The programme promoted knowledge sharing and cooperation while avoiding organisational rigidity, which generally advances innovation. Such free and dynamic talent flows further supported the development of key businesses and departments within the company, especially during periods of organisational transformation, which helped the organisation remain agile and adaptive.

1.2.5 Chapter 6: 'Building an Open and Inclusive Ecosystem: WeChat's Rise to a Super App'

Chapter 6 focuses on WeChat, an all-in-one super app with over 1.3 billion active monthly users. Launched in 2011, WeChat has expanded beyond instant messaging and social media to include voice messaging, WeChat Pay, Moments, Mini Program, and video channels, making it a super app for daily needs. This chapter examines WeChat's development, key sources of innovation success, and the ecosystems it created. We argue that WeChat's emergence as a super app benefited from the evolution of functions, its connective nature between internal functions and with external users, and reactions between product features. One distinctive feature of WeChat's innovation was its depth; this *deep innovation* is captured in the 'first principles' orientation of its product design. At the same time, the WeChat team also had a deep understanding of the essential needs of the app's users. The team continues to design products and explore functions from a long-term perspective of those needs. The success of WeChat as a super app arguably also benefited from *invisible, compound, and continuous innovation* that promotes the interaction of multiple innovations and amplifies the overall value created. Finally, WeChat established an open, decentralised, and inclusive ecosystem for co-growth through three main approaches. The first approach involved enhancing product capabilities internally. The second was to empower players in the WeChat ecosystem, which included individual consumers and business enterprises. In doing so, the company was able to provide services and create value for players based on the principles of fairness and decentralisation. The third approach was to support third-party service providers, offering them space for growth.

1.2.6 Chapter 7: 'Developing Leading Products through Continuous Innovation: The Case of QQ and Tencent Docs'

A strong product gene has been embedded in Tencent since its birth and the company has developed a wide range of superior products over the past two decades. Chapter 7 examines how Tencent achieved leadership in relevant fields for both old and new products. What approaches did Tencent adopt to maintain the vitality of its original products, while also ensuring that its new products remained competitive in the market? Through a comparative study of an old Tencent product, QQ, and the much newer Tencent Docs, we identified differences and similarities in the company's approach to developing each product.

We found that QQ differentiated itself from foreign competitors (e.g. ICQ and MSN) and similar internal products (e.g. WeChat) through iterative innovation and radical innovation. This prompted a self-transformation led by the product development team in order to adapt to contemporary youth culture. The overall approach helped QQ to overcome growth bottlenecks, generate substantial revenue, and retain a high user percentage. Developed in 2017, Tencent Docs became a leading file collaboration product in China by leveraging Tencent's user base and experience in social media. Initially adopting a Business-to-Consumer (B2C) strategy, Tencent Docs switched to a Business-to-Business (B2B) approach to gain a competitive market edge. The success of Tencent Docs can be attributed to strategic innovation and technological catch-up. Teams for both products focused on creating user-oriented product value and actively capturing user needs. Their focus was enabled by strong technological capabilities accumulated in-house, internal collaboration, and an open, intrapreneurial, and inclusive culture fostered by Tencent.

1.2.7 Chapter 8: 'Maximising the Value of Platforms: Social Innovation and Social Value Creation'

Chapter 8 examines how, as a leading internet-based platform company, Tencent created social value and fostered social innovation to maximise platform value. It highlights key aspects of Tencent's social innovation and social value creation, including its motivation, manifestations, approaches, and mechanisms. Social innovation at Tencent is driven by strategic upgrades based on social needs with an emphasis on social value creation on a strategic level. Tencent has established a mechanism for social innovation to create social value that involves three key approaches: First, the involvement of various business departments in social innovation, leading to the integration of social value creation into daily business operations – social innovation benefits from the interplay of technological, product, and business model innovations; second, the co-creation of social value within the Tencent ecosystem – Tencent leverages its digital capabilities to build platform ecosystems and facilitate connections and collaborations among a diverse array of external stakeholders; and third, use of the so-called CBS trinity, which is crucial for social innovation – Tencent aims at creating value for customers (C), industries/businesses (B), and society (S). As a result, Tencent has created multifaceted social value across diverse scenarios involving social inclusion and the promotion of industry digitalisation, and, in service of the public interest, rural revitalisation, disaster response and relief, and carbon neutrality.

1.2.8 Chapter 9: 'Conclusions: Tencent's Innovation Model'

Chapter 9 summarises the key features of Tencent's innovation, which we call DDIC. Much like a towering sequoia tree, Tencent's innovation is anchored in deep and expansive roots which are interconnected and mutually reinforcing, and is guided by a strong sense of direction. This foundational strength extends outward, supporting the growth of a broader ecosystem. This tightly integrated innovation system gives Tencent exceptional resilience, allowing it to withstand market uncertainties – just as a sequoia endures the storms of nature. We then present an overall model for Tencent's innovation mechanism: OCEAN. Tencent is a market-type organisation with an OCEAN ecosystem in that it pursues *Openness*, encourages *Coopetition*, focuses on *Empowerment*, promotes employee *Autonomy*, and values the *Needs* of users, employees, and society.

We connect OCEAN to each chapter to reveal how the model works. In this way, Tencent provides ample resources for competition and collaboration, fostering creativity and viability. Tencent supports and motivates employees through autonomy while creating an open and inclusive platform ecosystem that empowers various stakeholders and facilitates co-growth. Aside from strong in-house R&D, Tencent's competitiveness stems from *deep innovation*, namely, first-principles product design, a deep understanding of user needs, product features, and keen market awareness. We show how Tencent excels at developing superior products and creating social value through *invisible and compound innovation*, or the integration and interaction of process, product, strategy, and business model and social innovations that users may not notice. Tencent's digital-enabled management innovations serve and create value for employees, managers, and the organisation. Tencent's *value-directed innovation* development then aims to create business value and broader value for customers, the market, industry, government, and society.

Combining these findings, we also propose how these important factors and mechanisms work with an open corporation innovation system framework. Finally, the chapter closes with a discussion of the contributions and managerial implications for related fields.

1.3 Contributions

In today's era of technological transformation, research into the mechanisms for innovation created by enterprises is of crucial importance. After all, innovation drives economic growth. It does so by increasing productivity and efficiency along with creating new industries and subsequent job opportunities. Through learning about the successes and experiences of leading companies, other companies can identify ways to foster a culture of innovation, encourage their employees to think creatively, and collaborate effectively to generate new ideas and nurture innovation. Beginning at this starting point, our book digs deep into Tencent's internal and micro-mechanisms for innovation. We focus on its distinctive approaches to innovation in order to provide implications from which other companies can learn.

This book contributes to the academic literature and business management in the following ways. First, this book fills a gap in the study of China's leading internet companies, particularly Tencent, by providing a systematic analysis of its multi-dimensional innovations – technological, product, managerial, social, and so on. Unlike existing works focusing on leadership or corporate development, it explores how Tencent emerged as a global tech leader and reveals that Tencent is a market-type organisation with an OCEAN ecosystem.

In terms of the research content, this book provides deep insights into Tencent's culture, organisational structure, incentive policies, product development, talent management, platform ecosystem, and social value creation, and highlights Tencent's overlooked innovation drivers, including coopetition, talent mobility, and social value creation, offering valuable insights for both scholars and business leaders. Existing research on Tencent often relies on secondary sources or limited first-hand data, which restricts its depth and reliability. Our book stands out as the first academic study to analyse Tencent's innovation management through a four-year, mixed-methods case study, combining extensive fieldwork and individual-level survey data, offering comprehensive insights and advancing the field with micro-level analysis.

Additionally, this book advances the concept of a corporate innovation system (Granstrand, 2000; Lundvall and Rikap, 2022) by offering theoretical and empirical insights into its construction and interconnectedness. Using Tencent as a case, it introduces an open corporate innovation system, where innovation performance is shaped by capabilities, incentives, and internal organisational policies and institutions. These elements interact to drive co-growth between Tencent and its ecosystem partners, enabling the company's DDIC innovations over the past two decades.

Overall, this book adds greater depth to insights into Tencent's mechanisms for innovation, challenging existing stereotypes of Chinese IT companies and extending our understanding of the micro-mechanisms of innovation management within a world-leading internet-based platform company in China. We show that Tencent's uniqueness is its DDIC innovations driven by a market-type organisation and OCEAN ecosystem. We examine how it achieves value creation through the innovative application of basic technology and the development of an innovation-empowered ecosystem, and how an orientation towards social impact drives inclusive innovation at the new development stage. We believe that this book offers valuable managerial insights regarding innovation in the digital era to other companies in both developing and developed countries.

2 | *Tencent*
A Rising Technology Giant in China

The Chinese technology giant Tencent provides internet users worldwide with a huge number of products. An exact number is difficult to pinpoint, as even Tencent itself does not keep count. The company thus reaches billions of active users around the world through a vast portfolio that spans social media, gaming, fintech, and cloud services while continuously reshaping the digital landscape.

But how did Tencent evolve from a start-up with a single product into an internet titan amid fierce competition? Before delving into an in-depth analysis of Tencent's strategies and innovation model, this chapter begins with an overview of the innovation landscape in China. It then explores the historical development of Tencent along with the transformation of the company's corporate strategies, organisational structure, and other adjustments. Finally, it examines Tencent's endeavours in R&D, milestones in innovation, and the investment landscape – all within the broader context of the evolution of the internet industry in China.

2.1 The Development of Chinese Innovation

Over the past forty years, since the reform and opening-up of its economy, China has experienced rapid economic growth and witnessed a remarkable trajectory in the development of innovation (Fu, 2015). The Chinese economy initially relied heavily on manufacturing and low-cost labour but, over time, it gradually shifted gears towards fostering innovation-driven growth. Motivated by both domestic needs and global ambition, China is moving from a strategy of imitation to one of innovation. It has strengthened its indigenous innovation capabilities, establishing itself at the forefront of technological innovation and becoming a leading innovator country (Fu, 2015; Yip and McKern, 2016).

The Chinese government has played a pivotal role in this transition by identifying innovation as a national priority, investing heavily in R&D, establishing innovation hubs, and implementing policies to encourage entrepreneurship and technological advancement (Fu et al., 2021). According to the latest data from the National Bureau of Statistics of China, the R&D intensity (the ratio of R&D expenditure to GDP) reached 2.68 per cent in 2024 (up from only 1.3 per cent in 2003). Among this, the total amount of R&D investment exceeded RMB 3.61 trillion, a figure that ranks second in the world behind the US.[1] This concerted effort has borne fruit, propelling China to become a global leader in fields as varied as telecommunications, renewable energy, e-commerce, new energy vehicles, and AI.

Notably, initiatives such as the Made in China 2025 plan underscore China's ambition to become a powerhouse in advanced manufacturing and high-tech industries. With an unwavering commitment to innovation, China continues to chart new frontiers and shape the future of technology on a global scale. According to the Global Innovation Index (GII) published by the World Intellectual Property Organization (WIPO), China ranked thirty-fifth in 2013 but rose to eleventh in 2024 (see Figure 2.1; WIPO, 2024), first among the thirty-three upper-middle-income group of economies. All five top science and technology clusters are located in East Asia, with three in China. Clearly, China has become an important engine for technological innovation and creation globally.

Generally, patents represent new inventions and technologies. A high number of patent applications suggests a country is producing a significant volume of new technological solutions and advancements. The latest WIPO data show that China ranked first in international patent applications for three consecutive years beginning in 2019, arriving at roughly 70,000 Patent Cooperation Treaty (PCT) applications in 2022 – a figure that accounted for over one-quarter of total applications worldwide (WIPO, 2023), ahead of the US, Japan, and South Korea. Among the 16.5 million valid invention patents in the world, China ranks first with 3.6 million patents. This number surpasses the US, which held 3.3 million patents in 2021 (WIPO, 2022). The number of high-value invention patents per 10,000 people in China was

---

[1] Statistical Bulletin on National Science and Technology Funding in 2023: www.gov.cn/lianbo/bumen/202410/content_6978274.htm

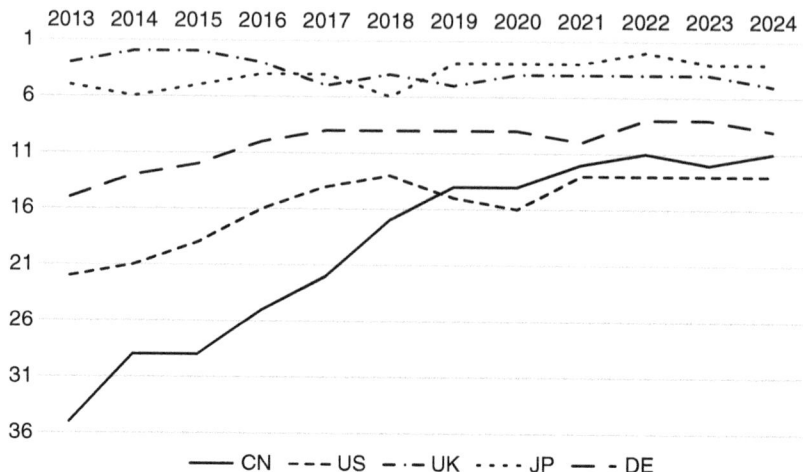

Figure 2.1 Rankings of main countries from the Global Innovation Index, 2013–2024.

fourteen by the end of 2024 (Ministry of Ecology and Environment of the PRC, 2025).[2] Among all of the entities leading innovation, private science and technology enterprises became an important driving force for the growth of R&D funds throughout Chinese society. They also became the primary force behind patent applications and contributed greatly to China's scientific and technological innovation.

Many of the large, leading internet companies we see today in China actually emerged in the late 1990s and early twenty-first century, and were thus relevant to the development of the internet in China. As a latecomer to the World Wide Web, China officially connected to the internet on 20 April 1994, becoming the seventy-seventh country in the world to enter the internet community (Xinhua, 2014). Access to the internet then began to spread in China at a relatively slow pace. In the global context for the internet, the American computer service company Netscape was first listed in 1995 on the New York Stock Exchange. The listing triggered a wave of entrepreneurship in China's nascent internet industry, and the establishment of the Chinese companies Sina, Sohu, and NetEase brought about an internet boom.

Figure 2.2 shows that in 2002, the internet penetration rate in China was only 4.7 per cent. By 2023, it had increased to 77.5 per cent.

2 www.mee.gov.cn/zcwj/zclcfh/202503/t20250329_1105003.shtml

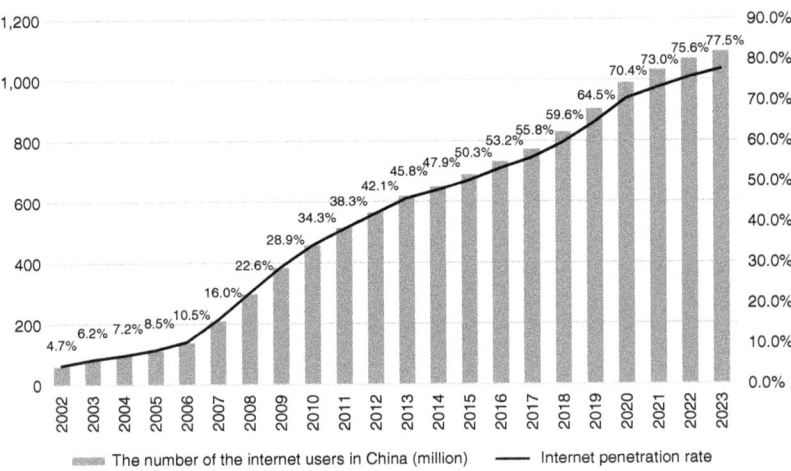

Figure 2.2 Number of internet users and internet penetration rate in China, 2002–2023.

This number increased to 78.6 per cent at the end of 2024. As more citizens gained access to the internet, the potential user base for digital products and services expanded exponentially and created vast opportunities for companies to innovate and scale. This surge in connectivity fostered the rise of e-commerce, social media, mobile payments, and online entertainment. Companies such as Tencent and Alibaba were at the forefront of this transformation.

In the meantime, China started developing a network security system that blocks users from accessing websites deemed inappropriate by the government in 1997. The system consists of an ensemble of social media regulations, intellectual property (IP) blacklists, keyword filters, data gateways, and human censors. To some extent, it limited the ability of foreign companies to access internet-based business (including cloud services) and favoured local companies, especially Baidu, Alibaba, and Tencent (Mueller, 2011). Today, these companies have become the digital forerunners in e-payment, social media, and other fintech solutions. They are also among the world-leading companies in multiple digital services and platforms.

The introduction of the internet to China inspired many popular products and services for personal computer end-users. China entered the mobile internet era around 2010. Figure 2.3 illustrates the development of the internet industry in China. The number of mobile internet

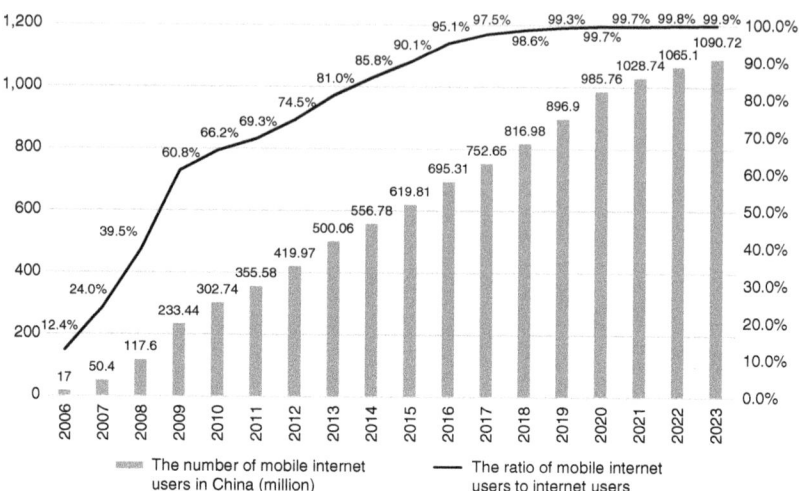

Figure 2.3 Number and ratio of mobile internet users in China, 2006–2023.

users has increased steadily since 2006, rising from seventeen million to over ten billion in 2021 (CNNIC, 2022). Many private companies were established in the 2000s, such as Baidu, Alibaba, and Tencent (collectively known in China as 'BAT'), and developed quickly alongside the progression of the mobile internet. Beginning around 2010, smartphones also grew in popularity in China. In the early 2010s, several start-ups, including Meituan, ByteDance, and Didi, entered the internet landscape to provide software services to China's internet users. Among these private companies, Tencent is the largest domestic social network and gaming company and one of the world's largest digital content providers.

2.2 The History of Tencent: An Overview

2.2.1 Company Founding

In November 1998, Tencent was founded in the city of Shenzhen in the province of Guangdong by Huateng (Pony) Ma and four other young entrepreneurs: Zhidong (Tony) Zhang, Liqing (Jason) Zeng, Chenye (Daniel) Xu, and Yidan (Charles) Chen. Pony Ma was born in October 1971 in Hainan province. Influenced by his family, he developed an interest in science, especially astronomy, from a young age. At age thirteen, Pony Ma and his parents moved from the island of Hainan to Shenzhen, where he met his future co-founders Daniel Xu, Charles Chen, and Tony Zhang in high school. In August 1980, Shenzhen was established as one of China's four special economic zones alongside Zhuhai, Shantou, and Xiamen. Stimulated by preferential policies, significant national investment, and international capital, the four southern regions experienced rapid economic recovery and development. This environment fostered innovation and an entrepreneurial spirit, paving the way for the creation of Tencent and its subsequent growth into a global technology giant.

In 1989, Ma joined the Department of Electronic Engineering at Shenzhen University alongside Xu and Zhang to major in computer science. Chen also attended Shenzhen University, where he was a chemistry major. To some extent, then, Tencent's founding began with Ma's personal interests. He had a passion for information technology and was among the first one hundred so-called netizens in China to gain access to the internet. Four of the five founding team members of Tencent – Ma, Xu, Zhang, and Chen – were high school and college classmates, with Jason Zeng being the exception. Known for his sales expertise, Zeng was brought on to complement the technical skills of the others. All five entrepreneurs shared an enthusiasm for the internet.

Tencent's founders played a key role in different fields, contributing significantly to the company's growth and success. From the beginning, each had clear responsibilities. As CEO, Pony Ma was responsible for strategy and product development. Given his exceptional talent in computer science, Tony Zhang took charge of technology R&D as CTO. Familiar with the internet and telecommunications industry in China and regarded as the most open, passionate, and inspiring of the founders, Jason Zeng focused on market and operations as COO.

The other two founders joined the company full-time later that year: Daniel Xu took on the role of CIO, responsible for information management, while Charles Chen served as CAO, overseeing administrative and legal affairs. The management team remained relatively stable throughout Tencent's development aside from the departure of Jason Zeng, who left the company in 2007 to become an angel investor. As the core decision-makers at Tencent over a lengthy period of time, the founders guided the company through its various phases of growth and innovation.

When Tencent was established in 1998, the internet industry was rapidly developing around the world. In the US, companies such as Netscape, Microsoft, Apple, and Yahoo were already making significant strides. Google, too, was founded in 1998. Many entrepreneurs in China were also seizing the opportunity to develop various internet fields. In the web portal sector, companies such as Sohu, Sina, and NetEase emerged around the same time. In the online gaming industry, Lianzhong Game and Shanda became prominent. Alibaba, Dangdang.com, and JD.com were established in the e-commerce sector, while Baidu and 3721 were founded in the search engine domain. These developments marked a significant period of growth within the Chinese internet landscape.

When Tencent began, the main business focused on expanding the wireless network paging system. This sort of software development project for enterprises or organisations was the best choice for all small and medium-sized network service companies at the time. As a start-up, Tencent was initially unclear about its next product, and in the late 1990s, China's internet was only on the cusp of a vigorous phase of development. But as the number of Chinese internet users rapidly grew, demand for instant messaging tools followed. Tencent launched its first popular product OICQ (Open ICQ), an instant messenger tool, in February 1999. The name OICQ originated from an Israeli company's product ICQ (derived from the English phrase 'I seek you'). But after receiving threats of a lawsuit from ICQ and its owner, America Online (now AOL), Tencent officially renamed the product QQ in 2000.

OICQ was among the first generation of instant messaging products in China's internet industry. Within four months of the launch of the original version of OICQ, it had one million registered users, and people began to use OICQ to communicate with friends online. In the early stages, QQ aimed primarily at the market of young consumers, offering basic functions such as text chat and file transfers. The launch of this instant messaging software reduced communication costs for individual users, and Chinese netizens began to experience a range of new features on QQ.

During the first three years of operations, Tencent remained unprofitable and even faced bankruptcy because of a lack of funding.

Several of the technically oriented founders conducted outsourcing projects to earn money to support the company. In 2003, Tencent entered the field of gaming, and in June 2004, five years after the company was founded, Tencent Holdings Limited was listed on the main board of the Hong Kong Stock Exchange, becoming only the second Chinese internet company to be thus listed. A few years later, in June 2007, the establishment of the Tencent Foundation marked the creation of the first charitable organisation by an internet enterprise in China. The Foundation would go on to develop Tencent Gongyi, one of the world's largest online fundraising platforms. In 2011, Tencent launched one of its most successful and popular products, WeChat, and by 2016, the company's market capitalisation exceeded HK$2 trillion.

As an internet-based technology enterprise, Tencent has developed rapidly over the past twenty-six years. Today, it is one of the top five internet companies in the world and the largest internet service portal in China,[3] offering products and services in a variety of fields that lead a number of industries. Tencent is one of the largest online gaming companies, ranking first among both personal computer and mobile phone users in China, as well as first in the world in terms of operating revenue. Tencent Music is the top music service provider in China. In terms of mobile payment, the number of both monthly active users (MAUs) and daily active users (DAUs) of Tencent rank first in China. Tencent is also the second largest provider of public cloud services within the Chinese market.[4] The story of Tencent's development and success has become an instructive case study at many business schools.

Over time, Tencent gradually constructed a complete, self-developed system that included providers, operating systems, chips, software as a service, and other components. This self-developed ecosystem provided a solid foundation on which the company could then serve the real economy. Figure 2.4 captures the range of the most successful and popular products or services developed by Tencent over the past two decades, for example, WeChat, Tencent Meeting, and so on, as well as its recent strategic focus on sustainable value creation.

---

[3] By total market capital: https://companiesmarketcap.com/internet/largest-internet-companies-by-market-cap/

[4] The public cloud ranking is based on the LaaS and PaaS revenue by IDC, as of 31 December 2021.

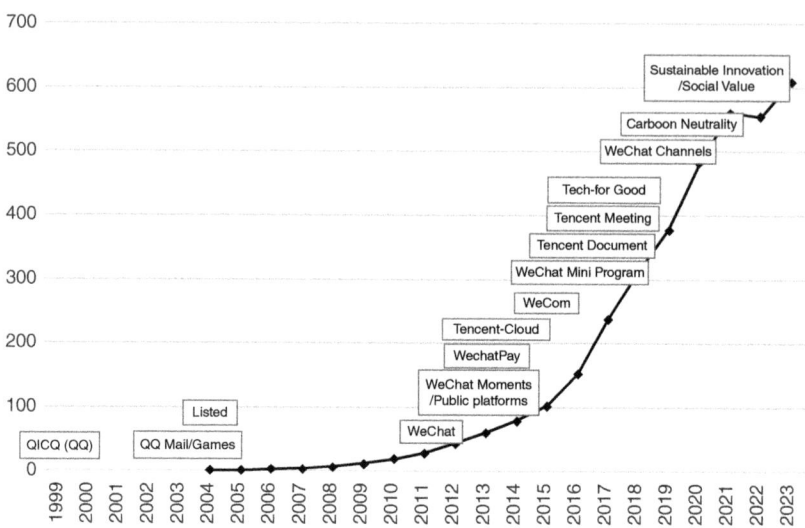

Figure 2.4 Tencent's major milestones and annual revenue, 1999–2023 (in billion RMB).

2.2.2 Profile of the Organisation

Alongside the rapid expansion of its product offerings, Tencent has stressed technological R&D, and the past decade in particular has seen a rapid growth in the number of employees. In 2021, Tencent Group had over 110,000 employees; more than half of whom were R&D personnel. By the following year, this ratio had risen to almost three-quarters (Tencent, 2022a). Based on the Tencent Annual Report, we attempted to draw the development of the employees and its revenue in the past two decades. Figure 2.5 compares the number of employees with Tencent's revenue growth for the period between 2003 and 2023, showing how both increased rapidly over the past two decades.

According to a 2022 annual report, Tencent generated RMB 554.6 billion of annual revenue with a net profit of RMB 188.24 billion, a year-on-year increase of 16 per cent. Tencent's revenues mainly derive from three primary sectors: value-added services, online advertising, and fintech and enterprise services. Of these, revenue from value-added services reached RMB 287.57 billion in 2022 to account for over half (52 per cent) of its total revenue. Revenue from the online

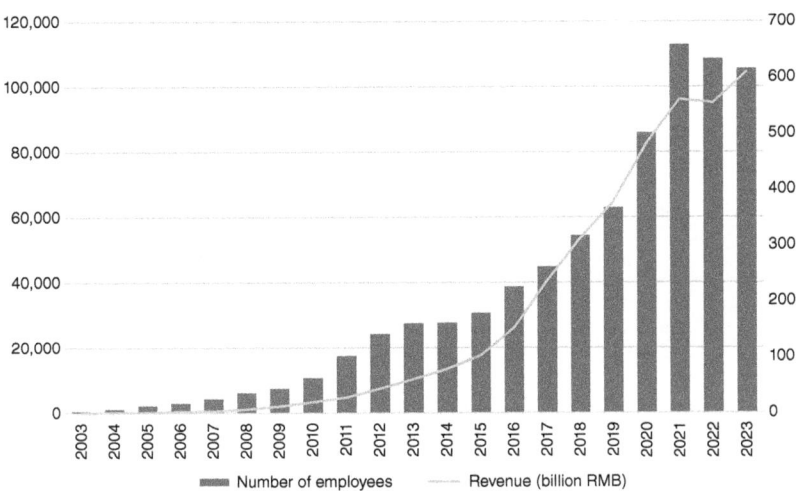

Figure 2.5 Number of Tencent employees and revenue growth, 2003–2023.

advertising business amounted to RMB 82.73 billion, accounting for 15 per cent. In terms of value-added services (including for gaming and social networks), revenues from the domestic gaming market reached RMB 123.9 billion. That same year, revenues from the international gaming market increased by 3 per cent, rising to RMB 46.8 billion. Figure 2.6 shows Tencent's annual revenue and market capitalisation (cap) over the past two decades.[5] According to Companies Market Cap (2024a), Tencent's market cap was over US$550 billion in October 2024. This makes Tencent one of the world's top twenty most valuable companies by market cap (CompaniesMarketCap, 2024b).

Our internal interviews established that by 2021 Tencent had more than 60,000 regular employees. Their average age was about thirty years, which is relatively young compared with other internet companies such as Baidu, Alibaba, and Didi. There are five main types of 'families' at Tencent based on the primary areas of expertise among staff: technicians (T), marketing (M), product (P), design (D), and skills (S). Over 40 per cent of employees were technicians, while about 20 per cent fell within the P family, working for product design and development.

---

[5] Market cap calculated based on the last day of each year.

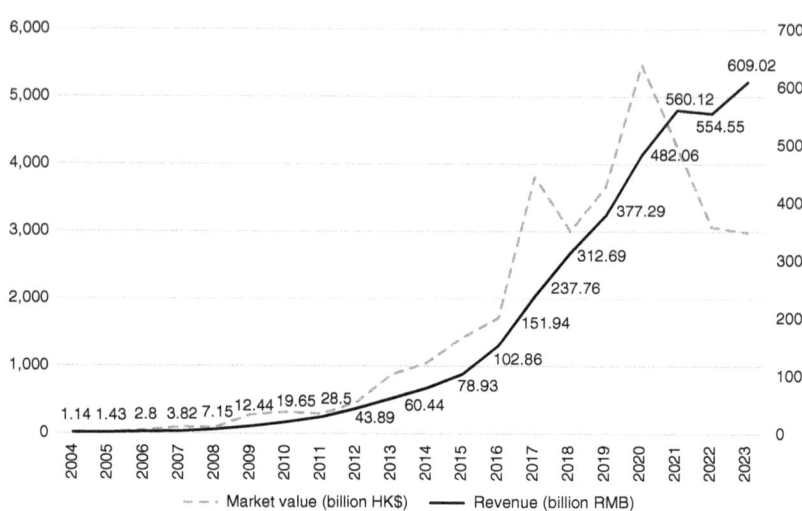

Figure 2.6 Tencent's annual revenue and market capitalisation, 2004–2023.

2.2.3 *Restructuring within the Organisation*

Over the past few decades, Tencent has been restructured several times to better serve the changing goals of the company. The first restructure of the organisation occurred in 2001, when the business department was divided into three large departments for marketing (M line), research (R line), and the functional department. On 24 October 2005, the company announced that it would adjust its organisational structure once more and all of its departments would be divided into eight units consisting of five business departments and three service support departments.

With the rapid development of WeChat (also called Weixin in Chinese) and more mergers and acquisitions, Tencent made a third major adjustment to its organisational structure in May 2012, when the company announced that it would upgrade the business unit (BU) system into a business group (BG) system (Wu, 2016). Two years later, in May 2014, Tencent restructured its internal organisation so the BGs were recombined into seven groups: The Corporate Development Group (CDG), the Interactive Entertainment Group (IEG), the Technology and Engineering Group (TEG), the Weixin

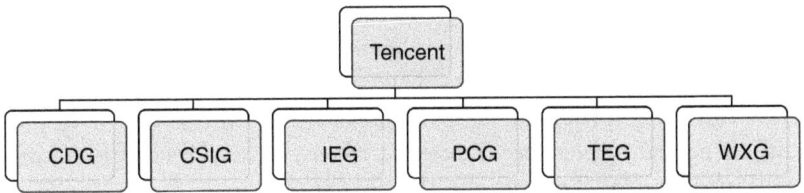

Figure 2.7 Tencent's business group structure, 2023.

Group (WXG), the Social Network Group (SNG), the Mobile Internet Group (MIG), and the Online Media Group (OMG).

On 30 September 2018, Tencent upgraded its strategy to embrace the industrial internet and conducted a radical adjustment to organisational structure that was internally referred to as the 930 Reform.[6] The four original BGs – the CDG, IEG, TEG, and WXG groups – were all retained while the remaining three BGs were reorganised into two new groups and one business line. A new Cloud and Smart Industry Group (CSIG) was created to promote the Business to Business (B2B) service based on Tencent Cloud, along with a Platform and Content Group (PCG). Following this adjustment, Tencent's six groups included the TEG, WXG, IEG, PCG, CSIG, and CDG, as shown in Figure 2.7.

The CDG is responsible for promoting development and innovation in important areas, such as financial technology and advertising, as well as marketing services that include payment and financial applications. The IEG is responsible for the R&D, operations, and development of the company's interactive entertainment business, which includes games and eSports. The TEG is responsible for supporting Tencent's business groups in terms of technology and operational platforms as well as for the construction and operations of R&D and data centres. It provides a full range of customer services and leads the Tencent Technology Committee in strengthening infrastructure through internal open-source collaboration, constructing new platforms, and supporting business innovation. The WXG is responsible for the construction and operations of the WeChat ecosystem and leveraging WeChat's open platforms, such as official accounts,

---

[6] Titanium Media, 'Tencent's Second Venture: Ten Years of Cloud Development behind to B': www.sohu.com/a/431034087_116132

mini-programs, WeChat Pay, and the search function. It provides solutions and connectivity for intelligent upgrades across all industries and is also responsible for the development and operations of QQ Mail and other products. As president of Tencent, Martin Lau has said, 'We need to be sober-minded, crisis-aware and forward-looking at all times to lead Tencent into the next era.'

After several rounds of organisational restructuring, Tencent now operates based on the BG mechanism. There are three functional support groups (S1, S2, S3) for administration, accounting and finance, and HRM, respectively.

Within its six BGs and three support groups, the team is the fundamental unit that enables staff to work together towards the same goal. Figure 2.8 shows the number of teams within each of the various groups as of 2021. The number of teams is highest in the IEG (over 1,000), while the TEG and WXG have a relatively low number of teams (around 300). Moreover, there are six types of teams within Tencent (technician, product, marketing, skill, design, and mixed teams). According to an internal document, the TEG has the greatest proportion of technician teams (about 65 per cent), followed by the WXG. The IEG has the greatest proportion of product teams (about 25 per cent), and the CDG is primarily made up of marketing

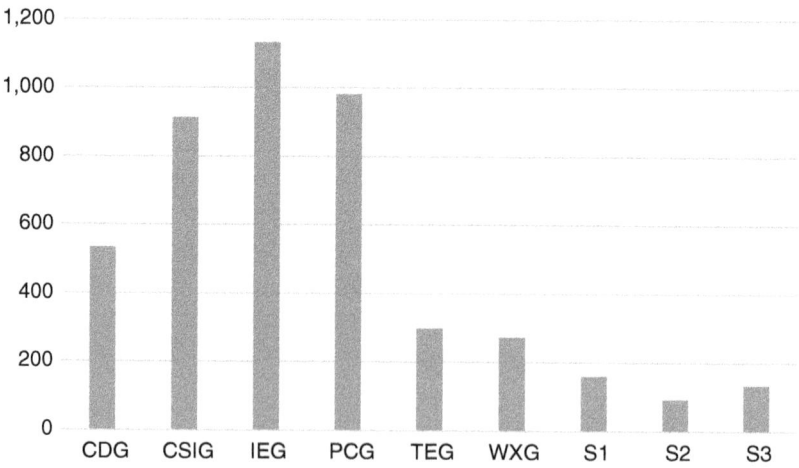

Figure 2.8 Number of teams within Tencent's business groups, December 2021. (Source: Tencent)

teams. The number of technical teams within each business group is the largest of any team type. It is also worth noting that each business group has mixed teams with various areas of expertise, which account for about 20 per cent of total teams on average. These different teams all support the hundreds of products and services offered by Tencent.

2.2.4 Milestones and Timeline of Strategic Transformation

Over time, Tencent was transformed from a small domestic company into an international entity with billions of dollars in assets. Alongside the development of technology and products, the strategic transformation of Tencent unfolded rapidly. The company experienced three major strategic transformations over the course of its development and updated its vision several times.

2.2.4.1 Timeline of Strategic Upgrades

In 2003, five years after Tencent was established, the company released its vision and mission for the first time: 'a friend who users rely on, a happy and energetic university, a leading market position, a partner worthy of respect, stable and reasonable profits', and 'creating a first-class internet enterprise'. This list of characteristics could be called Tencent Culture, Version 1.0. In 2005, the vision and mission were updated to 'improve quality of life through internet value-added services' and to become 'the most respected internet company', setting the company's values as 'integrity, responsibility, cooperation and innovation'.[7] This could be called Tencent Culture, Version 2.0.

In June 2011, Tencent announced its new open platform strategy, and the value of 'responsibility' was updated to 'proactivity'. March 2012 then saw the proposal of the Pan-Entertainment strategy. According to Tencent vice president Wu Cheng, 'pan' referred to 'internet-enabled media franchises' and the strategy aimed at making 'intellectual property' the engine for pioneering cultural products.

In November 2013, Tencent launched the Connect Everything and Internet Plus strategies. Not long afterwards, in April 2014,

---

[7] Tencent internal email by Pony, Martin, and the general manager office in 11 November 2019.

a new version of the Pan-Entertainment strategy emerged that aimed at the creation of a fan economy for celebrity IP based on the multi-field symbiosis of the internet and mobile internet. This was intended to include areas such as online literature, comics and animation, games, films and eSports, and music, among other things. The approach was upgraded to the New Innovation and Culture strategy in 2018 at the Tencent Neo-Culture Creativity Eco-Conference (also called the UP Conference annually held by Tencent). Through the promotion of neo-culture and creativity, Tencent looked to strengthen cultural communication between countries around the world.

In September 2018, the company again upgraded its strategy to 'roots in the consumer internet while embracing the era of industrial internet', shortened internally to the 930 Reform. As previously mentioned, the company also established two new BGs: PCG and CSIG.

In November 2019, Tencent announced its new mission and vision of 'value for users, tech for good', changing its core values as follows:[8]

(1) integrity (uphold principles, ethics, openness, and fairness),
(2) proactivity (pursue positive contributions, volunteer for responsibility, and push for breakthroughs),
(3) collaboration (be inclusive and collaborative, strive to progress and evolve) and
(4) creativity (push for breakthrough innovations, explore future possibilities).

Together, these could be called Tencent Culture, Version 3.0.

On 19 April 2021, Tencent announced a strategic upgrade, proposing the Sustainable Social Value Innovation strategy and establishing a 'sustainable social value business group' to promote strategic implementation. The strategy itself aimed at accelerating investment in scientific and technological innovation, rural revitalisation, education innovation, and carbon neutrality, among other areas. Under this strategic upgrade, Tencent's service targets would advance from users (C) to industry (B) and then to society (S), with the ultimate

---

[8] Tencent's official website: www.tencent.com/en-us/about.html#about-con-2

goal of creating value for society. The CBS (Customer, Business/ Industry, and Society) Trinity strategy required a greater focus on user value, technological innovation, and fulfilment of social responsibilities. Figure 2.9 shows the timeline of Tencent's strategic and cultural upgrades.

2.2.4.2 Milestones in Tencent's Strategy, Product, and Service Innovations

Since its founding, Tencent has introduced many innovative products to the market and conducted several business model innovations, for example, the QQ show, QQ Games, Qzone, Tencent Video, and so on. We summarise milestones in the company's strategic, product, and service innovations since its foundation to 2021 in Table 2.1, with strategic upgrades and transformations listed in bold. Tencent had four organisational restructurings in its history in 2001, 2005, 2012, and 2014.

2.3 Tencent's Technological Innovation and Endeavours

On a list of the world's most innovative companies compiled by *Fast Company* (2018), Tencent ranked number four globally and number one in China. The company became a Derwent Top 100 Global Innovator for the first time in 2020,[9] and again in 2021 and 2024. Tencent owns many well-known platforms and products, such as WeChat, QQ, *Honor of Kings*, and *League of Legends*, which serve the needs of daily life and entertainment for hundreds of millions of users. It also has an in-depth layout and capacities for innovation in AI, cloud computing, big data, blockchain, and other fields, providing intelligent and digital solutions for all walks of life. Behind Tencent's provision of so many products and services to so many users is the company's continuous exploration and investment in R&D and achievement of a number of cutting-edge technologies.

---

[9] Published by *Pandaily*: 'China's Xiaomi, Huawei and Tencent Named 2020 Derwent Top 100 Global Innovators', 22 February 2020, https://pandaily .com/chinas-xiaomi-huawei-and-tencent-named-2020-derwent-top-100-global-innovators/

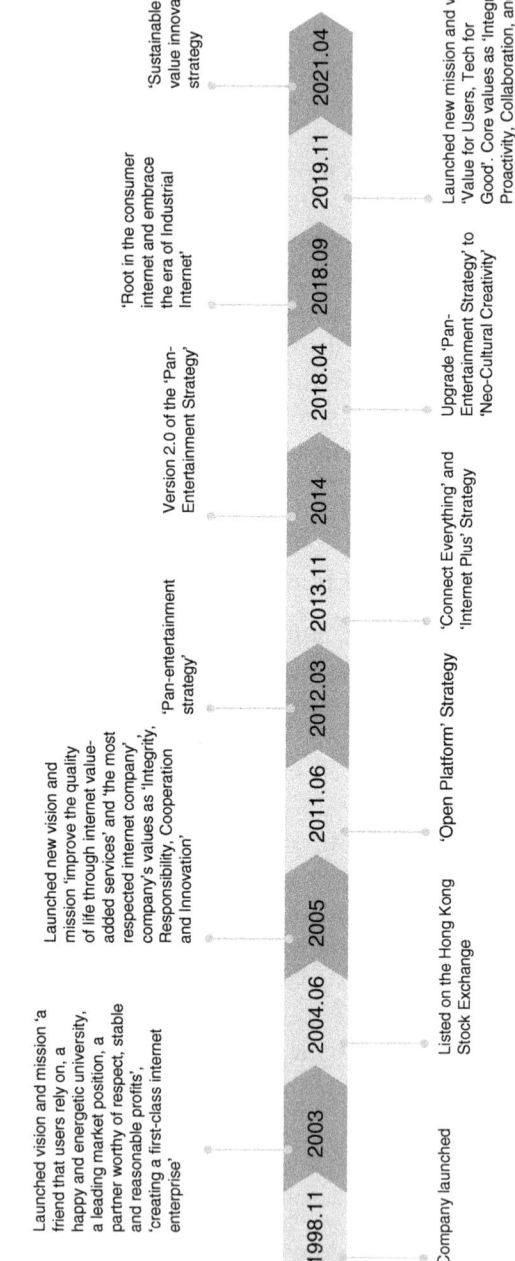

Figure 2.9 Timeline of Tencent's strategic and cultural upgrades, 1998–2021.

Table 2.1 *Milestones in Tencent's organisational development*

Time	Strategy, products or service innovation
April 2021	Launch of Sustainable Innovations for Social Value as a core development strategy
January 2021	Carbon Neutrality initiative
January 2020	WeChat Channels
December 2019	Tencent Meeting
November 2019	Corporate mission 'Tech for Good'
November 2018	Initiation of 'Xplorer Prize'
September 2018	Strategic upgrade and restructuring to embrace the industrial internet while maintaining roots in the consumer internet
April 2018	Tencent Docs
November 2017	Construction of a national AI open innovation platform for medical imaging
August 2017	Tencent Miying
January 2017	WeChat mini-programs
April 2016	WeCom
May 2014	Fourth organisational restructuring
April 2014	Pan-Entertainment strategy, version 2.0
January 2014	WeChat Red Packet and LiCaiTong (wealth management platform)
November 2013	Connection and Internet Plus strategies
September 2013	Tencent Cloud and cloud security
August 2013	WeChat Pay and mobile game centres at WeChat and QQ
May 2012	Third organisational restructuring
April 2012	Moments and WeChat public platforms
October 2011	Launch of Tencent Ads
June 2011	Open Platform strategy
April 2011	Launch of Tencent Video
January 2011	Weixin/WeChat
July 2011	Pan-Entertainment strategy, version 1.0
August 2009	Launch of QQ farm
August 2008	Public beta of QQ Alumni
June 2007	Tencent Charity Foundation
June 2006	Super QQ (updated to QQ membership in 2015)
December 2005	QQ Fantasy
July 2005	QQ Music
May 2005	Qzone
April 2005	Tenpay

Table 2.1 (*cont.*)

Time	Strategy, products or service innovation
October 2005	**Second organisational restructuring**
June 2004	**Listing on the Hong Kong Stock Exchange**
August 2004	Launch of mini homepage
November 2003	Web portal www.QQ.com
August 2003	QQ Games
May 2003	QQ Mail
January 2003	QQ Show
May 2002	Q coin
December 2001	**First organisational restructuring**
April 1999	Mobile e-mail
February 1999	OICQ (QQ)
November 1998	Founding in Shenzhen

2.3.1 Massive R&D Investment to Stimulate Innovation

To maintain a competitive advantage in technology and products, Tencent has invested heavily. As Figure 2.10 shows, in 2009, the company's R&D investment was RMB 1.19 billion; by 2016, the number had risen to RMB 11.85 billion, and by 2022 to RMB 61.4 billion. The investment accounted for approximately 50 per cent of the total after-tax net profit, ranking first among the top 500 private enterprises with a year-on-year growth rate of 18.3 per cent. In 2023, the total R&D investment increased once more to RMB 64.08 billion. According to public data, Tencent's total R&D investment over the past ten years has exceeded RMB 250 billion. From 2018 to the second quarter of 2023, Tencent's cumulative R&D expenditure maintained a double-digit growth for seven consecutive years.[10] For the past five years, Tencent has ranked second only to Huawei in terms of R&D investment among China's private technology companies. The massive amount of attention paid to R&D contributed directly to Tencent's capacity for innovation in scientific research and patent generation. Just as Figure 2.10 shows, the number of patents applied by Tencent has increased rapidly since 2015.

[10] Tencent internal document.

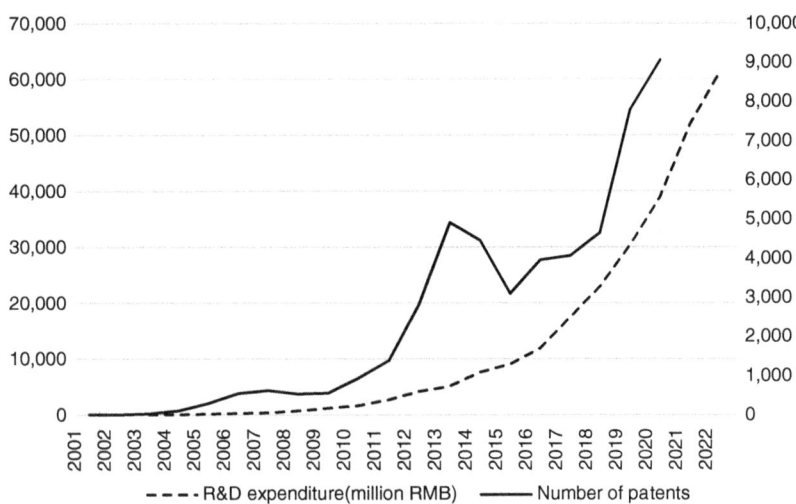

Figure 2.10 Tencent's R&D expenditures and number of patents, 2001–2022.

At the same time, Tencent's internal R&D staff accounted for 74 per cent of total staff in 2022, meaning that three out of every four Tencent employees were engaged in R&D. The company added over 6,000 new R&D projects in 2021, and the number of new R&D projects in 2022 was over 7,000 (a year-on-year increase of 19.8 per cent).[11] Tencent's innovation curve shows that the investment in innovation and the number of patent applications has developed in a positive direction.

From the perspective of global corporate R&D investment, according to the EU Industrial R&D Investment Scoreboard 2022–2024, Tencent's R&D investment scale in the past two years has been the highest among Chinese internet companies, ranking nineteenth in the world, second only to Huawei among all private companies (see Figure 2.11). In contrast, Google's parent company, Alphabet, along with Meta, Apple, and Microsoft, ranks among the top four in the world. In 2023, the R&D investment of Alphabet and Meta was 39.8 and 33.2 billion euros, respectively, while that of Tencent's was 8.12 billion euros in the same year. Compared to leading Western internet companies, the scale of R&D investment among Chinese companies still lags significantly behind.

[11] Tencent R&D Big Data Report 2022.

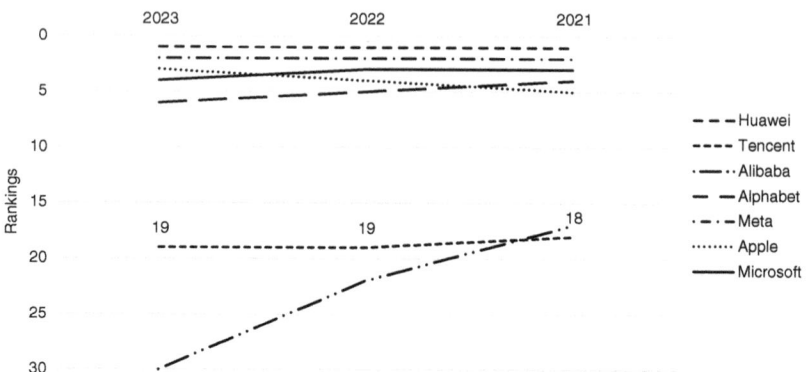

Figure 2.11 Rankings of R&D investment of top companies in China and the US, 2021–2023.

Tencent also globalised its R&D facilities, settling in innovation hubs. It has thirteen R&D centres in the US, South Korea, the UK, France, Germany, and elsewhere. The company opened an AI research centre in Seattle (Juro, 2017). At present, Tencent has branches in the Asia Pacific, North America, Europe, the Middle East, and Africa at sites including Seoul, Singapore, Tokyo, Los Angeles, Toronto, and beyond.

In the field of accessibility, Tencent has engaged in relevant R&D for sixteen years since the launch of QQ's information accessibility version in 2007. Currently, all products are optimised for accessibility and there are over forty specialised functions and products to provide services to users with disabilities. Tencent and the China Disabled Persons' Federation jointly established a barrier-free innovation laboratory to promote the application of next-generation internet technology in the field of accessibility and further lower the threshold for product upgrades and application innovation across the entire industry. Today, Tencent has released eight 'vibration feedback' technology patents to the public for free. Through open licensing, it promotes the broader implementation of cutting-edge technologies with lower usage thresholds and more reliable IP protection.

Tencent has always valued basic scientific research and original innovation. While the company increased its own investment in R&D, it also established an RMB 10 billion public welfare fund to support basic research. Tencent's New Cornerstone Investigator programme supports outstanding scientists in the fields of mathematics and physical, biological, and biomedical sciences with the aim of exploring innovative models for long-term and stable social funding for basic scientific research. Tencent aims to invest RMB 10 billion over ten years and provide steady support to between 200 and 300 outstanding scientists. Established in 2018, the Xplorer Prize is one of the most highly funded programmes for young scientific and technological talents in China.[12] It grants a merit-based, no-strings-attached award to outstanding scientists under forty-five years of age who hold full-time positions on the Chinese mainland, Hong Kong, or Macau. It is the most generous talent-funding programme for young scientists in China. Since 2018, the company has enabled approximately 250 outstanding scientists from universities and research institutes to push scientific boundaries in chemistry and new materials, astronomy, geoscience, life sciences, and more.

In terms of AI, Tencent states that it invests in all of its products and new endeavours in a strategy the company calls 'ubiquitous AI'.[13] Tencent comprehensively laid out important branches, such as machine learning, natural language processing, speech recognition, and computer vision. Regarding cloud technology, the company has accumulated leading technology and corresponding patents in security capabilities, big data processing, storage, networks, databases, and more.

2.3.2 Internal and External Collaboration for High-Quality Innovation

As early as 2006, Tencent began to promote the agile evolution of the R&D model, forming an enterprise-level agile R&D system that included the agile R&D collaboration platform TAPD, the code management platform TGitee (similar to GitHub), the intelligent continuous integration platform Tencent CI, and other R&D efficiency tools. Tencent's internal data shows that in 2022 the company completed an average of 8,050 requirements per day with an average iteration plan duration of fifteen days and an average of twenty-five requirements per iteration. Among these, 35 per cent of the requirements could be released and launched within a single day and 70 per cent of bugs could be resolved within two days.

[12] The official website of the Xplorer Prize: https://xplorerprize.org/#/index
[13] Tencent, *2017 Annual Report. Smart Communication Inspires.*

Driven by an open-source collaborative strategy, Tencent continues to promote the dissemination of more basic or key technologies to the outside world, and closely participates in the construction of the open-source community. The open-source rate of Tencent's internal code repository has remained above 80 per cent for four consecutive years. The total number of code contributors has reached 5,814, while the total number of departments participating in collaborative construction has reached 332.

Tencent summarises its patent management experience as 'IPO' linkage, wherein the letter I refers to innovation, P to patent, and O to operations and application. The company believes that it is only through an organic linkage between these three elements that Tencent can continuously produce high-value patents and applications that reflect the value of these patents, thus supporting the CBS strategy. The vice director of Tencent, Bo Jiang, points out:

Tencent has established a strict patent review mechanism and formulated full-process systems and guidelines to ensure that every patent is moving in the direction of high value and high quality. It is also actively exploring the use and operation of patents, using ordinary licences, free Open licencing, cross-licencing and other means to leverage the value of patents, improve user experience, solve industry pain points, and fulfil social responsibilities.[14]

As a private enterprise promoting technological innovation through industry–university–institution collaboration, Tencent established a laboratory matrix based on AI and cutting-edge technology for the next generation of the internet, covering fields such as cybersecurity, autonomous driving, robotics, and advanced medical care. It created joint laboratories with China's top universities, which include Tsinghua University and Peking University, among others, to integrate superior resources and explore pioneering achievements in cutting-edge fields.

In January 2018, Tencent and Google together announced they had signed a patent cross-licencing agreement for multiple products and technologies. Tencent remains the only Chinese company to have attained a patent licence agreement with Google; the milestone was also the largest patent cross-licencing agreement reached in the global internet industry to date.

[14] The keynote speech of Bo Jiang at the Twelfth China Intellectual Property Annual Conference: https://baijiahao.baidu.com/s?id=1777647798120204947&wfr=spider&for=pc

In 2022, Tencent and other companies jointly took the lead in establishing the Global Carbon Neutral Open Technology Alliance. Various companies contributed 221 carbon-neutral technology-related patents that were disclosed to the public in the form of free and open licences. This number continues to grow.

2.3.3 Technological Innovations and Achievements

Many studies measure innovation or technological progress using patent applications as they represent the actual creation and dissemination of knowledge in productive activities. Patents are the currency of business innovation. Some companies submit hundreds or even thousands of patent applications annually – not only to safeguard their innovations but also to generate significant revenue through licensing and related strategies. In this section, we mainly focus on Tencent's achievements in terms of patents.

The application and authorisation of patents captures a brief history of Tencent's engagement with technology. Tencent first applied for a patent in the spring of 2001, only three years after the company's founding. The first patent application was for a utility titled a 'single-window multipage browsing device' (CN2559055Y) created by Pony Ma.[15] The patent directly promoted a change in how browsers were used as multiple pages could be opened within a single window. Over twenty-two years later, we continue to enjoy the convenience extended by this patent.

During the company's early years, it obtained only a few dozen official patents. But after WeChat was released in 2011, the number of official patents applied by Tencent began to rise significantly. Once the company announced its deep dive into the industrial internet in 2018, the increase grew even greater. Over the next three years, the annual growth rate of Tencent's patents exceeded 45 per cent.

So far, Tencent has expanded its global IP portfolio to cover more than 100 countries and regions, showing a strong global expansion ambition and its IP protection strategy. By 6 March 2023, the

---

[15] The utility model enables the simultaneous browsing of multiple webpages in a single window of an internet browser; users can browse different pages by simply clicking on a page tab in the window.

company had acquired over 40,000 officially registered trademarks.[16] According to the 2022 annual report released by China's State Intellectual Property Office, Tencent ranked second in China with 4,076 invention patents granted; it was also the only internet company with over 4,000 granted patents, as shown in Figure 2.12. When a patent is granted, it gives the applicant 'an exclusive right to a product or a process that generally provides a new way of doing something, or offers a new technical solution to a problem', according to the WIPO. According to the latest official data, Tencent has made a total of over 75,000 patent applications in major countries and regions around the world. By December 2023, the number of patents granted to Tencent exceeded 37,000, ranking the company second among global internet companies in terms of patent applications and authorisation. In terms of the distribution of Tencent patents in invention, design, and utilities, statistics show that most of Tencent's applications are invention patents that lay the technical foundation for many of Tencent's products.

By a rough estimate, the number of invention patents granted to Tencent over the past three years was over thirteen per day. Among all patent applications, it is worth mentioning that roughly 22,000

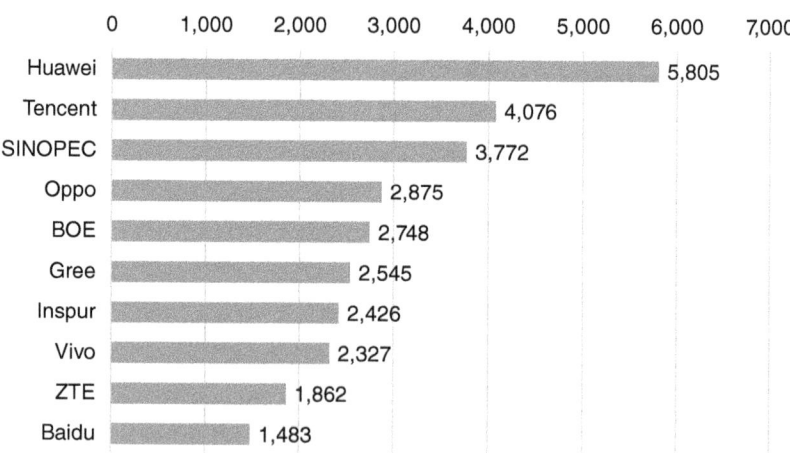

Figure 2.12 Top ten companies for number of granted inventions in China, 2022.

---

[16] From the Tencent's official website media article: 'Tencent Offers Enhanced Tools to Prevent Infringement and Strengthen Enforcement of IP Rights on Weixin', www.tencent.com/en-us/articles/2201537.html

patents involved female applicants; this accounted for over 35 per cent of the total number of patent applications. Tencent advocates for an equal and diverse innovation environment and encourages knowledge sharing. The company focuses on conducting R&D and improving the user experience, regardless of the gender of the developer.

Internal statistics from February 2021 also reveal the number of patents granted to internet companies in China as well as in the US Patent Office. Tencent ranks number two (second only to Google) in the number of patent applications (inventions, utility, and design) held by global internet companies in major countries and regions in the world. Tencent is far ahead of other peer competitors including Alibaba, Baidu, Qihoo 360, and JD.com in the domestic internet sector and in the number of inventions granted both in China and the US, showing a strong innovation capability and technological leadership in this sector.

Tencent's patents are distributed across fields that include cloud computing, social networking sites, AI, games, financial payments, security, social media, and internet browsers. In the area of network security, Tencent has applied for over 4,000 patents and secured over 1,000.[17] These patents support the company's products – from games, payments, and video conferencing, to social media software, QR codes, and so on.

The State Intellectual Property Office also disclosed statistics on applications for blockchain patents in December 2022. Unsurprisingly, Tencent was ranked first overall. The company had applied for patents in the areas of supply chain finance, fund settlement, electronic bills, and anti-counterfeit tracing, as well as the charity, medical and health fields, judicial deposits, and a variety of others. According to third-party data statistics, Tencent has ranked first in the industry over the past ten years in terms of the number of Chinese patents granted to inventions from technical fields such as cloud computing and big data services, AI software development, and internet security services.

So far, Tencent holds three patents that have won the WIPO-SIPO award for Chinese Outstanding Patented Invention and the China Patent Gold award from China's State Intellectual Property Office; one industrial design won the WIPO-SIPO award for Chinese Outstanding Industrial Design. In 2021, Tencent's Application Processing Method

---

[17] Internal document from February 2021.

and Device (ZL201610908829.0) won silver at the twenty-second China Patent Awards Review Results. This particular patent corresponded to a familiar name: the mini-program. The patent titled 'A Data Transmission Method, System and Related Equipment' won the twenty-second China Patent Gold Award in 2020; the patent was for one of the technologies behind Tencent Meeting (comparable to Zoom). In 2022, five Tencent technologies were awarded the highest honour (the Leading Scientific and Technological Achievement award) at the China International Big Data Industry Expo.

To illustrate, QQ is one of the most popular Tencent products. The birth of the earliest version of QQ was based on a patent granted for 'a system and method for instant messaging' (一种即时通信的系统和方法) (Tencent QQ, 2019). As subsequent patents were granted one by one, QQ's functions became increasingly powerful. Today, Tencent has applied for more than 3,000 patents worldwide for QQ. Over 1,500 patents, such as for large file transmissions within a QQ chatgroup, have been officially granted. In another example, there are over 2,000 patents for the many supporting technologies behind Tencent's most popular product, WeChat.[18] While developing the technological basis behind a patent is important, Tencent has valued the process of transforming innovations in technology to better serve society.

Although Tencent has a large number of pending patent applications, the company applies for most patents within China. This raises the question: are Tencent's patents both novel and effective at an international level? To answer this question, we dug deeper by collecting data supplied by the PCT, an international treaty with over 155 signatory states that enables companies to seek patent protection for an invention simultaneously across a large number of countries by filing an international patent application. Many professions thus use PCT data to evaluate the capacity for innovation within a country or company.

The WIPO releases the PCT annual review every year. As Figure 2.13 illustrates, Tencent entered the WIPO list for the first time when it applied for thirteen PCT patents in 2006, ranking 1,192nd among the applicants, tied with ninety other applicants. Fifteen years later, in 2020, the company ranked forty-second in the world with 470 PCT patents. Between 2017 and 2022, the annual number of Tencent's published PCT patents remained both high and stable.

---

[18] Interviews with a Tencent employee.

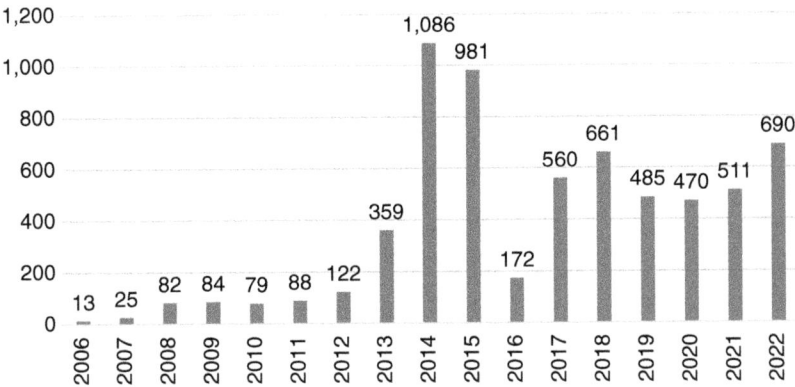

Figure 2.13 Number of published PCT applications from Tencent, 2006–2022.

Figure 2.14 shows the number of PCT patents of Google, Meta, Apple, Amazon, Alibaba, Baidu, and Tencent according to the WIPO Statistics Database. Tencent's number of applications for PCT patents can be compared to that of other domestic and foreign companies, and this number grew quickly after 2013, surpassing Google and Apple in 2014, and playing a leading role in the Chinese market. According to 2022 WIPO data, Tencent ranked eighth in the world with 2,127 PCT international patent applications for that year alone.

According to a survey we conducted at Tencent in 2021, over half (55.2 per cent) of the respondents replied 'yes' to the following question: 'Over the past three years, I have developed a completely new product/service or significantly improved an existing product/service.' Additionally, roughly half (50.5 per cent) of the respondents reported they had either developed new or significantly improved existing algorithms, processes, or management solutions over the past three years. In total, 63 per cent of respondents reported having achieved at least one of these two types of innovations, indicating a high level of innovation among Tencent employees.

The growth of Tencent's number of patents does not merely reflect the technological competencies of a private enterprise. Rather, it is a story of a company that adapts to the times, advances its vision and technical capabilities across the broader world, and expands benefits to encompass more people in more fields. This in turn stimulates its own innovation potential and delivers greater value.

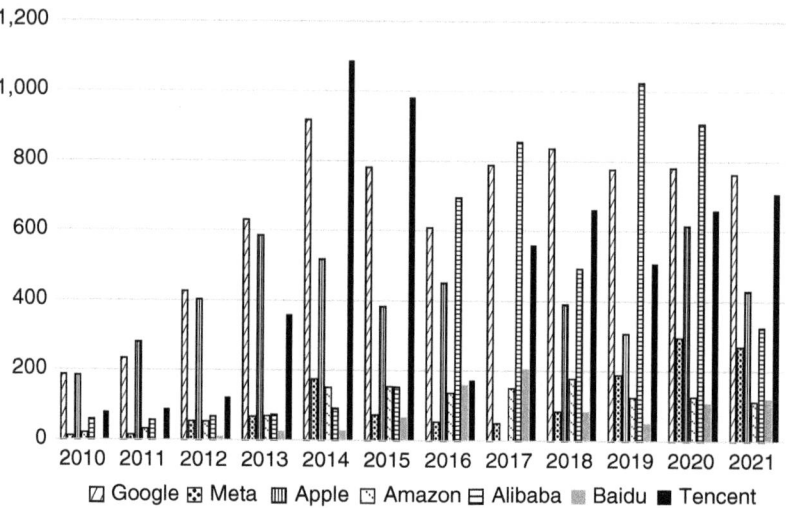

Figure 2.14 Number of PCT applications: Tencent versus other leading internet companies, 2010–2020.

2.3.4 *Not Always a Smooth Ride: Setbacks in Tencent's Journey*

Although we have seen that many of Tencent's products in the social and gaming fields have been very successful, Tencent has also experienced failures with many new product attempts and in competition with competitors, such as in the video live streaming, media, e-commerce, and social fields.

In 2009, Sina launched a Twitter-like product called Sina Weibo, which began the era of Weibo in China. Weibo is regarded as an important breakthrough in the transformation of mobile social networking. Traditional portals and social platforms such as Sohu Weibo and NetEase Weibo have followed suit. In order to cope with the competitive threat of Sina Weibo, Tencent launched a product, Tencent Weibo, to enter the Weibo track. At that time, Tencent QQ had accumulated a large number of active users. In the early stage, the number of users of Tencent Weibo increased rapidly through QQ diversion. The interface imitated Twitter and added functions such as 'broadcast' and 'comment' to encourage users to interact. At the same time, a large number of celebrities and media organisations were signed to create a content atmosphere. At one time, the number of registered users exceeded 300 million, surpassing Sina Weibo. However, starting around 2012, the user growth rate began to slow down. Although Tencent Weibo had a huge user base, the number of daily active users and content dissemination influence had always lagged behind Sina Weibo. In particular, some hot events and public topics fermented rapidly on Sina Weibo, setting off a wave of public opinion, while Tencent Weibo did not gain an advantage in this regard. Most users were zombie accounts which did not form a stable reading and interaction habit. In particular, social relationships on QQ were not suitable for users to express their ideas publicly, while Weibo was more inclined to information dissemination and public expression. In addition, Tencent was developing multiple Weibo-related projects at the same time, and early 'Weibo' and 'Taotao' were parallel, resulting in resource dispersion. At the same time, the research and development of WeChat was also being carried out. Internal resources were squeezed somewhat, and the company's strategic support was insufficient. After WeChat went online in 2011, it quickly became popular, and the company's resource focus further tilted towards WeChat. After 2014, Tencent Weibo stopped updating, and it was officially shut down in September 2020 after many years of operation. Subsequently, Tencent intervened in content platforms through capital rather than building Weibo itself, investing in such platforms as Zhihu, Kuaishou, and Bilibili.

The rise of WeChat led Tencent to understand that real social communication should be private, high-frequency, and based on acquaintance relationships, which is different from the 'semi-open public space' path of Weibo. These failed experiences also made Tencent pay more attention to quality at the strategic level, prompting Tencent to further clarify its own positioning, return to the essence of connection, avoid blindly copying competitors, and lay the organisational and strategic foundation for the subsequent success of WeChat.

Another product, Tencent Paipai.com, was launched in September 2005, when C2C e-commerce was rising rapidly in China. Taobao was established in 2003 and expanded rapidly. As Tencent's first official e-commerce platform, Paipai.com was positioned as a C2C transaction market, benchmarking Taobao.com. Tencent held QQ, a powerful social traffic portal, and hoped to use this advantage to enter the e-commerce field and create a new 'social + e-commerce' model. The website integrated the QQ account system, which made it easy for users to log in, and tried to use QQ chat as a communication tool for buyers and sellers. At the beginning, it provided incentive mechanisms such as free store openings, which quickly accumulated a large number of small and medium-sized sellers. However, in terms of core payment, logistics, and platform operation capabilities, it could not compete with Taobao. In 2010, Tencent established an 'e-commerce holding company' to integrate Paipai.com, QQ online shopping, and other businesses, intending to improve professional operation capabilities through corporate operations. Tencent's core advantages at the time were social and content, and it lacked experience in e-commerce operations and supply chain management. E-commerce platforms require strong product management, credit evaluation systems, and logistics guarantees, which Tencent is not good at. In addition, in terms of product experience, although Paipai. com integrates QQ accounts, the shopping process is complicated, and the page design and user experience are not as mature as Taobao. It lacks a perfect guarantee mechanism like Taobao's Alipay system, and user trust is low. In addition, there are many fake and low-quality products on the platform, and there is a lack of effective governance mechanism, which affects user stickiness. At the same time, the disadvantage of attracting users also stemmed from Tencent's failure to open up a closed-loop system from traffic to transactions to payment to services. Taobao had already formed a 'search-product-payment-evaluation' chain, while Paipai was frequently interrupted.

After realising that it was difficult to compete with its own platform, Tencent made a strategic shift. In March 2014, Tencent announced that it would package Paipai.com and QQ Online Shopping into JD.com, and at the same time, it invested in JD.com and became one of its most important shareholders. After JD.com took over Paipai, it tried to reshape Paipai into a second-hand trading platform, but the response was still mediocre. In 2016, Paipai.com was officially closed. Since then, Tencent no longer emphasises self-built platforms in the e-commerce field, but focuses on investing in and empowering leading companies (such as JD.com, Meituan, and Pinduoduo). Focusing on social and content ecology, the company handed over the monetisation of traffic capabilities to its partners, forming a platform-based role of 'connection + empowerment'. This has prompted Tencent to shift from an 'all-round enterprise' to an 'empowerment platform', and ultimately established the strategic idea of 'connecting everything'.

2.4 Diversification and Expansion: Tencent's Investment Strategies

Within the industry, Tencent is often referred to as a half-investment company. Over the past decade, Tencent has made numerous investments to expand its business landscape. Zhaohui Li, partner of Tencent Investment Management and vice president of Tencent Group, once said: 'Behind Tencent's substantial operating profits, most of the money has been transformed into the wings of investment, soaring high in search of more growth opportunities. This is how Tencent continues to explore and reach new heights.'

In 2011, Tencent established the Tencent Industry Fund at an initial scale of RMB 5 billion, marking its first professional investment and Mergers and Acquisitions (M&A) Department, as well as showcasing its openness and ability to cooperate. The inaugural Tencent Partner Conference was held in June 2011 and underscored strategic investment as a key component of Tencent's growth. According to ITJuzi, Tencent's investments have generally increased since 2011.[19] Figure 2.15 shows the number and volume of Tencent's investments between 2013 and 2022. Despite a significant decline in 2019 owing to the 9/30 Reform of 2018, which led to more cautious investment decisions, Tencent made a record 300 investment deals in 2021 to average one project every 1.2 days.

Tencent's strategic investments primarily follow the corporate venture capital (CVC) model, focusing on early-stage enterprises to support long-term growth. The company was China's most active CVC investor in the eight years after 2014, employing an 'open' strategy through investments and acquisitions. By November 2021, Tencent's portfolio included fifty-eight unicorn companies, and the company had made notable investments in JD.com, Dianping, Pinduoduo, Didi, Kuaishou, Zhihu, and Xiaohongshu. Tencent's investment team is known for sharp insights that have led to significant success and contributed greatly to the company's performance. In 2022, Tencent's other net income reached RMB 124.29 billion, up from approximately RMB 3.6 billion in 2016.

---

[19] Summarized by authors based on the leading data service provider of venture capital in China (ITJuzi): www.itjuzi.com/company_map/tencent

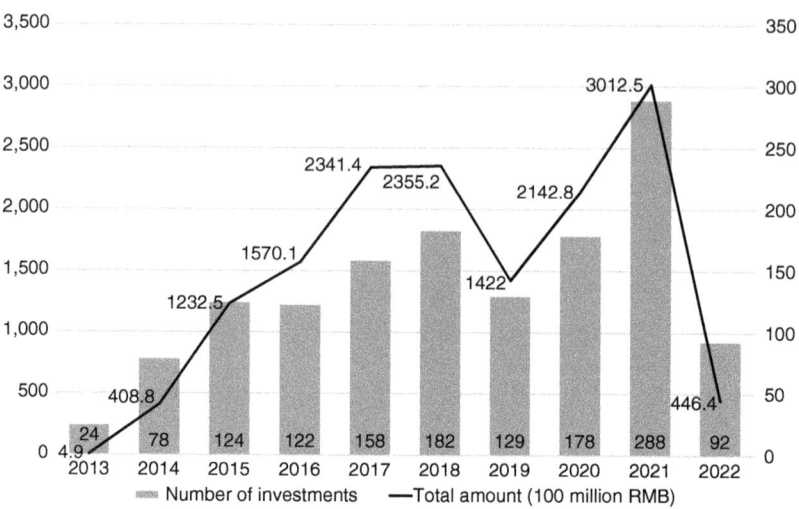

Figure 2.15 Number and volume of Tencent investments, 2013–2022.

While sustaining active investments over the long term, Tencent also maintains a low-profile and highly inclusive attitude externally. Since 2014, Pony Ma has repeatedly stated publicly that Tencent is willing to 'give half of its life to its partners',[20] preserving the decision-making power of the invested companies. For many of Tencent's target enterprises, the company's equity share is often less than 20 per cent. Tencent supports these companies unilaterally at the beginning, then aims to achieve mutual success through subsequent development. In 2018, Pony Ma published an article explaining Tencent's investment logic as a response to an online article which argued that Tencent does not have dreams and that it gradually became an investment company: 'Starting from Tencent's core advantages, we realised from the beginning with QQ that the core advantage of social products is traffic. In addition to developing multiple business lines ourselves to make good use of this traffic, we also invest in other teams that are more appropriate to handle non-core and non-specialised projects. This approach maximises resource utilisation and efficiency.'[21]

[20] Pony Ma's speech in China IT Summit 2015: www.tisi.org/3702/
[21] Pony Ma's response to an online article: www.thepaper.cn/ newsDetail_forward_2114128

Namely, Tencent helps other companies achieve growth rather than exerting direct control. This logic distinguishes Tencent from the rest of the industry.

Of course, such logic is also inseparable from Tencent's judgement of national policies and market trends. Since its strategic adjustment in 2012, Tencent has emphasised an open ecosystem in response to relevant state departments. The upgrade from PC to mobile internet was a response to a market trend at that time. Affected by the government's anti-monopoly legislation, especially restrictions on the disorderly expansion of capital, Tencent's investment speed has slowed down in the past two years as it has begun to cut some investment companies to optimise its asset portfolio.

Tencent's gaming business has long been its primary revenue source, and the company has maintained strong investments in this sector for over a decade. It has built significant competitive advantages in gaming, social software, and media and entertainment while continuously exploring emerging industries and making overseas investments. Tencent now invests in twenty-three sectors that include logistics, finance, healthcare, and real estate. Initially focused on software and media, the company's investments since 2019 have increasingly targeted advanced manufacturing, finance, and e-commerce. In 2023, Tencent invested significantly in AI. This strategy of diversified investment undoubtedly positions Tencent to capitalise on various new opportunities emerging in a rapidly changing business environment.

2.5 Facing Difficult Times

Since its founding in 1998, Tencent has grown into an internet giant and an 'everything online' company. It has not only witnessed the rise of the Chinese internet but also weathered countless storms. Along its path of development were several particularly noteworthy moments. It was through overcoming challenges and continually reinventing itself that Tencent became what it is today, acquiring the capability for sustained corporate growth.

2.5.1 Survival and Transformation

There were several moments in Tencent's history when the company's survival seemed uncertain. From the late twentieth to early twenty-first centuries, the global internet industry experienced a harsh winter that led many internet companies to collapse as a result of broken capital chains. During this period, China's internet industry was heavily impacted. As a start-up at the time, Tencent mainly relied on its QQ software to stay afloat and had not yet found a stable revenue model. With the burst of the internet or dot-com bubble, the entire industry plunged into a slump and the crash severely affected Tencent's financing and business development. Facing a severe cash shortage, Pony Ma and the other founders even considered selling QQ; however, they couldn't find a buyer after price negotiations failed (Wu, 2016). During this period, the company was on the brink of collapse. However, by actively seeking financing, securing investment from South Africa's MIH Group, and implementing internal cost controls, the company managed to overcome industry pressures and survive.

In 2002, in an effort to maintain operations and achieve profitability, Tencent attempted to implement a paid registration system for QQ. The decision triggered strong backlash from users, causing a significant loss of the user base. This crisis dealt a severe blow to Tencent's foundation, forcing the company to reconsider its business model. Afterwards, Tencent focused on continually optimising QQ and developing a series of relevant new products and business models, such as QQ Show, Qzone, and Q Coin. These innovations enhanced the user experience to solidify Tencent's market position once again.

Throughout its development, Tencent employed multiple adjustments to its business direction and strategic positioning. Starting from its initial instant messaging tool, QQ, to later ventures in the form of WeChat, gaming, payments, and cloud services, each transformation involved tests of the company's internal structure as well as external market challenges. Throughout, Tencent continuously sought new growth points and innovation in business models. Around 2010, during the shift to mobile internet, traditional PC internet businesses were significantly impacted. As a giant of the PC internet era, Tencent faced the daunting task of transitioning to the mobile internet. At the time, QQ remained Tencent's primary product, but the market had seen the emergence of a number of competitive instant messaging products for mobile users, such as Sina Weibo and Xiaomi MiTalk. Tencent encouraged innovation through an internal horse-racing mechanism (known as internal competition which allows several different teams to conduct parallel product development) that led to the successful launch of influential mobile internet products such as WeChat. That success enabled the company to cope with fierce market competition. At the same time, Tencent strengthened its collaborations with partners to jointly promote the development of the mobile internet ecosystem. These measures helped Tencent maintain its leading industry position within the mobile internet era.

2.5.2 *Conflict with Qihoo 360*

With the rapid advancement of the internet, Tencent achieved remarkable success in various domains that included social networks and gaming. In 2010, however, the company faced a significant challenge when it engaged in a fierce conflict with the cybersecurity company Qihoo 360 over market competition strategies and user privacy protection. Known in the industry as the so-called 3Q War, this incident became a defining moment in Tencent's history.

The conflict began when 360 introduced a software called QQ Guard, claiming it could protect users from alleged privacy invasions by QQ and accusing Tencent of monopolistic practices. This bold move directly threatened Tencent's core business. In retaliation, Tencent issued an ultimatum demanding that users choose between QQ and 360. The situation quickly escalated from product rivalry to a dramatic showdown that culminated in legal battles. Dubbed the first case of unfair competition on the internet, this dispute not only tested Tencent's crisis management skills but also forced the entire internet industry to rethink the dynamics between competition and cooperation.

Ultimately, the conflict was resolved with government intervention and resulted in a legitimate victory for Tencent. However, the 3Q War had a lasting impact on Tencent's reputation and business operations, and the incident marked a critical turning point for the company. In the aftermath, Tencent intensified its communication and public relations with the aim of rebuilding user trust. The company also began to place greater emphasis on the user experience and compliance, which contributed to healthier development of the entire internet industry. The episode underscored the importance of balancing competitive strategies with ethical practices, paving the way for Tencent's continued evolution and success.

2.5.3 Core Business Pressure

For a long time, Tencent's gaming division was a major contributor to the company's revenue and profits, underscoring its immense significance to the overall business. As a leading company in the global gaming industry, Tencent Games boasts hundreds of millions of active users worldwide. Tencent has successfully created phenomenal games such as *Honor of Kings* and *Game for Peace* (known internationally as *PUBG Mobile*), achieving massive success both domestically and internationally; the company has built a huge global ecosystem through independent research and development and global layout.

Self-developed products such as *Honor of Kings* and *Game for Peace* have long been at the top of global mobile game revenue lists, and in 2022, they won the global game company revenue championship with US$32.2 billion in game revenue. By investing in top international studios such as Riot Games and Supercell, Tencent has established a product matrix spanning multiple categories such as MOBA, shooting, and open world, and has formed a unique user stickiness based on the WeChat/QQ social ecosystem, ranking first in global game revenue for many years. China surpassed the US to become the world's largest game market in 2016, and many American, Japanese, and Korean publishers distribute their games in China through Tencent's platform. This segment not only brought substantial revenue to the company but also fostered comprehensive development in technology, content creation, user base expansion, and global strategic planning.

However, in recent years, with the continuous improvement of the industry regulatory system, China's supervision of online games has become increasingly strict. Tencent faces challenges brought by multiple policy regulations, such as restricting the gaming time of minors, tightening content reviews, and controlling game licensing, which have also had a negative impact on the growth of Tencent's gaming business. First, China's minor protection policies have imposed stringent requirements on real-name authentication and playtime restrictions – most notably, the 2021 regulation limiting minors to no more than three hours of gameplay per week. This directly impacted user engagement across the industry. Secondly, the tightening of game license approvals significantly lengthened the launch cycle for new titles, with the number of domestic game licenses issued in 2022 falling by 46 per cent year on year. Thirdly, heightened content review standards have required game developers to align worldviews, character designs, and narrative themes more closely with mainstream social values. Fourthly, strengthened anti-trust regulations have urged platform operators like Tencent to open up their ecosystems, mandating adjustments to long-standing practices such as exclusive publishing rights and preferential traffic distribution.

In the face of these mounting pressures, Tencent responded with robust compliance governance and a multifaceted strategic approach. As early as 2017, Tencent Games pioneered a 'pre-event, mid-event, post-event' framework for minor protection. Now entering its eighth year, the company's anti-addiction system has continuously evolved, incorporating tools such as real-name verification, facial recognition, gameplay and spending limits, referred to as the 'anti-addiction quartet'. On the technical front, Tencent was among the first companies to integrate with the national ID verification system, develop a parental control platform, and launch initiatives like the 'Healthy Gaming System' and real-time content compliance monitoring powered by AI and facial recognition technologies. By 2024, the proportion of total playtime spent by minors on Tencent's domestic titles had fallen to just 0.2 per cent – the lowest on record. In February 2025, Tencent once again led the industry by upgrading its minor protection system, launching a new model that combines technology, services, and public welfare to support the healthy development of young players.

At the product level, Tencent promotes the inclusion of traditional cultural elements in its flagship products such as *Game for Peace*, develops functional games, and explores social value scenarios such as education and medical care. On the ecosystem level, the company has accelerated its global expansion – by 2023, overseas revenues accounted for 33 per cent of its gaming income, with global products like *Tower of Fantasy* launched under the Level Infinite brand. Strategically, Tencent has taken a proactive role in shaping industry standards, collaborating with universities to research the positive social value of games, and investing early in frontier technologies such as cloud gaming and virtual reality to build a policy-friendly innovation ecosystem. Through a dual strategy of regulatory compliance and technological innovation, Tencent is actively enhancing its resilience to policy risks and pioneering a new paradigm for the sustainable development of the gaming industry.

As more gaming companies and independent developers enter the market, Tencent also faces stiff competition from companies such as NetEase, miHoYo, and ByteDance, particularly in popular game genres and emerging markets. Amid the backdrop of a shrinking gaming business, Tencent is under significant pressure to innovate and transform its operations.

At the annual meeting in 2024, Pony Ma emphasised the need for Tencent Games to innovate more and focus on user experience instead of relying heavily on a few established games that had once generated substantial revenue for the company. The founder cautioned against excessive commercialisation that could lead to player attrition, especially in blockbuster games and the anime-style game sector. With technological advancements such as cloud gaming, AR/VR, and the evolving preferences of players, Tencent faces heightened demands for technical upgrades and innovative content. Consequently, the company is again pursuing a diversification strategy that involves expansion into social networking, online advertising, fintech, and enterprise services to find new avenues for growth. The company has also increased investment in R&D of new technologies and models, driving industry upgrades and innovation.

This journey is fraught with numerous uncertainties and risks, such as the market acceptance of new ventures and technological challenges. But despite these hurdles, Tencent appears to be leveraging its keen market insights and robust capabilities for execution to overcome obstacles. For instance, Tencent is attempting to integrate its gaming business with other sectors such as eSports and live streaming to create a more comprehensive gaming ecosystem. While these initiatives are promising, it remains to be seen whether they will yield substantial results. Tencent is well aware that it must continue to increase its innovation efforts and focus on the quality of its gaming products and player experience in order to maintain its leading position in the gaming market.

2.5.4 Challenges with the Digital Era and Globalisation

2.5.4.1 Business Development and Data Privacy

With the rapid development of the internet and digital technology, all aspects of human life are inseparable from the internet, and a large amount of user data has become a core element of corporate productivity. However, affected by data leaks and cyber hackers, harassing calls for selling cars, houses, and insurance, telecommunications and financial fraud text messages, and various advertising bombardments have continued, causing users to suffer losses while enjoying the convenience brought by mobile internet products. Apple and Facebook have both been involved in information leaks due to insufficient supervision of personal information. How to protect user information and gain user trust has become an important factor in corporate competition. Many platform companies have also begun to upgrade measures and attach importance to the protection of user data. In June 2021, China promulgated the 'Data Security Law', which defined the responsibilities of corporate data security and then, in August, issued the 'Personal Information Protection Law', which defined the responsibilities of companies in protecting users' personal information, privacy, and sensitive data.

Internationally, in order to protect the security of personal information, the European Union officially implemented the 'General Data Protection Regulation' (GDPR) on 25 May 2018. The law raised requirements for companies to supervise user personal information and prevent companies from illegally misappropriating and selling personal information. Faced with heavy fines for failing to comply, this posed a challenge to the international development of many internet companies in Europe. According to the GDPR Preparedness Pulse Survey released by PwC US in 2017, 77 per cent of companies planned to allocate $1 million or more on GDPR readiness and compliance efforts – with 68 per cent saying they would invest between $1 million and $10 million, and 9 per cent expecting to spend over $10 million to address GDPR obligations. There is no doubt that privacy protection compliance will also bring huge additional costs to multinational companies such as Tencent.

Judging from the user inquiries received by Tencent's privacy consultation mailbox in 2018, personal information management, account management, and product security are the three major issues that concern users. User information security and privacy protection issues have become the focus of Tencent and the entire industry. Whether it is games, social media, or financial services, Tencent collects vast amounts of user data. According to Tencent's latest annual report, in 2024 the combined monthly active accounts of WeChat users is 1.385 billion, and the monthly active accounts of QQ mobile terminals is 524 million.

According to online sources, Tencent has experienced a user data theft incident in the past. In 2011, due to system vulnerability, the QQ group database was leaked. After Tencent discovered the problem, it promptly repaired it and the leak did not affect the normal use of existing users.[22] After that, no incidents of data leaks in Tencent have been reported to our knowledge. On the eve of the GDPR taking effect in 2018, Tencent QQ International's privacy policy was urgently updated. According to one of the GDPR clauses, 'When users request data deletion, the company needs to find the data in the database and delete it.' QQ International's privacy policy has also made it clear that if a user has been inactive for a long time or requests deletion, QQ International will also delete the user data in advance. Tencent Cloud also began to evaluate GDPR one year in advance to ensure that the company takes rigorous response measures and does not affect its own business.

On 27 December 2018, Tencent released the 'Tencent Privacy Protection White Paper' for the first time, which comprehensively and systematically expounded on Tencent's privacy protection concepts and principles and demonstrated to users the privacy protection functions of products such as WeChat, QQ, QZone, *Honor of Kings*, and Tencent Mobile Manager. In terms of privacy protection, Tencent adheres to the concept of 'technology for good, data with moderation', giving priority to personal information and data security and insisting on limited data collection, warm data services, attitude in data use, legal data management, and strong data protection. Wang Xiaoxia, general manager of Tencent Big Data Legal Compliance, said, 'Tencent has established a cross-departmental, cross-business, and cross-system data and privacy protection team. We hope to fully protect users' right to know and realise users' control over personal information through scientific and standardised security management processes and a sound security technology system, and create a safe and reliable online environment for users.'

Based on past experience, Tencent has built a privacy protection framework called PBD. P stands for Person, which focuses on protecting user privacy and improving the transparency of user privacy protection. B stands for Button, hoping to provide users with reasonable and efficient privacy protection through the 'privacy button'

---

[22] Tencent's response to the online report in terms of the data leak of QQ group in 2013: https://tech.huanqiu.com/article/9CaKrnJDg80

in product design, and to achieve user control over personal information by providing convenient information management functions. D stands for Data, which protects user data and privacy security through compliance management of the entire lifecycle of user data. This also includes security technologies such as data desensitisation, data watermarking, and anonymisation processing, as well as terminal security products such as Tencent PC Manager and Mobile Manager, and the Internet Security Laboratory Matrix, to create a safe and reliable online environment for users. Tencent incorporates the concept of privacy protection into all aspects of product development, function design, and operation and provides users with a better experience on the basis of ensuring that user privacy is safe and controllable.

In response to the needs of querying, modifying, and deleting personal information, Tencent has embedded the function of user management of personal information in product design, transforming the user's control over data into buttons that can be operated. In order to let users clearly know about privacy protection issues and maximise the protection of users' rights, Tencent has built a 'privacy protection platform'. Users can enter the platform to view the 'Tencent Privacy Policy' and supporting documents, product privacy protection guidelines, privacy protection FAQs, and other policy documents and make personalised settings according to the product guidelines. In terms of language, Tencent also tries to avoid obscure legal terms and vague expressions and uses concise and easy-to-understand expressions to facilitate user understanding.

Tencent's privacy policy compliance practices have also been recognised by regulators and the industry. In September 2017, the Cyberspace Administration of China and four other ministries jointly conducted a special review of privacy terms. Among the first ten products participating in the review, WeChat received the highest score. In November 2018, the China Consumers Association released the '100 App Personal Information Collection and Privacy Policy Evaluation Report', and Tencent products such as WeChat and QQ received good reviews.

2.5.4.2 Anti-trust Issues and Deglobalisation

With the rapid development of the internet industry, anti-trust issues have become a significant global concern. Starting in the early 2010s, the Chinese government began to intensify its regulatory scrutiny of large technology enterprises. As Tencent's business continued to expand, its prominent market position attracted heightened anti-trust oversight that resulted in unprecedented levels of scrutiny. In recent years, the State Administration for Market Regulation has conducted multiple anti-trust investigations into Tencent and other internet giants, imposing penalties for business concentrations not reported in accordance with the law. These measures not only require companies such as Tencent to strictly adhere to legal regulations in mergers and business expansion but also drive the entire industry to prioritise fair competition and consumer protection.

In 2021, the State Administration for Market Regulation fined Tencent for monopolistic practices related to music copyright acquisitions and mandated the termination of exclusive copyright agreements. The action compelled Tencent to adjust its strategy in the digital music market to align with a more open, competitive environment. In response to such anti-trust regulations, Tencent has actively strengthened its internal management and enhanced its compliance awareness to ensure the company remains on a lawful and compliant path. Through these efforts, Tencent aims to navigate the evolving regulatory landscape and continue its growth within a fair and regulated market.

Although Tencent has successfully shifted its focus to mobile applications, the rise of digital technologies such as 5G, AI, and big data presents new challenges. The emergence of competitors and ever-changing user demands are now at the forefront of Tencent's strategic considerations. For instance, short video applications like Douyin and Kuaishou have spurred new forms of entertainment that include short videos and live streaming, which pose significant challenges to Tencent's traditional media operations. These developments threaten Tencent's advertising business and social ecosystem, compelling the company to accelerate its innovation and continuously seek out new growth opportunities. As a result, Tencent embedded short video channels in its WeChat application in an attempt to capture a share of the market. According to the latest financial report, the first quarter of 2024 saw total user engagement time on the video platform experience a year-on-year increase of over 80 per cent. Such rapid growth also brought Tencent significant new advertising revenue.

In the context of globalisation, Tencent is also striving to expand its influence in overseas markets. Particularly in the gaming sector, Tencent is a dominant force globally. However, the path to internationalisation is fraught with obstacles that include cultural differences, policy restrictions, and localisation challenges. In the American market, recent years have seen Tencent's investments and business activities constrained by national security reviews thanks to ongoing trade frictions and geopolitical tensions between China and the US. These factors not only affect the pace of Tencent's international expansion but also underscore the need for the company to adopt more cautious and flexible strategies in its global endeavours.

2.6 Tencent's AI Ventures and Next-Generation Technologies

In the past several years, AI has experienced rapid growth worldwide and revolutionised various industries by enhancing automation, optimising operations, and enabling new business models. During the same period, Chinese enterprises rapidly increased their patent filings for AI products. The latest data from Statista in 2023 shows that by 2022, Tencent holds the second largest number of active patent families in AI and machine learning at over 13,000 (see Table 2.2). A family is a set of patents covering the same technical content. Competitors include the search engine provider Baidu ahead of the American company IBM, South Korea's Samsung, Chinese insurance provider Ping An Insurance, and former AI patent leader Microsoft. Tencent's number of AI patent families has increased rapidly since 2017.

Tencent's vision is to improve the quality of life for humankind through internet services. The company is now focused on emerging technologies and relentlessly exploring pathways for the technological evolution of various products. Tencent has built several labs, including for AI, quantum computing, and robotics X, along with one audiovisual and seven security laboratories. Tencent's AI has been applied in a range of business areas as well. In the area of content, Tencent AI provides users with more personalised recommendations to create a new service experience. In social media, it creates a more natural, interesting, and entertaining human–computer interaction experience. For gaming, AI is being used to bridge the boundaries between the virtual and real world in order to upgrade the gaming experience. In the meantime, Tencent is developing several AI projects in the healthcare, agriculture, and manufacturing industries, among others.

Table 2.2 *Number of AI and machine learning patents, 2013–2022*

Year	Baidu	Tencent	State Grid Corp	IBM	Samsung	Huawei	Microsoft	Alibaba Group	Ping An Insurance	Chinese Academy of Sciences
2013	147	125	255	1,528	836	205	3,350	90	0	695
2014	270	223	495	1,735	1,035	284	3,524	130	1	977
2015	494	332	861	1,985	1,664	398	3,671	170	1	1,312
2016	681	438	1,255	2,317	2,476	524	3,966	304	11	1,648
2017	1,141	713	1,792	2,900	3313	673	4,374	652	46	2,208
2018	2,176	1,550	2,442	3,806	4,322	924	4,865	1,107	534	2,886
2019	3,633	3,639	3,795	4,865	4,985	1,564	5,347	2,287	2,531	4,120
2020	5,885	6,921	5,667	6,566	5,879	2,512	5,740	3,022	4,207	5,660
2021	9,869	10,218	8,242	8,050	6,862	4,164	6,048	4,060	6,714	7,661
2022	13,993	13,187	11,555	9,497	8,690	6,510	6,356	5,429	9,142	9,909

Tencent Miying is the first AI product to use AI technology in the medical field. In 2017, the Chinese Ministry of Science and Technology released a list of the nation's new-generation open and innovative AI platforms. The list included Baidu, Aliyun, Tencent, and iFLYTEK. Today, many countries around the world are actively developing AI for medical purposes, but there are still many challenges within the process of popularisation. Tencent undertook the establishment of a medical imaging platform based on its AI capabilities. The project was led by the Tencent Internet+ Cooperation Division, which aggregates the capabilities of Tencent's internal AI lab, the Youtu lab, as well as the Architecture Platform Department and other top AI teams. Tencent integrated the strength of cloud computing, big data, user services, and other elements to launch the Miying Digital Intelligence Medical Imaging Platform. The platform enabled the interconnection of medical imaging data with business processes, providing integrated solutions for medical institutions. The product applied leading technologies, such as image recognition, big data analytics, and deep learning. Emerging from interdisciplinary R&D involving medical science, it assists doctors with diagnosis and screening of major diseases as well as in improving the efficiency of clinicians.

At present, the platform has opened up over twenty AI engines to help seventeen universities and research institutes, twenty-three public hospitals, and thirty-three technology companies carry out platform-based scientific research. Through 'cloud + AI', the platform has realised a range of digital imaging applications (e.g. for remote diagnostics, remote consultation, remote teaching, and auxiliary diagnostics) that help doctors complete multi-scene and multi-terminal diagnoses through mobile terminals. The end result accelerates the mutual recognition and sharing of examination results within medical alliances, boosting hierarchical diagnostics and treatment. In November 2023, Tencent won the 2023 World Internet Conference Awards for Pioneering Science and Technology.

In 2022, Bo Jiang, vice president and deputy general counsel of Tencent Group, said that as an internet technology company rooted in China, Tencent has always been anchored at the forefront of science and technology. The company has deepened innovative applications, laid out the next generation of internet technology innovation, maintained industry leadership in patents, and continuously consolidated the 'thickness' of technological innovation. Tencent uses digital technology to assist in the high-quality development of the real economy, promote industrial symbiosis and co-progress, and actively explore the 'depths' of innovation in the development of the digital economy. Finally, the company uses technological goodwill to enhance sustainable development and promote positive values in science and technology.

The launch of ChatGPT by OpenAI allowed the whole world to witness how large language models are increasingly shaping the future of AI by enabling more sophisticated natural language processing and generation capabilities. Following several Chinese technology companies (Baidu, SenseTime), Tencent entered this competitive field with its own AI model, HunYuan. The model has over 100 billion parameters and was trained with over two trillion tokens, demonstrating an advanced understanding and generation of human-like text. The HunYuan model is part of Tencent's broader strategy to integrate AI across various sectors, enhancing applications in customer service, content creation, and more. This move also aligns with the global trend of technology giants investing heavily in AI to stay at the forefront of innovation. According to a 2024 UN report, China has led the patents race for generative AI with 38,210 inventions, far surpassing the US (6,276). Tencent (2,074), Ping An Insurance (1,564), and Baidu (1,234) are among the top ten inventors in generative AI patents. Four Western companies in the race are IBM (601), Samsung Electronics (468), Alphabet (443), and Microsoft (377) (UN, 2024).

2.7 Summary

To date, Tencent has built a complex and open business ecosystem that includes over a dozen lines of business and hundreds of products. The company occupies a leading position in a wide range of fields. Tencent's roots lie in social media, but half of its revenue comes from gaming while its future growth lies in advertising, pan-entertainment, finance, and even investment. For this reason, it is difficult to characterise the company and perhaps inappropriate to classify it as an entity in a specific industry. Rather, it is a massive ecological enterprise akin to a forest – one of the most respected and powerful companies that has profoundly influence Chinese society.

Within the history of its development, there were times when the company found it difficult to survive, owing to a lack of funding or fierce market competition. In the end, however, Tencent persevered to become one of the largest internet companies in the world. This chapter has provided a detailed description of the development of the tech titan Tencent, whose history aptly illustrates the saying: 'Rome wasn't built in a day.' Tencent's current achievements are inseparable from the accumulation of its past successes, including the company's strategic adjustments, massive R&D endeavours, and continuous innovation in technology and products alongside the rapid development of China's internet market. Its success can be attributed to a proactive approach towards anticipating challenges and embracing a forward-thinking mindset.

Tencent has also proven its ability to align with and leverage the prevailing trends of the times. Whether facing technological advancements, shifts in consumer behaviour, or changes in the global business environment, Tencent has consistently demonstrated agility in adapting its strategies to remain at the forefront of industry developments. The company's impressive commercial instincts, proactive risk management, and agility in embracing contemporary trends all underscore its position as a dynamic and forward-looking player in the business world, setting a good example for other latecomer companies.

3 | Competition and Cooperation
Using Organisational Resilience to Foster Innovation

As one of the world's largest companies in the digital sector, Tencent boasts more patents in its portfolio than its most significant Western competitor, Meta, and other Chinese internet companies. Beyond the sheer quantity of patents it has amassed, Tencent has developed numerous groundbreaking products that enjoy widespread market popularity, playing a pivotal role in shaping the company's destiny. This begs the question: why Tencent? How did a company that was once dismissed as a mere copycat rise to such prominence? To answer this question, it is imperative to note Tencent's approach to innovation and notably to a mechanism known as 'coopetition', which combines cooperation and competition. This chapter sheds light on this intriguing and important phenomenon, which has often been overlooked in previous studies of Tencent and underestimated by leaders of other Chinese companies. It is indispensable to the company's innovation process, indisputably yielding remarkable products for the market. It generates excellent ideas and draws out concerted effort from employees. It also facilitates the combination of complementary knowledge between competing teams and across different functional areas. Surprisingly, the coopetition mechanism was not designed and imposed by executives in a top-down approach. Instead, it arose organically owing to the high level of autonomy and tolerance permitted within the company.

This chapter delves into the details of the coopetition mechanism at Tencent, discussing representative examples that demonstrate how it has driven innovation and high performance within the company. We detail the history of the 'horse racing' culture at Tencent, its implementation, and its evolution in the context of wider organisational transformation. We will explore iconic products, including WeChat, QQ Show, *Honor of Kings* (one of the world's most popular mobile games), and Tencent HunYuan, created in the era of large language models. We also touch on some examples of comparable practices within other companies. Finally, we discuss our findings and aim to extract valuable lessons for other companies, inspired by Tencent's example.

3.1 Internal Coopetition at Tencent: A Blueprint for Success

In his biography of Tencent, Wu (2016) mentions the 'horse racing' mechanism as one of Tencent's proprietary weapons. He notes that it has led to the development of many disruptive and innovative products. Derived from ancient practices aimed at selecting superior horses for warfare and transportation (known in Chinese as *Saima*), the term 'horse racing' was coined by external observers to describe Tencent's internal competition model. This strategy was implemented by Tencent approximately two decades ago to catalyse innovation within the company. The 'horse racing' culture has unquestionably played a significant role in Tencent's success, but questions remain about its efficacy and whether competition trumps cooperation within the company. In this section, we examine the nature of Tencent's horse racing culture in detail and investigate its true impact.

3.1.1 Unravelling the Origins: The Birth of Tencent's Horse Racing Culture

The company has leveraged internal competition to drive innovative product development, which inevitably emerges as a central theme in discussions of Tencent's innovation culture. The roots of competition within Tencent can be traced back to 2003, coinciding with the launch of QQ Show and the introduction of a new profitable model for the company. In 2001, three years after Tencent's establishment, its founders made a strategic decision internally to restructure it into three primary business departments: Marketing, Research, and Administration. At that point, QQ was Tencent's flagship product, and the company was exploring various avenues to monetise it further, such as selling special QQ ID numbers to users.

In 2002, China witnessed a significant milestone in its online gaming industry as paying users surpassed four million, with the sector's industrial chain maturing rapidly. Sales channels and agents proliferated and online game recharge cards gained popularity. At the same time, the number of registered users on Tencent's QQ platform exceeded 100 million, reflecting the widespread adoption of online gaming and the allure of QQ's social features to Chinese netizens. Despite this rapid user growth, Tencent still faced the challenge of monetising its platform effectively and generating sufficient profits to sustain daily operations. Consequently, in 2002, it embarked on the development of a virtual currency called QQ coin.

Towards the end of 2002, a product manager at Tencent proposed a novel system that would allow users to purchase virtual decorations for their profiles with QQ coins. These decorations included clothing, accessories, and backgrounds. This branching out led to the creation of QQ Show, which by 2003 had established a profitable model for internet value-added services, opening up new horizons for Tencent. The author Xiaobo Wu (2016) asserts that QQ Show was a revolutionary paid product both in Tencent's history and in the broader context of the Chinese internet. It epitomises what Wu calls 'Eastern application innovation' within the global internet industry.

Tencent subsequently underwent a significant strategic evolution, abandoning the separation between technical development and marketing within its QQ Show team and adopting a project-based product manager system. Two informal rules emerged inside Tencent: 'Whoever proposes, executes' and 'successful products may lead to the formation of independent teams'. This paradigm shift marked the inception of the horse racing mechanism. Within this dynamic environment, product developers enjoyed greater autonomy. Tencent empowered its employees to pursue product development independently and proactively, and they began to initiate original projects spontaneously across various Research and Development (R&D) areas and teams. Units that succeeded in this internal competition were rewarded with more resources and higher priority for development opportunities (Du and Chen, 2018).

In 2012, Pony Ma wrote an open letter to Tencent's partners in which he addressed topics ranging from internet innovation to corporate management. He encapsulated Tencent's internal transformation and the lessons learnt over the past fourteen years in what he termed 'grayscale rules' for establishing an efficient and resilient organisation. These rules encompassed seven dimensions: demand, speed, flexibility, redundancy, openness and collaboration, innovation, and evolution. Ma emphasised the necessity for internal redundancy within the company, advocating for tolerance of failure, acceptance of moderate amounts of waste, and encouraging internal competition alongside trial and error. He noted that success often results from experimentation and emphasised the importance of allowing multiple teams to work on similar products simultaneously if they were related to a project with strategic significance. Even in cases in which products 'fail' in competition, they can serve as sources of inspiration for others. Ma referred to this process as 'internal trials'. He emphasised that not all redundancy within the system equates to waste, because experimentation and failure are integral to innovation and success. Tencent provides an environment that cultivates employees' imagination and inspiration. Many of the company's most popular products are not the result of top-down strategic directives but originate from grassroots work. A director in Tencent's social networking business group once remarked: 'We embody the spirit of a start-up. At Tencent, there are no clear prohibitions on what can't be done.'

Over the past two decades, internal competition has shown itself to be one of the most successful mechanisms within Tencent, yielding a plethora of triumphant products. Examples include QQ Zone, QQ Show, WeChat, *Honor of Kings*, and QQ Game. These products have predominantly emerged from the independent development efforts of business units at the lowest level, a far cry from being the outcome of top-down directives, as one might assume. Each team is free to conceptualise and execute similar products using distinct approaches, before launching them online to compete until the most popular product emerges in the end market. Tencent's top executives then determine resource allocation based on the outcome. This process encourages the generation and selection of novel ideas and rewards the integration of the best ideas, delivering superior products to the market. Bottom-up innovation propels Tencent forward in multiple ways. A strong engineering culture, commitment to multiple iterations, and the relentless pursuit of continuous improvement are all deeply ingrained in the company's DNA.

3.1.2 WeChat: Born in Horse Racing, Achieving Success through Coopetition

Most people know of WeChat for its user-friendly interface and micro-innovation. Over time it has evolved into a super-app with a wide range of functions. An online survey of nearly 2,000 Tencent employees at the end of 2021 showed that WeChat was regarded as the most successful product in the company's history. It is particularly popular with employees largely because it emerged through internal competition, as Pony Ma confirmed on 6 December 2017 at the Guangzhou Fortune China Global Forum.

When WeChat was developed in January 2011, Tencent already held the leading market share in the instant messaging industry with its successful and popular product, Mobile QQ. At the end of 2010, active users of this IM platform had reached 647.6 million, a year-on-year increase of 23.8 per cent. Similar products in the market such as Mobile Fetion (developed by China Mobile) and Mobile MSN Messenger (from Microsoft) occupied only relatively small niches in the market. Before WeChat's launch, there were already a number of voice chat software applications in existence on the mobile internet. Examples included Talkbox, Kik, WhatsApp, and Kakao Talk abroad, and Gexin and Mitalk in China. These had carved up most of the market share between them. Meanwhile, Sina Weibo (now called Weibo) had been launched in August 2009 and was becoming increasingly popular as a smartphone-based product, regarded as the 'Eastern Twitter'. Just one year after its launch, its registered users had exceeded fifty million. A large number of Mobile QQ users were enticed over to Weibo, which became the largest threat to Tencent.

Like Facebook, QQ's development began in the PC era. Tencent's revenue was derived from online advertising and premium QQ users' membership fees. Alongside the continuous growth in the number of QQ users, however, smartphone use began to surge. More and more users began to rely on mobile apps instead of PC software. Pony Ma realised that a big change was coming, namely that mobile internet use would eclipse that of PCs. This challenge demanded an urgent response. When Ma was interviewed at the Fortune China Global Forum in Guangzhou on 6 December 2017, he said that he was deeply aware that the internet world was shifting from PC to mobile. QQ, the most popular IM software, faced this same challenge. Faced with the threat of losing market share to competitors such as Weibo, and in reaction to the incipient dominance of the mobile internet, Tencent executives decided to encourage its IM product teams to create a more attractive product to enter the mobile internet market.

In 2010, Pony authorised two R&D units within Tencent to work on new IM networking apps for mobile phones, just like their competitors, WhatsApp and Kik, thereby beginning the shift to mobile. At the same time, a team leader located outside headquarters spotted the same opportunity and volunteered to develop the product. This was Xiaolong (Allen) Zhang, the current head of WeChat. The three teams developing similar mobile IM products were Mobile QQ team, QQ Mail team, and QQ Address Book team. Each team had a different design philosophy and implementation approach. The Mobile QQ team (based in the Shenzhen headquarters) focused on optimising the design of the existing Mobile QQ to be friendlier to smartphones. The QQ Address Book team (based in Chengdu) was trying to combine the phonebook with IM features. Both teams belonged to the Wireless Internet Business (WIB) division. In contrast, the QQ Mail team, at the Tencent R&D Centre based in Guangzhou, was trying to develop a smartphone-based IM product from scratch.

At that time, the WIB division was in charge of all IM products except for the computer-based QQ. Pony Ma claimed that the WIB department would have an unlimited budget for this project (Yang et al., 2016), but the QQ Mail team received only 100 million RMB to develop WeChat. The teams were competing to outperform each other and get more resources from the company to launch the product successfully. Xiaolong Zhang's team in Guangzhou was responsible for QQ Mail, which emerged as the final winner. Surprisingly, WeChat was not the brainchild of Tencent's core team or mature WIB team, who had an unlimited budget for their products. The team responsible for WeChat did not belong to the QQ Mail department. The products developed by the two teams that were part of the WIB department were very similar to QQ in functionality because they had been developed as improvements on original QQ products.

When executives came up with the idea of developing a smartphone-based IM product, Xiaolong Zhang took the initiative and told Pony Ma that they wanted to develop an IM software product similar to Kik. This was established as a special interest project on 18 November 2010. Zhang led a team of fewer than ten people in a 'little dark room' to develop the product. Most of these team members were recent graduates with barely any experience in the mobile phone industry. Under Zhang's guidance, they worked day and night. The first-generation product was completed for three mobile systems in under seventy days. Zhang claimed that at that point dozens of people were transferred from the QQ Mail department and divided into different development groups, each responsible for functionality, UI, backend system, and so on. Zhang mainly played the role of a product manager.

On 21 January 2011, the first iOS version of WeChat was officially launched, followed by the Android and Symbian versions. When Zhang was asked about WeChat's team and several others doing the same work at the same time, he said: 'This is indeed a bit abrupt and conflicting, but it depends on whether Pony thinks this conflict is acceptable. For a new product, from the company's point of view, it is more important to be able to seize such an opportunity, rather than thinking about how to spend resources.'

In fact, cooperation among otherwise competitive departments led to the success of WeChat. After the first version of WeChat was launched, other teams that were originally developing similar products within Tencent collaborated to improve WeChat instead.

In just one year, WeChat far surpassed almost all its rivals in this field. Pony Ma once commented: 'Because of WeChat, we ended the battle for market with Weibo.' WeChat is by far the fastest-growing online instant messaging system in the history of the internet. By the beginning of November 2011, less than ten months after its launch, the number of WeChat users exceeded thirty million; a month later, this number had reached fifty million, orders of magnitude more than its forerunners and competitors. Competition in the mobile internet industry was incredibly intense at the time. When Tencent launched WeChat, competitors were continuing to enter the market, including Mitalk (developed by Xiaomi), Yixin (co-developed by China Telecom and NetEase), and Feixin (developed by China Mobile in 2007). In 2010, Feixin had over 500 million registered users and over 100 million active users. WeChat developed extremely fast and maintained a high degree of user 'stickiness' or loyalty. WeChat's success is inextricably linked to its superb design concept and rapid iterative innovation, both of which are centred around improving user experience. The explosive growth of user numbers was undoubtedly also related to WeChat's origins in QQ, meaning that new users could conveniently register using their QQ ID. However, today's WeChat may not have been created had Tencent not encouraged internal competition, empowered its subunits, and given them sufficient freedom. Between 2011 and 2013 WeChat gradually became the most impactful social networking tool in China. Nowadays it is completely integrated into the life and work of China's mainstream consumers.

Xiaolong Zhang, now the senior executive vice president and president of Weixin Group, once stated that an internal horse racing mechanism enables the company to stay unified in the face of competition. Pony Ma once posted in his WeChat Moments: 'Mobile QQ has contributed most of QQ's active users, and it still has a strong stamina. QQ and WeChat oppose each other but also complement each other. Both competition and cooperation coexist at the same time, each has its own mission and goals, and it is more stable to walk on two legs.'

WeChat is a popular product that now influences over 1.2 billion people worldwide. It is one of the outstanding examples of products made possible by internal coopetition. Some scholars even regard WeChat as a new-to-the-world innovation (Murmann and Zhu, 2021). As a successful IM product with innovative features, WeChat has been imitated by other popular foreign products such as Facebook and Kik Messenger (Murmann and Zhu, 2021; Livingston, 2014). It pervades all areas of the daily life of Chinese people. 'If you're in China, you kind of live on WeChat, it does everything. It's sort of like Twitter, plus PayPal, plus a whole bunch of other things, and all rolled into one great interface. It's really an excellent app.' This was said by Elon Musk, the CEO of SpaceX, in an interview in May of 2022. Some have suggested that X (formerly Twitter) will be turned into a WeChat-style super-app with payment features under Musk's ownership, given the excellent example it provides (Bleach, 2023).

3.2 Everywhere You Look: The Reach of Internal Competition

WeChat is just one of the many internal competition success stories from Tencent. Many other popular Tencent products were created and refined through the horse racing mechanism. In addition to owning WeChat, Tencent is also the world's largest video game vendor. In 2023, Tencent Games boasted impressive revenues of $26.5 billion and commanded 33.2 per cent of the market share. Tencent has developed and invested in many popular PC and mobile games to date. When it first entered the gaming industry, Tencent would set up a studio with a single game as an independent unit. If that studio succeeded, it would be greatly rewarded. If it failed, it would be dismantled and rebuilt. An internal horse racing mechanism was thereby formed in the Game business group. Given the fierce competition in the gaming market, it was considered easier to produce the right product by allowing multiple teams to compete on the same track. As a result, Tencent established Quantum, Lightspeed (later merged into Guangxi Studio), Mofang, and many other studios, backed by QQ's traffic and cash support.

League of Legends (LOL), a multiplayer online battle arena (MOBA) video game, was developed and published by the American company Riot Games in October 2009. Riot Games had made a deal with Tencent allowing them to handle the game in the United States. It was introduced to the Chinese market in September of 2011 by Tencent Games. At the beginning of that year, the co-founders of Riot Games had sold a majority stake in the company to Tencent. By 2015 it was 100 per cent controlled by Tencent.

LOL was available only on PCs when it was published. At the same time, Quan Min Chao Shen (全民超神) had received many market resources from Tencent Games and was very popular. It was one of the first MOBA mobile games published by Tencent, but its market share started to decrease when *Honor of Kings*, another mobile game developed by Tencent, entered the market. When *Honor of Kings* surpassed Quan Min Chao Shen in market share, Mobile QQ, WeChat, and various other resources began to be diverted towards it. This helped push *Honor of Kings* to further success.

Honor of Kings was independently developed and maintained by Tencent Games TiMi Studio Group to be a MOBA mobile game with well-designed maps, diverse heroes, and captivating gameplay. It works on Android, iOS, and NS platforms. It was officially tested on Android and iOS platforms on 26 November 2015. Arena of Valor, the European and American version, was released on the Nintendo Switch in 2018. Between its release in 2015 and October 2021, the cumulative revenue of *Honor of Kings* exceeded $10 billion. According to Statista, the global revenue of *Honor of Kings* reached $1.48 billion in 2023, underlining its financial prowess. As of December 2023, the daily active users have exceeded 160 million, the maximum number of concurrent online users has exceeded three million, total number of downloads has exceeded 3.8 billion times, becoming one of the most downloaded MOBA mobile games in the world.[1] Notably, this mobile game was developed by the R&D teams in Chengdu rather than the

---

[1] www.statista.com/statistics/1231125/tencent-global-mobile-game-revenue-of-honor-of-kings/?srsltid=AfmBOorMoogAFzJ-HJSNbvQvHMrghlbb9D8hCotih fpZtoVtyCrtoecX

core teams in the Shenzhen headquarters, which might be expected to have more access to company resources.

Tencent Games is a leader across the entire game industry, with *Honor of Kings* and *LOL* occupying half of the domestic market in China. Since *LOL* announced its entry into mobile gaming in 2019, the competition between *LOL* and *Honor of Kings* has become fiercer. No one can tell what the next disruptor will be, but it will likely come from within Tencent itself.

Many of Tencent's successful products had internal competitors early on. As Tencent moves into livestreaming, at least six of its subsidiaries are competing in the industry. Tencent is making great efforts in the field: its livestreaming products include QZone Live (QQ空间直播), Huayang Live (花样直播), NOW, eGame, Inke, Douyu (斗鱼), We Sing (全民K歌), and Penguin Live (企鹅直播). Each of Tencent's livestreaming teams has a different focus, including sports, karaoke, and games. Before Tencent commits to spending more money on a specific product and its promotion, developers must build it themselves first. In addition to its livestreaming services, Tencent currently operates at least four music apps, three companies developing virtual reality technologies, and two film companies (Tencent Pictures and Penguin Pictures). In terms of Tencent's advertising business, it once provided the Chitu advertising platform (赤兔广告) before Guangdiantong (广点通), however, the latter stood out definitively in the competition. Tencent's senior management team leaves a certain amount of leeway between groups because they never know which group will come up with the best product.

In the current era of dominance by large language AI models, numerous Chinese enterprises of various sizes have embarked on developing their own general-purpose models. Tencent's own model, named 'HunYuan', was officially launched in September 2023. Tencent showcased HunYuan's impressive capabilities, boasting over 100 billion parameters and training with more than two trillion tokens. It has since become the cornerstone of over fifty products and services, seamlessly integrated with collaborative Software as a Service (SaaS) offerings such as Tencent Cloud, Tencent Marketing Solutions, Tencent Games, Tencent fintech services, Tencent Meeting, Tencent Docs, Weixin Search, QQ Browser, and other core offerings.

During our interviews with Tencent, we discovered that the development of the Tencent HunYuan began as early as 2018 and stemmed from an internal horse racing initiative. More than five teams, hailing from different departments under various managers and employing diverse approaches, simultaneously undertook the development and training of the model. These R&D teams opted to keep their leaders at arm's length from their decision-making processes, preferring to present the formal model without providing input or expressing their positions beforehand.

In the internet industry, markets and technologies change quickly and are full of uncertainty. Vitality is hugely important. In December 2015, Pony Ma confirmed that internal competition is a necessary driving force for innovation. In Tencent, competition between business units, teams, or individuals is common. As one of the interviewees at Tencent said: 'If you are conducting one project, there must be another team that is doing the same thing in our company at the same time.' Whether horse racing happens depends on the context and the development stage of the company overall, as well as specific business fields.

Internal competition emerged as a crucial feature of innovation, acknowledged by both insiders and outsiders as integral to Tencent's culture. To gain insight into Tencent employees' perception of internal competition, including their views on horse racing, we conducted a large-scale survey involving a questionnaire and online survey at the close of 2021. The survey also explored other significant aspects of corporate culture. A total of 1970 employees voluntarily participated. This was the first time that Tencent had allowed such a large internal study to be conducted by outsiders. Based on the existing literature (Birkinshaw and Lingblad, 2005), we posed three questions to assess the extent of similarity to other adjacent teams in terms of charter, capacity, and product market, employing a 5-point Likert scale (see Figure 3.1). The average scores provided by respondents were 3.45, 3.55, and 3.48, respectively. This indicated a higher level of internal competition observed in Tencent over the preceding three years. As of the end of 2021, internal competition continued to prevail within Tencent.

We inquired about employees' perception of situations where other teams within Tencent were working on similar projects. Specifically, we asked: 'If other teams in Tencent are highly similar to yours in terms of product or business area, how many such teams are there?' Of the 1970 employees surveyed, 1,132 respondents (57.5 per cent) indicated the existence of at least one team undertaking a similar project to theirs within Tencent (see Figure 3.2). This percentage is notably high. Among these respondents, 104 individuals also reported more than four teams with similar goals, suggesting a culture of intense internal competition.

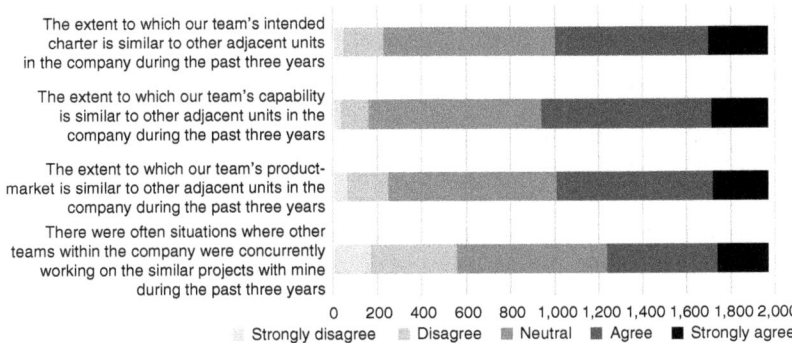

Figure 3.1 Internal competition at Tencent (survey results, N = 1970).

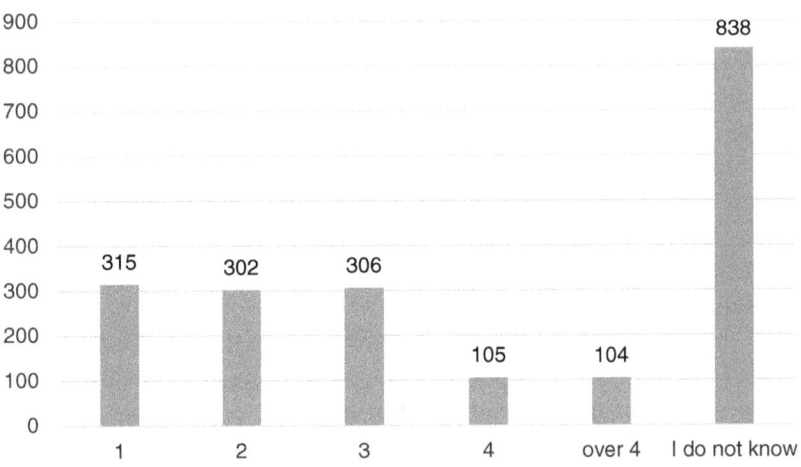

Figure 3.2 How many teams are doing a similar project to your team's?

3.3 Unveiling the Impact: The Influence of Internal Competition

In the historical stage of Tencent's rapid development, faster responses and stronger competitiveness were important to prevail over external rivals in the wider market. Tencent forms an open market where teams compete with each other to develop the best and most popular product for the market and obtain more resources from top executives. Alternatively, they can seek out and find collaborators within the internal market.

We conducted interviews to gain a better understanding of how employees at Tencent think about the horse racing mechanism and its effect on organisations and individuals. Many employees responded that competition and cooperation work concurrently to improve their performance. As one employee commented:

Although there is internal competition, there are some internal mechanisms that could ensure cooperation in the meantime. A typical example is that some team leaders are also acting as directors. They may be concurrently serving two or three potentially competing groups at the same time. Through their overall guidance, the positioning of each group will be more clearly and detailly assigned, thus avoiding such waste of unnecessary resources.

From the organisation's standpoint, horse racing embodies a strategic approach that involves significant investment of resources to capitalise on timely opportunities, mitigating the risk of missing out on potentially lucrative business prospects within a limited timeframe. For instance, during the mobile internet era, Tencent seized its opportunity amid fierce competition in the instant messaging sector and developed WeChat, which has since evolved into a pivotally important product and platform. Unlike top-down mechanisms that dictate and control every aspect of a company's existence, horse racing is a bottom-up approach, particularly conducive to fostering innovation, iteration, and even disruption when contending with external players.

At the team level, internal competition offers two distinct advantages. First, it serves as a platform for identifying and nurturing top-tier leaders and team members. Through the competitive process, organisations gain insights into their teams, leaders, and individuals. The most capable are characterised by their abilities to adapt swiftly, perform under pressure, and accurately gauge consumer demands while leveraging company resources. Second, horse racing enables multiple teams to accumulate relevant experience simultaneously. Even if certain directions prove to be fruitless and some teams falter in the process, the experience garnered remains valuable going forward, particularly when a standout product emerges in the market. Subsequent collaboration among teams facilitates product refinement and improvement.

Contrary to the common assumption that relative stability is often associated with joining a large company like Tencent, the horse racing mechanism ensures that no employee can remain complacent in their comfort zone. Employees cannot rely solely on their past achievements to secure their position indefinitely. With product teams and employees engaged in fierce competition within the same field, each individual must continually underscore the value of their contributions. This atmosphere fosters a culture of self-motivation, prompting employees to enhance their skills and explore new avenues. It also instils a sense of urgency, fuelling innovation performance. As everyone strives to outperform their peers and emerge victorious inside Tencent, a drive for excellence permeates the organisation. One interviewed employee commented: 'I can strongly feel that the internal competition could enhance the vitality of teams and organisations. When some of your work overlaps with others, maybe 10% or 20%, you will be more positive and proactive in conducting your work than your competitors.'

However, internal competition is not without its downsides, as it inevitably entails both success and failure. One significant drawback is the potential waste of resources, resulting in redundancy, imbalance, and internal discord. Allowing different teams to pursue similar objectives often necessitates additional resource allocation, which can be particularly challenging for small- and medium-sized companies. However, in the case of Tencent, horse racing represents an innovative approach to organising and incentivising innovation to a certain extent. One of the technical staff said in an interview: 'The cost of such systematic experiments in the internet industry is low, which may be different from traditional industries. In the internet industry, product and service innovation iterate very quickly. Usually there is no extra investment in infrastructure and no large-scale projects.'

When internal competition yields both success and failure, particularly at the individual level, it becomes imperative to offer protection and encouragement to those who have made sincere efforts but faced setbacks. Often, teams associated with failed projects are immediately disbanded, but Tencent's high tolerance for failure ensures that its employees remain motivated to invest continuous efforts in competitive activities.

However, the internal competition mechanism also introduces three types of discord within the organisation: business, data, and technology disharmony. Business disharmony arises when multiple departments engage in redundant business activities in the process of internal competition. Data disharmony manifests as the inability to share internal data between different teams owing to the strong departmental barriers needed for fair competition. Technology disharmony occurs when several R&D teams concurrently develop the same technology, such as Platform as a Service.

Despite the pros and cons of the horse racing mechanism, Tencent's experience and record of success confirm that it is a rational and valuable approach. And despite the challenges it presents, the evidence suggests that its benefits outweigh its drawbacks. An internally competitive environment is essential for fostering innovation and delivering outstanding products and is therefore central to the company's competitive edge.

3.4 Empowering Innovation by Stimulating Coopetition

3.4.1 Bottom-Up Autonomy Fuels Competition and Cooperation

The culture of competition is embedded in the daily work of Tencent employees. They are regularly encouraged to look for new products and opportunities emerging in the industry. If these are missed, they will be snapped up by other employees. Based on our interviews, this competitive environment is not generally driven by top Tencent executives. Because the company encourages the bottom-up generation of ideas, employees have more freedom to experiment or to change things if they feel that it is worthwhile. Innovations are less likely to be killed off at an early stage and can be upgraded more efficiently. Employees are encouraged to explore widely, based on their own fields of expertise. Business responsibilities overlap between different teams. One of the interviewees said:

The company is actually very decentralised and empowers employees quite a lot. As grassroots employees, we have relatively strong decision-making power. While we have such a competitive relationship with others, in fact, the communications between two teams are relatively smooth. We will come up with some cooperation plans or solutions from the bottom. Although the things we do are similar, we can still try to strive for a way that everyone can obtain a good performance.

Based on our interviews, Tencent differs from traditional enterprises, which tend to have internal plans, strategies, and unified arrangements. Tencent is a purely market-oriented enterprise, a federal-type organisation with a flat internal structure, a high degree of autonomy in each department, flexible management, and an emphasis on self-motivation, competition, and cooperation. The company resembles an organic market without a unified plan and strategy. To a large extent, Tencent's decision-making comes from the bottom up. Employees and leaders in business units have enough freedom to decide what to do and develop, which opens up more possibilities for internal competition and cooperation.

When we carried out interviews, many people said that Tencent has no overarching strategy. Instead, it has a bottom-up, self-driven, free coopetition, which creates a sense of ownership in each team, so that each team can have its own autonomy and be responsible for its own profits and losses. Once the market has determined the winner, Tencent can fully support it with all the technical, financial, and market resources at the disposal of such a large company. 'Competition trumps cooperation' becomes 'intense coopetition'. In practice, vertical collaboration is common. Although Tencent developed its internal open-source project later than its Western peers, such as Facebook, it has been a leader in promoting intrafirm cooperation in China.

3.4.2 Strategic Evolution: Igniting Innovation through Coopetition

As the consumer internet enters a mature stage, China's To Consumer (ToC) market is gradually becoming saturated, the demographic dividend has begun to dwindle, and leading internet companies such as Alibaba and Tencent have begun to target the To Business (ToB) market and enter the industrial internet. Over the years, Tencent has gained significant experience in dealing with individual consumers and knows how to attract them and meet their needs. Over the long term, horse racing has proven to be a net positive for Tencent. Without it, WeChat and *Honor of Kings* would not exist. During the past few years, the strategy has helped Tencent attract many users and become the internet industry leader. As previously noted, Tencent began by concentrating on ToC products, such as QQ, WeChat, and Online Games. In recent years, it has shifted its focus towards ToB. It has also started to develop social products and take up some charitable activities.

As mentioned in Chapter 2, Tencent has updated its strategies numerous times over the past twenty years. In September of 2018, the company announced that it was restructuring to embrace the industrial internet while maintaining its roots in the consumer internet. This was dubbed the '930 Reform' internally. Two new business groups, PCG and CSIG, were established to support the new strategy. PCG is responsible for the integrated development of Tencent's internet platform and its content and culture ecosystem. It integrates social platforms such as QQ and QZone with traffic platforms such as Tencent's AppStore and browsers, as well as content platforms including news, videos, sports, live broadcasts, anime, and movies, to develop a better growth environment for Tencent's content ecosystem. PCG also aims to promote the cross-platform and multi-modal development of IP, with the overall goal of creating more diversified premium digital content experiences for more users. CSIG is responsible for promoting the company's cloud and industrial internet strategy and creating solutions for smart industries through technological improvements such as cloud computing, AI, and network security. It explores innovative interactions between users and industries, connects upstream and downstream enterprises in the industry, links online and offline scenarios and resources, and drives the digitalisation of retail, medical, education, transport, and other industries. In addition, CSIG helps companies serve its users in smarter ways, building a new ecosystem of intelligent industries that connect users and businesses.

In 2005, Tencent announced that its corporate values were integrity, responsibility, collaboration, and innovation. Alongside the strategic upgrade, in 2019 the corporate values changed to integrity, proactivity, coordination, and creativity, further emphasising inclusive and collaborative development within the company. The switch to new values, from collaboration to coordination, was the idea of Mark Ren, COO of Tencent. In his opinion:

Coordination is different from collaboration. The former is a way of distributing the work to people who have the same goals and resources, the latter is a way where people have their own work already and people do part of the work separately and benefit from it partly. Namely, the nature of collaboration is to serve its own small goals, while coordination emphasises that all partners serve a common big goal.

After the launch of the new strategy and the organisational restructuring, Tencent has developed its business and product to individual consumers (C), business partners (B), and government (G). B and G customers have more complex needs and require longer value chains than those in the ToC business. Tencent spreads its ToB-applicable products and capabilities across multiple business groups. In addition to SNG's Tencent Cloud, this includes WXG's mini program, official account, payment, WeCom, CDG's Social & Performance Advertising (SPA), MIG's Location Based Services (LBS), security, medical care, OMG's brand advertising, and lower-level AI capabilities.

A product could feasibly be developed separately by two or more teams and the different versions could then be compared to determine which one better suits the ToC market. However, some issues that arise in the course of developing the ToB business cannot be solved through horse racing. They often require collaboration and the application and combination of functions and data from multiple departments. C-end users tend to be more impulsive, while B-end consumers tend to be more rational. Providing a ToB service therefore tests the company's service capabilities and operational capabilities and requires more focus on details, which horse racing cannot necessarily provide. After all, in a long transaction cycle, even the smallest problems will affect user experience.

Tencent realised that the methods it had used to contact users of ToC products were not suitable for this new strategy. For example, problems would arise if multiple departments in Tencent were to propose multiple different solutions to B or G customers. Allowing several individuals from different teams in Tencent to communicate with a single business representative or government official simultaneously is not a good idea. When dealing with business partners, each Tencent team represents Tencent's image and solutions to the outside world. Were each team to propose their own solution to each problem, each with a different budget and plan, this would cause confusion. Sometimes teams compete with each other, trying to win the order by proposing the lowest price. Tencent can then provide customers with a single, consistent solution. Division of labour within the company is therefore still required. CSIG was established in the hope of improving interactivity and collaboration between departments when developing its ToB business.

Pony Ma commented on the latest strategic upgrade:

This initiative is a new starting point for Tencent to move towards the next twenty years. It is a very important strategic upgrade. The second half of the internet development belongs to the industrial internet. In the first half, Tencent provides users with high-quality services through connections. In the second half, Tencent will build on this basis to help industries and consumers form a new, more open connection ecology.

After the adjustment of the organisational structure, there may be more opportunities for cooperation than competition. Cooperation within the company is increasingly being encouraged. Therefore, cooperation over the traditional horse racing and competition was prioritised internally. In the eyes of the outside world, Tencent has a strong ToC gene, but lacks a ToB gene. But just as China's industrial internet is still developing, Tencent is evolving to enhance its ToB capabilities. Tencent is also deeply aware that business customers will be willing to enter their ecosystem only if the company focuses on them and on solving their problems. The company is therefore implementing changes in different infrastructure layers to enhance the capabilities of different departments.

Tencent is doing three things on the 'back end'. The first is empowerment, which is achieved by pooling Tencent Cloud's experience, internal information sharing, and project support. The second is training, which involves collaborating with Tencent Academy to turn Tencent Cloud's experience into a formal curriculum to help peer departments build effective capability models. The third is benchmarking research. Tencent identifies and studies domestic and foreign competitors to understand their business models and how they build their sales teams. The results of this research are turned into courses and used to provide and improve internal consulting services to relevant teams.

Achieving improvement at the front end and middle layer is more difficult, as it requires more coordination across different business groups and departments. At the front end, Tencent's teams are accustomed to working in a 'closed loop' in which each department prefers its own team to contact customers directly. Business partners usually need an industry-specific solution, unlike individual customers. This is not problematic if only a single product is required by the customer, but if a complex solution is needed, multiple departments contacting customers separately would cause chaos. Sometimes a team might promise a solution to a customer that requires support from another department. Every team has different priorities, so this might cause such projects to be delayed. On occasion, teams might also compete with each other on quotes for the same customer.

Within the middle layer, large projects usually require multiple departments to work jointly towards tailored solutions for real-world scenarios. The same products and technologies are applied very differently to, for example, finance, public transport, and national security. As a result, a communication and decision-making system is required to organise products and capabilities into complete solutions. The core of middle development is improving problem-solving capacity, designing and establishing cross-team information synchronisation, joint decision-making, capability sharing, and a benefit-sharing management mechanism. To deal with cross-departmental coordination issues, Tencent is trying to become more agile by building rapid response teams to coordinate business departments and clarify each team's input. This breaks down internal boundaries, increases organisational flexibility, and serves the organisational strategy.

Tencent's existing ToB products, Tencent Meeting, WeCom, and Tencent Docs belong to three different business groups, all of which have large numbers of users. WeCom is a powerful underlying platform for internal business use and provides reliable, enterprise-standard data protection. It had served more than 5.5 million companies and had 130 million MAUs by December 2020. Tencent Meeting and Tencent Docs are core applications. The former was launched in December 2019, has more than 100 million users, and is available in over a hundred countries and regions. Tencent Docs is a collaborative online document product, similar to Google Docs, introduced by Tencent in 2018. These three parts are now becoming more and more synergistically integrated.

In January 2022 it was announced that the functions WeCom, Tencent Docs, and Tencent Meeting had officially integrated and connected. A new efficient collaboration function was jointly launched on WeCom. For increased user convenience, a unified external access point was created. Each team contributed core technical workers to the joint R&D of the new function. However, the three entities have not been completely subsumed into one department. Each unit retains some freedom to explore innovation from different perspectives and grow independently.

In 2018, when Tencent Docs was first launched, one of the tech leaders floated the idea of cooperation between the three teams. After a one-year run-in period, WeCom had integrated Tencent Docs and Tencent Meeting at the bottom of its technology, but the three teams still maintained independence in their development. However, owing to the rise in remote working during the pandemic, the three platforms began to receive increasing amounts of feedback on their collaboration. Each platform works superbly when used on its own, but users need to use a separate account to log on to each platform. Tencent attaches great importance to user experience. The second round of collaboration began at the end of 2020 after the top management team stressed the importance of improving user experience. Between July and October 2021, technical workers from the three business groups gathered in Shenzhen and jointly facilitated the development of the product.

One of the advantages of cooperation is that it allows different teams to play their own role in completing a single large project, which is highly efficient. In the process of cooperation, each team could focus on the tasks at which they are best and support each other; employees are also more likely to rely on each other. Communication becomes smoother. At the same time, technicians can acquire knowledge beyond their own fields more quickly, deepening their understanding of the project. One interviewee from Tencent Cloud told us: 'Cooperation is indispensable for us to reach commercialisation. We have to cooperate with colleagues from diverse departments along the value chain, such as R&D department, sales department, marketing, industrial ecosystem partners in education, government affairs, etc. Especially in the cloud computing area, we have to build such a system to obtain competitiveness in this industry.'

Another example is IEG. IEG's early objective was to find a cross-regional and cross-team co-construction project carrier, and a representative in the form of the TechFuture (TF) project. The TF project is led by the IEG Internal Research System Management Department and is jointly organised and operated by SG, NEXT, the public R&D operation system (CROS), and HR. This allows colleagues from different studios to cooperate on the basic underlying technologies of game development, including in-depth interactive environments, dynamic weather systems, plot systems, open-world water bodies, and other public game technologies that are required for high-quality 3A games in the future. Everyone contributes to the project, which breaks down the barriers erected by horse racing to a certain extent. This is the first instance of such cooperation in IEG's history.

Through these projects, Tencent provides a channel for inter-departmental communication and cooperation for technical personnel. Some projects are led by Guangzi Lab and some by Tianmei Lab. Each of them can recruit personnel to operate across the whole of IEG.

3.4.3 Shattering Barriers: Fostering Internal Openness at Tencent

In 2018, Tencent established a technical committee to foster open-source collaboration and transition internal R&D onto the cloud across the organisation. This initiative aimed to dismantle technical barriers, enhance the R&D environment, and foster internal openness and cooperation. The inaugural open-source collaborative project was the result of concerted efforts from four teams. Initially, some team members struggled to grasp the concept of combining R&D efforts. A few even considered giving up. However, the final outcome demonstrated significant potential for future organisational coordination from top to bottom. In May 2021, the newly formed CSIG Technical Committee established eight working groups, covering areas such as cloud native technology (云原生), standard formulation and implementation (标准制定实施), R&D efficiency enhancement (研发效能提升), quality and operational stability (质量和运营稳定性), technology frontier exploration (技术前沿探索), and technical collaborative co-construction (技术协同共建). CSIG aims to establish a 'technology club' that facilitates horizontal exchanges and cooperation, enabling the efficient reuse of valuable technologies and transforming internal technical potential into external productivity to drive business growth. These working groups collaborate closely with Tencent Group's technical committees to provide them with a robust platform and support mechanism, fostering a culture that champions innovation.

According to the Tencent R&D Big Data Report,[2] as of the end of 2021, Tencent's internal open-source rate had consistently exceeded 80 per cent for three consecutive years, with over 72,000 new internal open-source code bases introduced, which was 26 per cent more than the previous year. More than 20,000 Tencent developers actively participated in internal open-source contributions. By March of 2023,

---

[2] https://blog.csdn.net/qq_29166327/article/details/123650509

Tencent had established and nurtured 147 company-level Open-Source Collaborative Teams (Oteams), encompassing key internet technology domains such as computing, storage, databases, and AI, and involving all of Tencent's core business sectors such as WeChat, QQ, and Tencent Cloud. The total number of code contributors reached 5,814, with 332 departments engaged in collaborative construction. The largest Oteam involved a total of sixty-eight departments. Many Oteams within Tencent have been independently and voluntarily established. Until 2022, approximately 80 per cent of the teams fell under the purview of the newly established domain committee, which is sector-managed, with a technology-savvy expert serving as the committee chair. This organisational structure aims to enhance technological prowess within Oteams. Internal open-source collaboration has significantly bolstered Tencent's R&D efficiency by consolidating similar Oteams. Moreover, it fosters knowledge sharing and cross-departmental learning, thereby enhancing the organisation's innovation capabilities. It is notable, however, that in 2018 it was almost impossible to access another team's code within the same business group, let alone across different groups.

When discussing internal competition at Tencent today, most employees would acknowledge its pervasive presence between individuals, teams, and business groups alike, particularly given the overlapping responsibilities within the company. Such competition is particularly prevalent in business units, while departments like the Group Brand department, which offer numerous cooperation opportunities with business units, experience relatively little competition. Despite the significance of competition, the degree of cooperation outweighs it. While this cooperative culture has been a longstanding norm in the past, it has significantly changed in recent years. One employee stated:

When our business has competition with other units, it is more likely to promote cooperation as we have some similar goals. We all want to achieve value from our own perspective to obtain recognition from the leadership, thus, we would try to understand each other and find a balance after negotiation and communication. Finally, our company will benefit from this cooperation.

3.5 Inside the Arena: Exploring Chinese Internal Competition Practices

In the internet era, we have witnessed the rapid growth of Chinese companies such as Alibaba, Meituan, Bytedance, and JD.com. Their valuations are among the highest in the world. However, pinpointing the precise characteristics and representativeness of the innovation models they adopt is challenging. Tencent stands out as a pioneer in fostering and supporting the internal competition mechanism. There has been limited discussion of the phenomenon of internal coopetition in China. To the best of our knowledge, several Chinese companies have embraced internal competition to drive innovation, viewing it as a proactive response to external competition.

Alibaba employs a horse race strategy-letting teams compete and then backing the winner. Business units like Taobao and Tmall once competed for merchants and users. This spurs rapid innovation and market responsiveness, though sometimes it causes internal fragmentation. In 2010, Professor Julie Wulf of Harvard Business School produced a case study based on Alibaba,[3] summarising her findings as follows: 'Competition trumps cooperation, and distributed decision-making by individual business units trumps universal strategy.' She continued: 'Alibaba does not adhere to an overarching strategy, with each business department granted autonomy to formulate strategies independently.' Alibaba's governance model has empowered its subsidiaries to become leaders in their respective industries. Founder Jack Ma emphasised the importance of autonomy, stating: 'The presidents of business units must have the freedom to do what is right for their business. I hope business units will compete with each other and focus on being the best in their fields.' Wulf's case study also showed: 'When internal competitive conflicts arose among Alibaba's businesses, the company's culture tended to favour individual subsidiaries over the group.' Jack Ma consistently repeated to subsidiary heads that they had the freedom to make decisions that benefited their businesses.

Internal competition is widespread in Chinese internet companies, driven not only by the desire to seize opportunities in the digital era but also by intense competition in the Chinese market. Many large internet companies have adopted internal competition to incentivise the development of products and services, pushing their R&D teams to accelerate their pace. Some of these companies, including Bytedance and Pinduoduo, have been influenced by the success of Tencent's model. Bytedance, in particular, has experienced rapid growth and

---

[3] https://store.hbr.org/product/alibaba-group/710436?sku=710436-PDF-ENG

was valued as the world's largest unicorn in 2023.[4] It has incubated numerous apps, starting with Jinri Toutiao, a news and information content platform. Sub-channels within the platform that perform exceptionally well are upgraded to independent apps. Despite focusing on different topics such as life, sports, entertainment, and society, these sub-channels are operated by distinct teams and are independent. This complementary competition is a cornerstone of Bytedance's own horse racing strategy. Apps such as Douyin, Huoshan Video, and Xigua Video are exemplary products of this method.

Recently, Douyin Group launched the micro-short play applet 'Paopaoxinxuan' on Douyin, while Pipi Xia introduced the independent app 'Pipi Xia Lite', focusing on free micro-short plays. Tomato Fiction, a reading app published by Bytedance in 2019, expanded into the micro-short play realm with the launch of the independent app 'Hongguo Free Short Plays' last year. Micro-short plays, typically consisting of eighty to 100 episodes lasting one to two minutes each, are characterised by dramatic narratives, numerous plot twists, and powerful climaxes aimed at engaging users. In 2024, the micro-short play industry experienced significant growth, with multiple products from Bytedance exploring various approaches to the micro-short play track. While it is still uncertain which company will dominate the market share and emerge as the winner in this track, internal competition remains a vital strategy for companies seeking to capitalise on opportunities in the rapidly evolving business landscape.

Huawei, as a leading global provider of information and communications technology (ICT) infrastructure and smart devices, also runs multiple research programs simultaneously, focusing on near-term product improvements, medium-term technological advances, and long-term fundamental research through its large research institutions called '2012 Labs', which resulted in R&D excellence but mainly follows a top-down and disciplined structure. As CEO, Ren Zhengfei wrote some articles to convey crisis awareness to employees, so that they could feel the pressure from external market competition. At the same time, the company also implemented a last-place elimination

---

[4] 'Unicorn' refers to a startup company valued at over US$1 billion which is privately owned and not listed on a share market (https://en.wikipedia.org/wiki/Unicorn_(finance)).

mechanism in HRM. Through the four mechanisms of 'cadres can be promoted or demoted, work can be left or right, personnel can enter or leave, and compensation can be increased or decreased', the company's internal competition pressure was increased. In this context, employees must continue to work hard and perform at a high level in order to obtain more opportunities and resources. At the same time, under the guidance of the company's overall strategic goals from top to bottom, employees need to make commitments to the completion of established goals, while maintaining teamwork and collaboration in the process of pursuing goals.

3.6 Discussion and Conclusion

In today's business landscape, companies' strategic behaviours have undergone dynamic shifts owing to globalisation and digitalisation. In discussions about competition, the focus is often on competition between companies. These companies employ diverse strategies to vie for a larger market share and strive to deliver the best products to customers. Since the early 1980s, intrafirm competition has become increasingly prevalent in large organisations where multiple units frequently overlap in their organisational charters (Birkinshaw and Lingblad, 2005). This phenomenon spans various industries, including automotive (Peters and Waterman, 1982), IT (Galunic and Eisenhardt, 1996), and fast food (Kalnins, 2004). Companies leverage internal competition strategies to stimulate innovative idea generation and drive product development.

Previous literature on Tencent and WeChat has predominantly emphasised internal competition or horse racing as drivers of innovation (Birkinshaw et al., 2019; Wu, 2016). However, the significance of cooperation among different departments has been overlooked and underexamined. In this chapter, we have presented numerous examples illustrating the pivotal role of simultaneous competition and cooperation within Tencent in fostering critical innovation.

Organisations are increasingly leveraging internal competition by facilitating parallel development across different units or divisions. This approach is often employed to inspire new product development teams, encouraging them to exert more effort and strive for more innovative ideas and performance differentials, thereby enhancing organisational flexibility and challenging the status quo (Theeke, 2016).

Intrafirm competition involves numerous teams and individuals vying for internal resources and attention from top executives within the organisation. The selection process determines which ideas are deemed viable while others may be abandoned. When similar teams compete for internal resources, individuals are confronted with competitive threats from their peers, motivating them to work harder to generate novel ideas and achieve team goals.

However, it is important to acknowledge that intrafirm competition for internal resources may lead to trust issues, knowledge protection concerns, and hinder knowledge sharing within the organisation (Bouncken and Kraus, 2013; Tsai, 2002). Intense competition is not always productive and may waste resources. Organisations need to consider whether they can tolerate this kind of waste. The extent to which a company promotes internal competition also depends on its development stage and strategic orientation. Internal competition can arise from bottom-up initiatives or top-down mandates. For instance, multinational company headquarters often task subsidiaries in different locations with developing similar products or services. However, this approach may lead to innovation becoming a pressurised task rather than a self-motivated endeavour.

Competition and cooperation are not mutually exclusive. They often coexist in a phenomenon called coopetition. Teams collaborate to expand opportunities and then compete to secure a larger share (Brandenburger and Nalebuff, 1996). Coopetition, extensively studied in an interfirm context, has proven to be an effective strategy for enhancing organisational innovation (Ritala, 2012). However, coopetition also manifests at the intrafirm level, involving different functions, departments, business units, or project teams (Strese et al., 2016). Innovation inherently entails significant uncertainty, and embracing diverse possibilities is crucial for genuine innovation. By keeping technological options open and diversifying investment, competition helps to keep a broad perspective for uncertain future scenarios in a dynamic market landscape. When functional teams or business units vie for limited resources or external market share, companies can simultaneously encourage cooperation to facilitate complementary knowledge sharing and learning between different units or teams, leveraging economies of scope efficiently to achieve organisational goals and enhancing innovation. Encouraging concurrent competition and collaboration encourages individual creative efforts, enables employees to acquire diverse knowledge, reduces information asymmetry, and facilitates innovation activities.

Innovation is a result of integrating existing knowledge with new ideas, a process interwoven with the acquisition of additional knowledge and ideas (Teece, 1998). These two processes coexist and are interconnected. Through empirical studies, we have identified coopetition as a potential strategy to drive innovation within Tencent. Our research elucidates the dynamics of internal coopetition and its antecedents and consequences. It also underscores the critical role of a democratic and inclusive organisational culture in fostering individual and organisational innovation. Remarkably, the competitive environment at Tencent did not originate from top executives but emerged organically from a democratised organisational culture, coupled with empowering leadership. WeChat and Tencent Games provide examples that illustrate how subsidiaries located far from headquarters can develop successful products with sufficient autonomy and support.

At Tencent, employees value the bottom-up innovation mechanism and the inclusive culture that affords them the freedom to create and innovate. Internal competition has spurred the enthusiasm of technical workers, leading to the development of numerous excellent product prototypes. It is internal cooperation, however, that ultimately drives the market success of these products. Through collaboration with upstream and downstream teams, individuals can access new knowledge, skills, and resources, realising mutual benefits. When multiple teams concurrently develop similar products and services within Tencent, they tend to propose integrated cooperative plans that benefit all parties and align with the organisation's mission. Each team contributes its capabilities and expertise to the final product, facilitating knowledge flow and sharing internally. This, in turn, creates more opportunities for knowledge combination and innovation generation. Over the past five years, Tencent has changed its focus from independent R&D and internal competition to a culture of collaborative construction, openness, and sharing, shifting from horse racing to open-source collaboration. This evolution reflects the company's commitment to encouraging organisational innovation.

Many Chinese companies and their Western peers have practised internal competition to spur innovation and efficiency, but some differ based on whether they prioritise technology, market share, or organisational agility. For example, Google emphasises experimentation and freedom, pioneering large-scale A/B testing for product development. They make decisions based on extensive user data rather than intuition, often running thousands of experiments simultaneously. At Meta, teams always compete by launching overlapping features (e.g. Stories in Facebook, Instagram, and WhatsApp) and racing for user engagement, while being empowered with autonomy and valuing product performance as the key metric. Meta's culture of 'move fast' and 'be bold' encourages internal rivalry and risk-taking. Microsoft also encourages product groups to compete with each other, but under strategic alignment. Recently, Microsoft has started shifting toward collaborative innovation and reducing toxic rivalries. However, in China, when it comes to horse racing or internal competition, many people think of Tencent first, as this has resulted in many popular products, such as WeChat and the HunYuan Model. Tencent's horse racing mechanism promotes coopetition, characterised by competition under flexible coordination and tempered by a shared platform.

Tencent's practice provides valuable lessons for large incumbent companies, especially for companies exploring product and technological innovation in nascent markets. Large incumbent companies often face the innovator's dilemma (Christensen, 1997), excelling at sustaining innovations-incremental improvements that serve their existing customers. However, they tend to ignore disruptive innovations, which are usually brought by start-ups or cross-industry enterprises. Serving their most demanding customers often leads them to overlook emerging threats. Many successful companies-despite vast resources-struggle to adapt to radical shifts. Tencent recognises the importance of seizing opportunities early, particularly in emerging markets where no dominant player yet exists. Internal coopetition generates more innovation opportunities and increases the likelihood of success, enabling the company to move swiftly, grasp the opportunity window, and gain a competitive edge. In addition, to contribute to this sort of coopetition atmosphere, companies and executives must build supportive mechanisms by empowering frontline employees with sufficient freedom, granting autonomy even to marginalised departments and affiliates, thus allowing them to make decisions independently. Competition naturally occurs when employees have the freedom and autonomy to carry out their work instead of being micromanaged. Creating a free internal market without barriers fosters greater cooperation, resulting in enhanced efficiency and significant innovation. Finally, it should be noted that internal competition may not be suitable for startups, as it requires adequate resources to hedge bets, run parallel experiments, and room for error tolerance. Start-ups usually have limited resources and a need for strategic focus. They primarily need fast, unified execution and high efficiency. Team cohesion and trust are very important at this stage. Internal rivals can hinder collaboration and create misalignment. But in large companies with enough resources and time to allow experiments, internal competition can be used to build a collaborative organisational atmosphere. When companies deploy internal competition mechanisms, they have to be prepared that it can cause duplicated effort, redundancies, and sometimes lead to conflict.

4 | Serving Talents through Digital Human Resource Management
Motivating Great Creativity

The importance of innovation to companies, especially knowledge-intensive companies like IT companies, cannot be overstated, as innovation is not only related to organisational performance but is also linked to an organisation's competitive advantage (Anning-Dorson, 2018; Damanpour et al., 2009). The capacity of an organisation to innovate depends on employees' skills, abilities, and motivation (Seeck and Diehl, 2017). HRM practices help to develop employees' skills, knowledge, and motivation so that employees' behaviours can contribute to the implementation of organisational strategies, including strategies for innovation. Moreover, HRM is involved in the process of innovation as the development and implementation of innovation requires employee input and engagement. Viewing talents as one of the keys to innovation, Tencent has been placing great emphasis on HRM practices to support and motivate employees. Moreover, over recent years, as a 'born digital' (Monaghan et al., 2020), Tencent utilises digital technologies and products as an enabler in HRM practices, with the aim of serving employees and stimulating employee creativity. Although there is some research regarding the relationship between HRM and employee creativity or organisational innovation, prior literature has not explored how the use of digital technologies in HRM, or digital HRM, supports employees and promotes employee creativity and organisational innovation. Therefore, the objective of this chapter is to explore how Tencent leverages digitalisation of HRM to stimulate employee motivation and creativity. In particular, we shed light on the productisation of HRM as a novel approach adopted by Tencent to deliver HR services and support and motivate employees. This chapter also presents the mechanism of the HRM productisation and highlights the distinctive features of this approach. This chapter not only contributes to the literature on digital HRM but also adds knowledge to the literature on the relationship between HRM and innovation against the backdrop of digitalisation of management.

This chapter is structured as follows: firstly, an overview of Tencent's HRM system is introduced, covering the company's HRM values, structure, and system; secondly, we analyse a novel approach adopted by Tencent – productisation of HRM – and explain its mechanism. Thirdly, we elaborate on how this approach supports and motivates employees. Finally, we discuss the findings and provide some lessons based on Tencent's approach to its HRM practices.

4.1 HRM Value and System at Tencent

The components of an HRM system include value, policies, practices, and processes (Bowen and Ostroff, 2004). HRM philosophy or value is defined as 'how the organisation regards its human resources, what role the resources play in the overall success of the business, and how they are to be treated and managed' (Schuler, 1992, p. 21). HRM philosophy highlights the value and role of human capital in an organisation, while HR processes explain how philosophy (via practices) is implemented in an organisation. Thus, HRM philosophy or value, which is based on how human resources should be treated, plays a crucial role in the operation of an HRM system through shaping HRM practices and processes. For example, managers who believe that employees seek responsibility and can be self-driven are likely to design an HRM system with more autonomy and less control. Managers with an employee-centred philosophy (which places a high value on employees) might focus more on investing in human capital, improving employees' work experience, and prioritising employees' benefits and welfare (Lepak et al., 2004, 2007). This is strongly reflected in our case company – Tencent, which has a distinguishable corporate and HRM value.

Tencent's rapid development benefits from its corporate value, namely 'user-oriented value'. Tencent has adhered to this 'user-oriented value' principle since its inception. When designing products and providing services, Tencent puts the user first and maintains constant interaction with users, to capture and gain a better understanding of their needs. Based on users' needs and feedback, Tencent undertakes product iteration to improve users' experience and create value for them. Such user-oriented value is not only rooted in its product design and business operations, but it also affects Tencent's HRM value. One of the co-founders of Tencent, Charles Chen, pointed out that 'Tencent is rooted in users and based on employees.' Users and employees are the two main drivers for Tencent's development. For the HR department, employees are users of HR services. Therefore, the core HRM value at Tencent is about serving and creating value for employees. Employees are treated as users of the HR department, and the HR department is a service provider. As the senior vice president and head of the HR department, Dan Xi suggested that employees are the most valuable resources at Tencent, and the HR department is not managing employees but serving them. This is different from more traditional HRM ideas, which assume that employees work towards reaching a goal only if they are closely supervised and controlled (Monks et al., 2013).

Furthermore, the management team at Tencent holds the view that employees can be self-motivated. After Tencent upgraded from consumer internet to industrial internet and restructured the organisation into six business groups, businesses among different groups and teams vary with high complexity and huge diversity. This includes content business in the PCG, advertising business in the CDG, and game business in the IEG. The more different and complicated businesses are among teams and groups, the more challenging it is for the HR department. Facing such complicated business operations, the HR department believes that self-motivation is the best way for an organisation to develop. Once employees are self-motivated, they can exhibit their skills, showcase their talents, and fulfil their own career ambitions, which contribute in many ways to the organisation. Therefore, what the HR department must do is provide an HRM system for employees in order to serve, stimulate, and motivate them. An HR manager explained, 'At Tencent, we believe in the self-motivation of employees. Employees' self-motivation is about everyone really wanting to contribute to the organisation. Self-motivation is not likely to be achieved by managerial control. Instead, we provide services and give them support so that they are willing to be more engaged and more self-motivated.'

Similarly, a member of the HR staff stated, 'In other companies, it is more likely to be top-down management and authoritative control. However, in our company, it is not about managerial control. We are serving and supporting employees.'

Therefore, the notions of 'employees are HR's users' and 'employees can be self-motivated' foster the service-oriented value at Tencent, which is deeply embedded in the HRM system. As a result, a service-oriented HRM value leads to a service-oriented HRM system at the company. To some extent, such a service-oriented value echoes the employee-centred approach in a high-commitment HRM system, which places a high value on employees. Different from a high-commitment HRM system (Park et al., 2019), a service-oriented HRM system not only places a high value on employees but it also creates value for employees. Bearing in mind that employees are its users, the HR department is committed to improving employees' experience, promoting employee involvement, satisfying various needs of employees, and providing a more friendly and convenient service and support for employees. Such a service-oriented HRM value affects the HRM policies, approaches, and practices in the HRM system at Tencent. There are three shared values set by the HR department, namely professionalism, service, and partners. These values are also related to the notion of the 'three pillars' of HRM and influence the structure of the HR department. The main functions of HRM have been divided by Ulrich (1997) into three directions: SSC (Shared Service Centre), HRBP (Human Resources Business Partner), and COE (Centre of Expertise). In 2012, Tencent officially created a service-oriented HRM structure supported by three pillars: COE, SSC, and HRBP. In 2014, Tencent upgraded the SSC to a Shared Delivery Centre (SDC) to further productise HR services and provide end-to-end services to internal employees and even external customers. As shown in Figure 4.1, the COE teams are mainly responsible for making HR strategies and policies and setting management guidelines for the whole company. Moreover, they fulfil the HR functions and projects, including recruitment (external and internal), training and development, compensation and welfare, corporate culture, and so on. In 2020, an HR tech centre was established to apply more digital technologies to HRM practices. The SDC teams are responsible for developing digital products and platforms to fulfil HR functions and deliver HR services. The HRBP teams usually work as partners in different business groups and have very strong relationships with business groups. They usually act as business groups' HR advisors and provide personalised HR services and solutions to cater to the needs of different business groups.

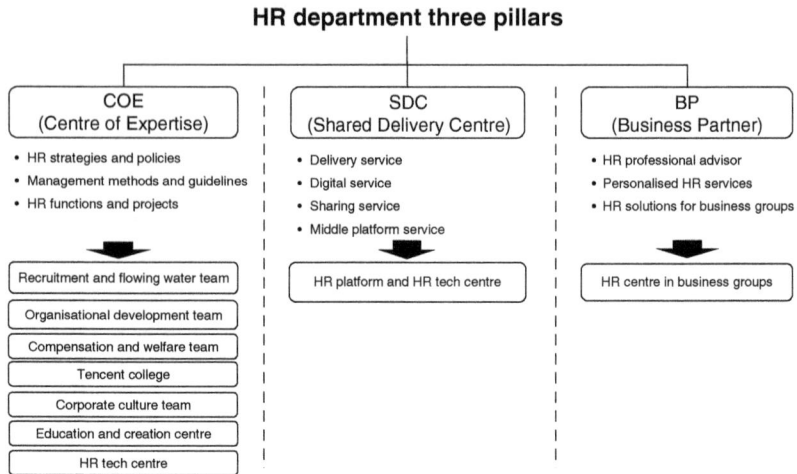

Figure 4.1 Three pillars of the HRM system at Tencent.
(Source: Tencent)

4.2 Productisation of HRM and Delivering HR Services to Talents

At Tencent, the service-oriented HRM value has catalysed a novel HRM approach: digital productisation of HRM. This entails the systematic integration of digital tools and products into HRM processes, facilitating the effective delivery of HR services to employees. The term 'productisation' refers to the process of analysing a need, defining, and combining suitable elements, tangible and/or intangible, into a product-like defined set of deliverables that is standardised, repeatable, and comprehensible (Flamholtz, 1995; Harkonen et al., 2015). The concept of productisation provides a product-centric focus and has a distinct role in the interface of product development and marketing considerations, involving activities from the initial product idea to the interactions and commercialisation with customer focus. The existing literature largely focuses on four types of productisation, namely productisation of products, productisation of services, productisation of software, and productisation of technology (Harkonen et al., 2015). While productisation is mainly discussed in business operations, so far very few studies have examined productisation in management activities. Based on its advanced capabilities of product development and its service-oriented HRM value, Tencent applied this concept to its HRM practices and claimed that digital products provide a pathway for Tencent to transform the fulfilment of HR functions in the delivery of HR services to talents.

In early 2012, Tencent purchased and introduced an external e-HRM tool called 'PeopleSoft' into its HRM practices. However, PeopleSoft did not work well at Tencent. This is because PeopleSoft was mainly designed to follow managerial procedures and could not support the strategic orientation of HRM, especially during the rapid development of the organisation. In addition, the e-HRM system was not in line with Tencent's HRM value to serve employees, and did not focus on employee experiences and engagement (Ma, 2022). In August 2012, WeChat introduced its 'official account', a public profile, which allows individuals or organisations to publish content, attract followers, and offer interactive services. In March 2013, WeChat added a new function – 'menu' – on its official account and invited internal departments (including the HR department) to test its function. The HR department realised that this could be a good opportunity to set up their official account as a service platform to offer HR services and interact with staff. Following that, HR teams have considered whether and how HR functions can be realised by products, whether and how employee experience can be improved by products, and whether and how HR policies can be implemented by products. Since then, the HR department embarked on the journey of productisation in the HRM system through developing its own digital HR products, and more HR products have been designed and developed for employees and the organisation.

By 2022, the HR department had designed and developed more than 150 digital HR products. These products cover the main HR modules or functions, including recruitment and selection, performance management, training and development, employee benefits, and well-being. The following list shows seven main types of digital HR products which are widely used in the company and cover the main HR functions.

(1) **External recruitment tools**
   - Digital procedures
   - Self-service
   - Automated talent selection and identification
(2) **Internal recruitment tool (Flowing Water platform)**
   - Digital procedures

- Protection of staff privacy
- Alignment with internal mobility policy

(3) **Objective and performance management (OKR tools)**
- Co-involvement in objective management
- Goal alignment
- Progress tracking

(4) **Talent PivotTable**
- Comprehensive staff profiles
- Information exchange
- People analytics

(5) **HR assistant**
- Comprehensive HR services
- One-stop services
- SaaS (software as a service), accessible across the ecosystem

(6) **Training system (Qlearning)**
- Interactive platform with user-generated content
- Personalised and customised training resources
- Multiple channels (internal and external)

(7) **Employee benefits and well-being**
- Various programmes (physical, psychological, financial)
- Digital procedures
- Personalised services for specific groups (e.g., mothers, interns)

The first one is external recruitment tools. Both recruiters and applicants can easily follow all the recruitment procedures online, with little in-person instructions and interference. In this way, the HR teams are less likely to rely on labour/manual input. For example, applicants' assessments, remote interviews, and background checks can be conducted online instead of on-site. In addition, due to AI technologies, the products can automatically select, allocate, and recommend suitable candidates for recruiters based on job descriptions, thereby increasing the efficiency and accuracy of resume screening. The second one is an internal recruitment tool called the 'Flowing Water platform'. This product is designed for the internal mobility policy at Tencent. To encourage employees' internal mobility and protect their privacy in the process, this product allows staff to apply for an internal post without notifying his/her current line manager. The objective and performance management tool helps teams and individuals set challenging goals in a measurable way. In addition, employees and managers are able to align objectives and goals and collaborate to fulfil them. Talent PivotTable is an HR product based on data presentation and people analytics. Managers can access personal information (such as personal profile, performance information, etc.) of employees easily and quickly. In addition to information presentation, Talent PivotTable provides analytical results for managers. Thus, managers not only have access to performance analysis of their team but can also gain a better knowledge of its performance level in the whole business group or even in the company. Such information and analysis provide a foundation for managers' decision-making.

HR assistant provides comprehensive HR services for staff, which cover induction, payslips, absence management, social insurances, and so on. HR assistant is built into the WeChat app as a form of Official Account, and employees can easily access its functions on their mobile phones. Qlearning is an online training platform at Tencent which contains a wide range of external and internal learning resources. Based on individuals' needs and preferences, this platform provides more personalised and customised training resources and contents for staff. Moreover, employees are encouraged to produce training content and courses on the Qlearning platform themselves using their own expertise and skills. With the help of Qlearning, a digital interactive platform was built for knowledge sharing at Tencent. In addition, Tencent provides various products for employees' benefits and well-being, and these cover physical, psychological, and financial programmes, including sports programmes, counselling, housing plans, and so on. Some products are designed and developed for particular groups, such as mothers, interns, and so on, to cater to their needs at work and in life.

Furthermore, Tencent has established a mechanism for the productisation of HRM (see Figure 4.2). In this mechanism, the service-oriented value in HRM is a driving factor for the productisation. With such service-oriented value, the HR department puts more emphasis on delivering HR services to employees, while digital products provide a pathway for Tencent to transform the fulfilment of HR functions to the delivery of HR services. As an HR manager explained, 'The rapid development of digital technologies is not the main reason that we adopted productisation of HRM. It is our management philosophy that motivates us to apply suitable technologies and develop products in HRM.'

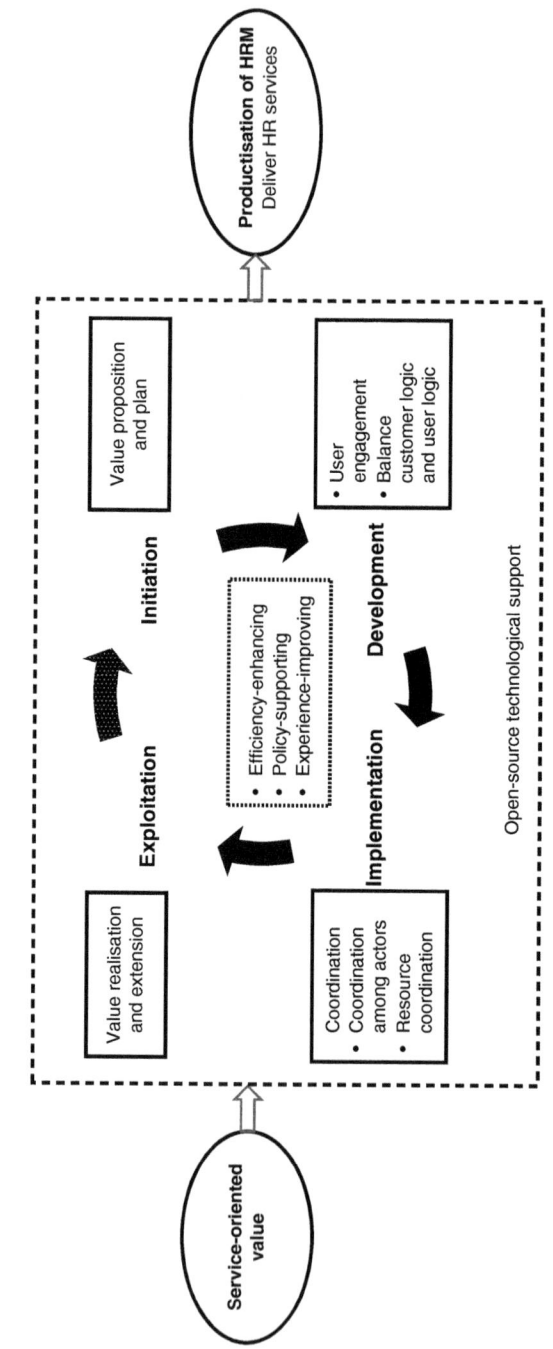

Figure 4.2 Mechanism of HRM productisation.

In the initial step, the HR team sets the value proposition for the products, which focuses on three main areas, namely managerial procedures, employee experience, and organisational policies, which are targeted at serving managers, employees, and the organisation, respectively. Based on the product value, there are three main types of HR products, namely efficiency-enhancing, policy-supporting, and experience-improving products. In contrast to traditional companies where digital HR tools are targeted more at senior management and the HR department itself (Bondarouk, Parry, and Furtmueller, 2017), Tencent's HR products are accessible to both managers and employees and to both the HR department and business groups. However, the productisation of HRM does not mean that products need to be developed to meet all needs from employees or managers, which would most likely lead to an excess of productisation and resource waste. To achieve a feasible and sustainable productisation in HRM practices, a clear plan is needed. Tencent established a committee for project planning and resource allocation in the HR department. The committee members need to take into account the demands of both customers and users. They estimate the cost and the benefits of each product, calculate the life cycle of products, evaluate product needs, and then decide which products should be developed as a priority and how much money and resources should be allocated.

4.2.1 'Employees Are Our Users': Developing the Best Products for Employees

During the stage of development, employees are seen as 'users' of the digital HR products, while HRM teams and staff act as product managers and build productisation capabilities to design and develop the best HR products for employees to both serve and motivate them. User engagement is a cornerstone of Tencent's products and has been considered a 'must-do' in product development at Tencent. Also, user engagement has been embedded in the process of product development. 'User engagement' refers to the fact that users are involved in the process of product ideation, design, and development in different ways, with the aim of understanding users' needs and improving users' experience. Every employee, including HR staff, receives training on user engagement when joining Tencent. User engagement is also applied in the design and development of HR products. In contrast to other products that are designed in business groups for the external market, HR products are primarily designed for internal users, mainly employees. More importantly, they put more emphasis on employee experience, not just focusing on efficiency enhancement or cost reduction. As one HR staff commented, 'At Tencent, all the products are based on user-oriented design thinking. We put much emphasis on our employees' experience and values. We follow these when designing the products and these are integrated into every detail of HR products.' Similarly, 'Our HR products are used internally, and we really care about our employees. This is different from HR products in other companies where they just develop products to follow procedures but ignore users' experience. We care about our employees, for example, whether they use them ok or not, whether they use them happily or not. Very important for us.'

The HR department has set up an internal user engagement programme called 'voice program', where users' voices can be heard through various channels. In the voice program, there are various methods, such as one-to-one interviews, focus groups, surveys, and usability tests, that aim to gain a better understanding of users' needs and problems. User engagement is involved in all phases/stages of product design and development. At different stages, different methods of user engagement are applied. Before the launch of products, HR staff would invite a small number of employees to conduct a product test so that they could identify problems that employees encounter when using the products and understand employees' expectations. After the products are launched, HR teams usually get employees' feedback and ask them to rank HR products by means of an employee survey. When products are to be upgraded, frequent users are selected to test the new version of these products and give constructive feedback. This is evidenced by the experiences shared by HR staff who are responsible for the design and development of employees' benefit and well-being products.

In other companies, when they developed products for employees' benefit and well-being, they did not pay much attention to employees' needs and voices. Very often, HR department develops and launches products based on the product proposal agreed by management, even without a test. And they seldom revised the project even though some employees made suggestions or comments. In contrast, we appreciate employees' voices and needs. Especially before the launch of products, we are happy to adjust our proposal based on employees' suggestions as we reckon employees as our users.

Our HR staff who designed the products will do user engagement, which is very important. We will ask for their opinions, their experience and suggestions on our products. We even used their feedback or scores to decide whether a product is successful or not. At Tencent, thinking about users is always very, very important.

In addition, HR staff adopt different methods for 'user engagement', based on the targeted users and product scenarios. For example, when designing a product for managers in business groups, they usually conduct one-to-one interviews with managers so as to gain an in-depth understanding of their needs and also the rules of the departments. HR teams also integrate their own participant experiences in the product design. For example, based on their own experiences at the graduate job fair, HR staff designed a queuing calling system to match recruiters and applicants more efficiently.

Moreover, such internal 'user engagement' offers opportunities for employees to get involved in HRM practices. At Tencent, the HR department built a programme called 'experience officers'. Experience officers are volunteers from different business departments. They are given particular tasks or scenarios and asked to provide some ideas about what they expect from the products. Most experience officers are experienced product managers or designers in business groups, so they integrate their knowledge and experiences into the development and ideation of HR products and offer some valuable and creative ideas.

4.2.2 Balancing Customer Logic and User Logic

As HRM products are targeted at different actors, such as managers and employees in the business department, the HR department, and the organisation, Tencent differentiates customers from users among these actors in the process of developing HR products. For HR products, *customers* are those who make decisions and invest in digital HR products at the organisation level, such as senior managers and HR managers on behalf of the organisation; they put more emphasis on operational needs, value creation, and return on investment (ROI) of products. *Users* are those who use the products, which mainly include managers and employees in business departments; they care about the user experience. Furthermore, as two groups of actors (customers and users) are involved in the productisation of HRM, two main logics emerge for the development of HR products.

Customer logic refers to the perspective and needs of the HR department and organisation (as customers) who make decisions and invest in HR products to create value and improve ROI, while *user* logic refers to the perspective and needs of the staff and managers in the business department (as users) who are more concerned with the usability of the products. On the one hand, HR products serve the staff and managers in the business department (as users) to cater to users' needs and improve their experience. On the other hand, HRM products need to meet the operational needs of the HR department and organisation (as customers) with a good ROI. It is crucial to balance the two logics in the productisation of HRM to address any potential conflicts or concerns. For example, in the process of developing employee benefits and well-being products, a large number of product needs emerge from different types of staff (full-time/part-time/interns) among different business departments. However, some needs are not common or involve only a small number of staff; in such cases, the cost of product development outweighs the benefit, and thus the HR department prefers to provide offline or manual services to cater to staff needs rather than developing specific digital products.

4.2.3 Coordination in the Process

At the stage of implementation, some challenges might emerge at the organisational level as complex phenomena might arise at the interface of human and digital products. Arguably, coordination is the key at the implementation stage, including among actors in the HRM system and resource coordination. As mentioned, multiple actors are involved in the process of productisation of HRM, including HR teams as developers, and managers and employees in business departments as users. The HR department needs to coordinate with managers in business departments for product adaptation so that the products align with the business departments' operations and prevent any mistakes and conflicts. In addition, the HR department needs to coordinate with employees in business departments to get staff involved in product scenarios to increase employee participation and product utilisation. For example, the usage of Talent PivotTable relies on clear rules on view permissions in business departments in order to protect data privacy and the security of staff and departments. However, in some business departments, relevant rules are vague, or not established; in other words, with inadequate and vague rules, it is very likely that users' data privacy is violated. Therefore, HR teams need to communicate and coordinate with business departments to help them establish relevant rules and adjust the product so that it can adapt to business departments' operations.

Furthermore, with the increasing number of HR products, it is very likely to lead to a waste of resources if there is a lack of coordination. This issue has been brought to light at the implementation stage, taking into account achieving higher ROI in the process. To address this issue, the HR department adopted an approach of 'central platforms', including an operation central platform, data central platform, and technology central platform, which enable the coordination of operation, data, and technology-related resources and activities. The operation central platform is designed to support the reuse of product development resources. Although HR products are designed for different groups in different scenarios, there are some common operations involved in the process for the same HRM functions. For example, in order to reuse the resources of product developments in external recruitment, HR staff decouple similar user behaviours from various scenarios or recruitment channels, such as recruitment demand, job application, CV scanning, interviews, negotiation, and reference checks. The development resources for similar user behaviours are extracted and integrated on the operation central platforms so that these resources can be reused for developing different types of recruitment products. Such operational central platforms are innovative in the digital HRM field. One HR manager commented: 'In this way, we can utilise our resources for developing products more efficiently and also meet various needs of different groups in different scenarios at the same time. This approach has been developed very well, and we are applying this to the whole digital HRM system.'

Similarly, the data central platform is built to gather data generated from different HRM modules so that HR data can be shared and applied for all the HR functions, while the technology central platform is built to provide and share one technological architecture for developing HR products.

4.2.4 Open-Source Technological Support

Our findings suggest that the productisation of HRM benefits from the application of advanced digital technologies. Tencent took the lead in applying digital technologies and digital products in the HRM area. For example, virtual reality is applied in training products to provide an immersive virtual experience for employees; blockchain technology is applied to build digital qualifications in the recruitment and training system in order to identify talent more efficiently. Such advanced technology capabilities benefit from the internal technological cooperation at Tencent. To strengthen the internal technological cooperation, Tencent has established Oteams with the aim of fostering knowledge/technology sharing and learning between different teams and departments that specialise in different technological areas. The HR department is actively involved with other teams to obtain and enhance their technological capabilities or reuse the relevant capabilities of other departments in the process of productisation. Oteams offers technological support and solutions to make product improvements. For example, some functions of Tencent Meeting and Tencent Docs are integrated into external recruitment products to provide better online recruitment experiences for applicants. As one HR manager commented: 'When we are building our technology roadmaps and seeking technological solutions, we rely on our internal open-source technological cooperation. Oteams is just like an open-source platform with various interfaces, and we can just assemble or connect the technological components to develop our products.'

4.3 Serving Talents and Creating Values through Digital HR Products

Digital HR products cover the main HR modules and fulfil the HR functions, including recruitment, performance management, training and development, and employee relations, which contribute to talent identification, recognition, and development at Tencent. More importantly, these products not only serve actors in the HRM system, including employees and managers, but they also create value for them. First of all, the products greatly improve employee experience. This is highly related to the 'user-oriented' principle of product development and the service-oriented HRM value. A majority of interviewed staff spoke highly of the HR products and thought that such products are very user-friendly and easy to access in their daily work.

I used to work in the media industry. There was no such HR product to support us when recruiting a new employee. When we had any questions in terms of recruitment procedures, we needed to contact the HR team, which was time-consuming and caused shorthandedness for the HR department. At Tencent, you just need to follow the tips on the recruitment product. It is very easy to use, very handy and efficient.

HR assistant is very handy, as we can use it whenever and wherever we want and need. For example, if I had an accident and went to see a doctor, I would need to ask for leave. I can easily do it in no time on my mobile phone, instead of carrying my laptop.

Second, HR products not only deliver a better experience for employees, but they also enhance employee engagement and empowerment within an organisation. Arguably, digital HR products empower employees by providing them with digital tools that are said to enhance their autonomy at work. This is because these products, such as Qlearning and recruitment tools, autonomously perform the functions of information access and processing, effectively promote the fulfilment of HRM activities, and foster employee self-management and autonomous collaboration. Also, products such as OKR tools and employee well-being programmes provide personalised knowledge sharing and career development, as well as customised rewards and well-being initiatives that recognise and acknowledge individual employee contributions. Therefore, for the knowledge staff at Tencent, these products are not managerial control tools but rather support employees and create a channel for them to get involved in the daily operations as a means of self-management, which leads to 'self-motivation' among these knowledge staff at Tencent. Such findings resonate with Edwards et al.'s (2024) study, suggesting that when employees perceive algorithmic HRM systems as supportive rather than controlling, they experience better intrinsic motivation. As some interviewed employees commented:

These products are not like some cold-hearted tools for us, or something that companies impose on us. I feel that these products are truly supporting us, not only in our work but also in our lives.

In an IT company, everyone has their expertise and managers are not everywhere. When we are fulfilling the goals for a team, it needs everyone to get involved, because this relies on each person's engagement and development. Such things can be achieved by our OKR tools and training platform. I think these products empower us because there is less control from line managers. So, we can concentrate on our own tasks and fulfil them by self-motivation.

Third, the digital products help managers in their decision-making and improve their managerial efficiency. These products provide people-analytic functions for managers so that they can gain a better understanding of their jobs and team management based on data-driven analysis. Talent PivotTable and recruitment products are two typical examples, as evidenced by our interviews with managers from business groups.

The data [on Talent PivotTable] presents detailed information about my team members and gives a clear picture of the performance in our team. I can obtain the information whenever I need and there are some analyses for us. This is very straightforward and helpful for us, so I know what we need to improve in our team.

The recruitment products are like self-service tools. Also, it can recommend some CVs based on my needs and it can present the applicants' information in a better and quicker way, which help me to choose.

These digital products provide a new pathway for the HR department to deliver HR services. With the productisation of HRM, the traditional fulfilment of HR functions has been transformed into delivering HR services, and the one-way implementation of HRM, or management from the top, has shifted into interactive relationships between 'service providers' and 'users'. This approach not only improves employee experience but also empowers employees with 'user-oriented' digital services. One interviewed HR staff member in a financial company explained that such an approach was not only related to the technological superiority in IT companies but was also suited to the knowledge staff in this sector. 'IT companies have the capabilities for developing digital products. More importantly, compared to other sectors, the IT sector is more competitive and demanding. So, their employees need more and better services, such as a better digital HRM system, to cater for their needs, serve them, stimulate them, and retain them.'

Furthermore, Tencent has been leveraging these HRM products to create value externally. For example, The HR assistant has been applied in partner companies in the ecosystem and external market of Tencent as a SaaS (Software as a Service) product. The HR assistant can be linked not only to WeChat but also to apps of other companies so that users in other companies can access HR assistant easily. Moreover, the HR assistant provides customised solutions and services to meet the needs and follow the rules of external companies. In addition, the HR assistant provides application programming interfaces (APIs) for other third-party service providers so that they can contribute more functions and services to the product. In this way, Tencent has been building an open HR ecosystem. In this ecosystem, the external application of Tencent HR products is able to provide personalised digital HR services for other companies in different industries. One HR staff member who was responsible for the HR ecosystem commented: 'When we developed our HR products, we followed principles and procedures of product development to meet the standard of industrial application. Initially, it focused on our staff's needs; once the products are mature enough, we would like to extend these products to our ecosystem to create more value.'

4.4 Discussion and Conclusion

This chapter explores how Tencent utilises the digitalisation of HRM to effectively serve, support, and motivate employees, unveiling a unique approach of HRM productisation. At Tencent, digital products are systematically developed and applied for all the functions of HRM, and productisation provides a pathway to transforming HRM functions into delivering HR services for actors in the HRM system. The traditional goals of HRM are mainly to follow and support the organisational strategies and fulfil the HR functions. However, in the digital economy and in an organisation that pursues innovation with a high proportion of knowledge staff, the traditional HR practices are not enough and cannot be adaptive. In contrast to digital tools in other companies largely targeted at management, digital HR products at Tencent focus on managerial procedures, organisation polices and strategies, and employee experience, with three main product values, namely, efficiency-enhancing, policy-supporting, and experience-improving products. In doing so, employees' needs – not just managerial needs or organisational needs – are taken into account. Therefore, in addition to enhancing managerial efficiency, digital products are also used as empowering tools to improve employee experiences and engagement. In addition, digital products provide self-service and self-management channels for employees, which allows considerable autonomy for employees, stimulates self-motivation, and empowers them to be more creative.

Such an approach to productisation of HRM is driven by its HRM value. The user-oriented value, which is part of Tencent's genes, is not only rooted in the business operations but also deeply affects its HRM system; accordingly, Tencent has built a service-oriented HRM system. Different from well-recognised HRM systems, such as a high-commitment one (Park et al., 2019), a service-oriented HRM system not only places high value on employees but also creates value for those employees. At Tencent, employees are treated as the most valuable resource. In contrast to the control-style management, an employee-centred approach is a distinctive feature of the HR system at Tencent. Moreover, the service-oriented HRM system is aimed at providing services and creating value for employees, as the HR department holds the view that employees are HR's users, and employees can be self-motivated, which then fosters the organisational HRM value.

We argue that such a service-oriented HRM system and productisation of HRM are suitable and feasible at Tencent. First, after the strategic reform and organisation restructure, the HR department was faced with a more complicated and challenging organisational environment with various businesses and a fast-changing external market, which called for a more agile system. The traditional control-based HRM system cannot be adaptive and might restrain the creativity of employees, especially with a high proportion of knowledge staff at Tencent. Only when an organisation places value on – and creates value for – employees can employees contribute to organisational innovation with their abilities, skills, and self-motivation. Second, as a leading IT company, Tencent not only has advanced technological capabilities but can also develop dynamic capabilities to sense and seize the opportunities of applying digital technologies to its HRM system. The productisation of HRM benefits from its user-oriented value and rich experience of product development.

Furthermore, the approach of productisation of HRM adds a product-centric lens to HRM practices, especially in the digital era. This is different from a data-centred approach, which puts more emphasis on HR analytics. At Google and Microsoft, by applying digital technologies, HR analytics have been widely used for prediction and calculation in HRM functions. For example, the recruitment teams at Microsoft use data analytics to explore where great employees come from. 'Power BI', the data analytics tool at Microsoft, can turn information into visuals, which help HR teams to better understand a business situation (Microsoft, 2017). In Google's 'oxygen project', the internal data has been analysed to identify the eight characteristics of great leaders (Sullivan, 2013). Google's HR analytics have been used for calculation and prediction, such as calculating the value of top performers and predicting which candidates had the highest probability of succeeding after being hired (Sullivan, 2013). At Tencent, even though employee analytics play an important role in the digitalisation of HRM, the HR department puts more emphasis on product development and makes sure that digital HR products can satisfy the needs of employees and improve their experience when using the products.

In addition, HR products at Tencent are internally oriented and designed for internal employees. This is different from Alibaba and ByteDance, whose HR products are more like accessories to their commercial products such as DingTalk and Lark. In other words, these HR products were not developed for their own HR departments and are more targeted at external business needs. In contrast, at Tencent, the HR department largely focuses on the needs of internal users and pays less attention to external business needs or commercialised needs, although they are working on one such HR SaaS, namely HR assistant. As a result, employee experience and interests are deeply considered throughout the development of HR products. Viewing internal employees as users, HR departments not only fulfil HR functions but also deliver HR services through digital products and stimulate the self-motivation of employees while empowering them to be more creative.

Tencent provides several valuable insights into the application of digital technologies in HRM. First, Tencent's service-oriented HRM model serves as a compelling example for IT companies and knowledge-based organisations. It illustrates how treating employees as key stakeholders in HR services can enhance motivation and engagement. Traditional control-based HRM systems, which offer limited autonomy, often suppress creativity and innovation. To fully unlock employees' potential – including their skills, capabilities, and intrinsic motivations – organisations must not only value employees but also actively create value for them.

Second, as digital technologies evolve, managers must explore their application beyond business operations and into HRM practices.

When integrating digital solutions, it is critical to consider employee needs alongside organisational and managerial goals. Digital tools should not only improve operational efficiency but also empower employees, enriching their overall experience and fostering greater engagement.

Third, adopting best practices from product design and development can enhance the creation of digital HR solutions. Techniques such as strategic planning and user engagement – anchored in the 'voice of the user' approach (Cooper, 2019; Kahn et al., 2012) – are particularly useful. By involving employees in the co-creation process and responding to their feedback, organisations can ensure that HR products are truly aligned with user needs. However, productisation should be approached with caution. HR products should not attempt to meet every individual demand within the HRM system. Over-productisation risks wasting resources and diluting value. A tailored value proposition and a clear resource allocation plan are essential starting points. Moreover, balancing customer logic (organisational priorities) with user logic (employee needs) is vital, as these groups often have distinct concerns.

It's also important to recognise that productisation goes beyond developing digital tools. In practice, organisations often face implementation challenges – such as aligning digital products with departmental operations or managing employee reactions to new systems. Active managerial involvement and cross-functional coordination are crucial for successful adoption.

Fourth, the success of digital HRM relies heavily on the awareness, skills, and capabilities of HR professionals. Beyond core HR expertise, they must understand employee needs in digital contexts and acquire competencies in product development. While large organisations often have access to these capabilities, small and medium-sized enterprises (SMEs) may struggle due to resource limitations. Nevertheless, even under constraints, SMEs should prioritise employee feedback and active involvement when deploying digital HRM solutions.

5 Flowing Water for Dynamism
Internal Mobility to Boost Innovation

Under conditions of fierce competition for talent, skilled workers are encouraged to move between countries, organisations, and units (both internally and externally). The mobility of talent is common among large multinational companies such as Google, Facebook, and Microsoft. It arguably contributes to the transfer of information and capabilities, as well as the promotion of knowledge building for organisations. Talent mobility thus enhances the innovation of an organisation (Singh, 2005; Agarwal et al., 2004; Shipilov, Godart, and Clement, 2017).

In recent years, a growing body of research has focused on the subject of interfirm mobility (Agrawal, Cockburn, and McHale, 2006; Cirillo, Brusoni, and Valentini, 2014). Less attention has been paid to internal mobility (Choudhury, 2020; Ray, 2023), however, which refers to employees moving from a subunit to a peer subunit at the same parent company (Madsen, Mosakowski, and Zaheer, 2003). Internal mobility helps build up an internal labour market in which talented employees can steer their own career path within an organisation. Through knowledge transfer, internal mobility enables employees to cultivate a more diverse perspective and a broader range of expertise that in turn stimulates creative thinking (Benson and Rissing, 2020; Rodan and Galunic, 2004; Mannix and Neale, 2005). In practice, however, it is often challenging to establish an internal labour market and implement an internal mobility policy, partly owing to cultural resistance and a lack of clear policies.

In the early 2010s, Tencent adopted a set of internal mobility policies in the form of the Flowing Water programme; these policies were specifically designed to effectively allocate and develop internal talent. The programme was highly valued by both internal and external talent, making it very attractive to prospective employees. In this chapter, we detail how Tencent carried out its internal mobility policies with a focus on how internal mobility promotes dynamism, stimulates employee self-motivation, sustains organisational agility, and ultimately drives innovation. In the first section, we introduce the Flowing Water programme as the basis for internal mobility policies at Tencent. The next section presents the benefits produced by the Flowing Water programme to individual employees and organisations. The final section discusses the findings and highlights the most salient implications for management.

5.1 Flowing Water at Tencent

This section presents the origin and development of Tencent's internal mobility policies. Specifically, we explain how Tencent implemented the Flowing Water programme and addressed challenges within the process of promoting its internal mobility policies.

5.1.1 *What Is Flowing Water?*

Tencent's Flowing Water programme is an internal talent mobility mechanism that allows for mutual selection between employees and hiring departments. The programme imposes only basic conditions on employees: so long as they have worked in their current position for a year and have met the performance threshold, and if the new department confirms acceptance after an interview, the employee transfer will be approved. The programme is open to internal applicants only and transfers are voluntarily initiated by employees, who can apply to positions in other departments without informing their current department leader. Throughout the interview process, all parties involved are required to maintain confidentiality. The employee's original direct supervisor is informed of the transfer only during the transfer-out phase of Flowing Water. Even if their supervisor opposes the transfer, the employee will automatically complete the transfer within a maximum of two months because of the guarantees provided by the Flowing Water programme.

A simple example illustrates how the Flowing Water programme works. Perhaps an employee has worked in a particular position for over one year and his/her most recent performance rating is two stars or above (out of a maximum of four stars), which meets the basic criterion of the Flowing Water programme. For whatever reason, the employee wants to change his/her job position. Then the employee can visit the company's Flowing Water platform to see whether there are any internal recruitment opportunities at the department he/she is interested in. If there is a suitable position, the employee can apply through the system. From there, he/she waits for notification of an interview. A successful interview means that the employee has passed the Flowing Water application. The employee can then choose a time to inform their current supervisor of the transfer and complete the handover within a maximum of sixty days, reporting to the new department thereafter.

To encourage manager rotations, Flowing Water implemented specific rules and mechanisms. Staff with at least one year of experience in management positions are eligible to apply for a transfer, provided the new position is either at the same managerial level or lower than their current role. To apply for a new job at the same managerial level, managers are required to have a performance rating of two stars or higher. No performance rating requirements are necessary for applying to positions at a lower managerial level.

5.1.2 *The Origin of Flowing Water*

Tencent experienced rapid growth in the early 2010s, which led to the establishment and expansion of numerous new business departments across various sectors. As a result, there was significant demand for new talent. By 2010, Tencent had over 10,000 employees and many began to seek internal transfers especially to the newly created business departments. The company saw retention of top talent within the organisation as an optimal choice from both a business and talent development perspective.

Despite Tencent's rapid growth and the establishment of new business departments, the lack of an effective internal mobility system made it challenging for employees to transfer within the company. The HR department acted as an intermediary to match job vacancies with employee aspirations. This process relied on e-mail exchanges, resulting in low overall efficiency. Employees further encountered significant barriers to transfer in the attitudes of line managers. Owing to the high cost of internal training or high demand for talent, line managers sometimes refused to approve transfer applications. Employees who had applied for internal positions may receive unfair performance ratings from their current departments ahead of the transfer.

To promote internal mobility, Tencent introduced a new policy in 2011: employees who had been in their current position for at least one year and had a performance rating of at least two stars (meeting expectations) were eligible to apply for other internal positions. If an employee received an offer for a new position, their current line manager could negotiate to retain them but was not allowed to impede the transfer during the transition period, which could last up to ninety days.

Despite the changes imposed by the new internal mobility policy, its effectiveness remained limited owing to negative attitudes among managers regarding employee transfers. Employees applying for internal positions often faced interference from their line managers during the process. This sometimes resulted in the loss of talent. For example, an employee based in Shenzhen applied for a position at the WeChat Group in Guangzhou, hoping to reunite with his girlfriend. Although he passed the interview and received an offer, his line manager assigned him urgent tasks to complete over several months – thereby delaying and effectively blocking his transfer application. Frustrated, the employee eventually resigned from Tencent and found another job in Guangzhou. The incident indicated to the top management team that the internal mobility policy was not being effectively implemented. They recognised the need to change the mindset of line managers and to better address employee needs in order to establish a more effective internal mobility system (Tencent, 2022b).

5.1.3 The Development of Flowing Water

At the end of 2012, Tencent launched a special programme for its internal mobility policy called Flowing Water (活水 *huoshui*). Inspired by a Chinese poem, the name signifies the idea that employees should be able to move freely within the organisation to maintain its dynamism. To implement the programme, the HR department established a dedicated team. Thanks to employee feedback, they realised that the internal talent market was insufficiently active because employees had various concerns stemming primarily from three issues:

(1) worries about their current supervisor's views on internal applications and transfers, including fears that their supervisor would disapprove or even block their transfer;

(2) concerns about receiving a lukewarm response from the recruiting department during the internal transfer application process, and fears that their application would go unnoticed; and

(3) worries about the difficulty of adapting to and integrating into a new department after the transfer.

Given these concerns, the leader of the Flowing Water team established a so-called highest principle: that 'the Flowing Water programme should be employee-centred, serving the highest organisational goals and promoting full mobility across the company' (Tencent, 2022). To address and alleviate employee concerns, the team decided to promote a shift in culture that encouraged management to maintain an open attitude towards employees applying for and transferring to new positions. Consequently, the team adopted various approaches to adjust the Flowing Water programme with the aim of overcoming previous obstacles and creating a more fluid and responsive internal mobility system.

The first step in implementing revisions was to cultivate a culture of internal mobility within the organisation. In 2013, the Flowing Water team initiated a reform aimed at changing manager's mindset regarding internal transfers. Co-Founder and former Chief Technology Officer Tony Zhang and Dan Xi, senior vice president and head of HR, played active roles in this reform. During a meeting in which employees and managers were invited to discuss Flowing Water, Tony and Dan encouraged employees to participate in and managers to support the programme. Tony emphasised that internal staff should be prioritised for good opportunities and urged managers to be more open and supportive of employee career development. At the meeting, middle managers shared their opinions and provided feedback on Flowing Water. Employees who had successfully transferred through the programme also shared their experiences, discussing how quickly they had adapted to and were integrated into their new departments. At the 2013 Tencent Strategy Conference attended by all middle managers, the Flowing Water team showed short videos to introduce and promote the programme.

Alongside formal meetings, the Flowing Water team created a comic strip titled 'Mr T's Story of Internal Mobility' and circulated it among staff through the company's online forum (Tencent, 2022). The comic strip detailed the entire process of Mr T applying for an internal job to pursue personal growth and career development. It highlighted where to find internal recruitment positions as well as how Mr T overcame challenges, passed the interview, and communicated with his current line manager. The comic strip was well received, helping more staff – including managers – understand the workings and benefits of the Flowing Water programme to both employees and teams.

A digital product was also developed to promote and improve the internal mobility policies. In 2012, the HR department introduced the Flowing Water digital platform that enabled staff to seamlessly search and apply for internal positions. The platform significantly streamlined the mobility process. Importantly, the iteration of the product also contributed to refining internal mobility rules. Because the HR department saw employees as the end users of their products and considered employee feedback, they continued to optimise internal mobility rules through product iterations. At the outset of the product launch, when applicants clicked on 'I want to apply' within the online system, a prompt would appear with two buttons and ask applicants to choose whether or not they wanted to inform their current line manager of the job application. A majority of applicants chose not to inform their current line manager. The application was then sent to the interviewer who would schedule the interview with the candidate. Once the candidate passed the interview, a notification bar would appear on the system of the interviewer to remind them that the candidate had not informed his/her current line manager of the internal transfer. Only when the candidate had informed his/her line manager could the system move on to the next step and advance the transfer process.

The two buttons and notification bar placed considerable pressure on applicants who were not ready or willing to inform their current managers until they had been offered the job. This pressure was one reason for the low number of applications for internal mobility in 2012. In 2013, the Flowing Water team reviewed the rules and interviewed some staff members (including managers and employees) about their experiences with the product and application process. As the flowing water culture grew more prevalent, managers became more likely to accept internal talent flows. Eventually, they suggested that it was unnecessary for applicants to inform them about applications for internal mobility. As a result, the HR department updated the policy, removing the requirement for applicants to notify their current line managers. Correspondingly, the two buttons and notification bar were removed from the online system.

In 2015, some employees commented on an internal online forum about the inconvenience of having to browse internal recruitment websites at the office owing to the lack of mobile access. In response, the HR department designed and developed a mobile application that was even more effective at maintaining applicant privacy during the application process than the PC-based version. Employees provided survey feedback suggesting that the ninety-day transition period was too long and unnecessary. The Flowing Water team thus adjusted the maximum retention and handover period for the original department from ninety to sixty days on the online system; after sixty days, successful candidates would be automatically transferred to their new post in the online system. This sped up the handover process and reduced any risks to employees in the transfer process.

The Flowing Water team also focused on enabling information sharing and transparency to increase employee engagement with the programme. Since 2013, Flowing Water strategies and policies have been published on internal network bulletin boards, providing all staff with easy access to the details of the programme. The team actively collaborated with groups handling key projects to launch a communication platform called Linkshow. Through Linkshow, team leaders of major products and projects could share their plans, describe the work atmosphere, and demonstrate how they supported employee development. Sharing was aimed at attracting more talent via on-site workshops and live broadcasts.

This approach expanded employee access to a wealth of information about available positions and teams, enabling employees to develop a better understanding of strategically important projects supported by the organisation. The Flowing Water team regularly sent out internal recruitment schemes via e-mail that included descriptions of open positions, especially those within key businesses, to ensure that employees could easily and quickly access information.

With support from the top management team and through the dedication of the Flowing Water team, the programme saw significant improvements. The changes garnered increased attention and positive feedback from staff, as confirmed by our fieldwork. As one interviewed staff member commented: 'The system is designed properly and protects our privacy very well. Even though the original line manager did not approve [of our transfer], we were still able to transfer after the transition period. The system guarantees the freedom of our mobility within the company. There are no more worries or risks for us now.'

5.2 Flowing Water for Dynamism

Following the promotion of internal mobility policies, a growing number of staff members began to participate in the Flowing Water programme. From 2012 to 2020, over 60,000 employees applied for internal positions through the programme and over 12,000 were able to successfully transfer jobs internally (Tencent, 2022). The success rate of applicants in the Flowing Water programme was 20.1 per cent, which meant that one in five moved to another position within the company. Drawing on our fieldwork at Tencent, we discovered that Flowing Water not only enhanced the skills of individual employees, empowered them with the autonomy to shape their professional paths, fortified their self-motivation, and mined their capabilities for innovation. It also provided dynamic talent flows to support the sort of agility and adaptability that drives innovation at the organisational level.

5.2.1 The Individual Level

At the individual level, Flowing Water brought positive outcomes to employees. It did so partly by allowing employees to transition into new roles or departments, enabling them to develop a broader skillset and gain exposure to new perspectives. Such an internal mobility policy encourages employees to explore new roles, responsibilities, or departments within their current organisation. This breadth of experience builds a more versatile skillset, making employees more well-rounded. Employees are exposed to a diverse range of learning opportunities and can explore different aspects of the business, strengthening their adaptability. By doing so, they learn to view challenges from different perspectives. This often leads to creative problem-solving and innovation, as they can bring fresh ideas to each new role they take on.

In our survey undertaken at Tencent, 32.9 per cent (648/1,970) of employees successfully transferred positions through Flowing Water. We asked these 648 respondents to evaluate their situation following the internal transfer. A total of 62.6 per cent of respondents reported they had gained a more diverse body of knowledge and skillset after the transfer, while 61.4 per cent of respondents stated that their existing knowledge and skills were better utilised on their new team. An interviewed staff member recounted:

I originally came from a media background. After working in the media field for over three years, I had accumulated some experience in this area. But to further improve my skills, I knew I needed to get closer to the business side and this was why I chose to move to the advertising team. Now, my primary responsibility is handling public relations in the online industry. In this role, I work closely with business operations and sales, which helps me better understand our key business activities and allows me to participate in them. This has helped strengthen my skills.

Flowing Water has thus supported the career development of employees. Through internal mobility, employees were able to find roles that better matched their interests and aspirations. Because internal mobility allows employees to explore different roles, departments, or projects without leaving the organisation, employees can expand their skillsets and gain new experiences that align with their long-term career goals. On the whole, this makes their careers more dynamic and diverse. Our survey revealed that 55.8 per cent of respondents who had successfully achieved internal job transfers felt that they were responsible for the incubation and development of new products or new business. A total of 57.6 per cent of respondents who had successfully achieved an internal job transfer stated that they had been transferred to a team responsible for key products and projects within the company.

Our interview data also suggested that the main reason why applicants applied for internal jobs was to secure a position that better aligned with their personal interests and career development. As one interviewed staff member who transferred from the CDG to the IEG through Flowing Water commented:

My job is about marketing. When I joined Tencent, I did some general work in my area, but I am interested in the game industry and spent some time studying it. I found an opportunity on the Flowing Water platform and then joined the IEG. Now I can combine my marketing expertise and my interest in my current job position, which I think is more focused and enhances my skills for the long term. I think it is good for the organisation as well, as this position is now filled by a person who is more motivated.

The Flowing Water programme not only guaranteed freedom of mobility to employees but also empowered them by extending the opportunity to actively select their next roles – especially during times of organisational restructuring. As an employee commented: 'Internal recruitment at Tencent is actually somewhat sensitive, but there is a well-established mechanism in place to protect it. This ensures employees can move freely without burdens or risks.'

Instead of simply assigning employees to new roles without their input, Flowing Water extended the freedom for employees to select their next positions based on personal interests, strengths, and goals. This approach replaced the traditional model of passive job transfer with one that valued employee choice, allowing individuals to steer their own career progression. One interviewed member of the IEG successfully applied for internal posts on two occasions following the restructuring of the business group that disbanded her previous teams. Flowing Water helped her find better job opportunities, and she was able to join the teams of her preference:

I applied twice through the Flowing Water programme. With Flowing Water, I could proactively choose to join a new team rather than just passively accept a reassignment from above. This approach offers more flexibility. Internal communication is also smoother; when reviewing job requirements or talking to interviewers, for example, you can directly learn about the role's future tasks. This means that interviews and transfers only proceed when both parties have a clear understanding, giving you better insight into both the projects and the company's overall goals. So the transfer is based on mutual understanding and willingness between the team and me. In this sense, it feels more like a mutual choice, which aligns well with my expectations.

Such an internal mobility policy offers employees autonomy and fosters a more supportive and flexible environment as employees are able to take an active role in shaping their own professional journeys even amid organisational changes. As a result, employees tend to be more motivated and valued, which generally promotes creativity. A performance-tracking analysis across four assessments conducted by Tencent before and after role transitions found that employees who had changed roles in the second half of 2019 experienced an average performance improvement of 3 per cent in their first two post-transition assessments compared with their two pre-transition assessments (Tencent, 2022). Similarly, a survey-based study by Fu and Ding (2022) suggests that voluntary mobility has a more substantial and positive impact on individual innovation performance than passive mobility (e.g. sudden organisational restructuring). To sum up its effects at the individual level, internal mobility allows employees to enrich their capabilities and skills, acquire diverse perspectives and expertise, pursue career progression, and fulfil personal development with autonomy, thereby stimulating their creative thinking.

5.2.2 The Organisational Level

The successful implementation of the Flowing Water programme also yielded several advantages for organisational development and innovation. First, it ensured a continuous and dynamic supply of talent, fostering knowledge sharing and cooperation within the organisation. This approach keeps the talent pool fresh and adaptable as employees bring their experiences and insights from one role to another. Moreover, employees who apply for internal positions are already well-versed in company policies and culture, thereby reducing the need for basic selection and induction training. As an interviewed manager stated:

Tencent's external recruitment is quite strict so when employees participate in the Flowing Water programme, they have already undergone a basic screening. After spending a few years [in the company], your abilities are recognised and trusted. In the Flowing Water programme, department managers are more focused on whether your current experience is a good fit and if you can bring your experience or skills to the new position.

Employees are further inclined to share their accumulated experience from previous departments with current colleagues, promoting knowledge dissemination and enhancing cross-departmental cooperation. Internal mobility brings more connections and collaboration opportunities for departments, mitigates coordination failures in the organisation, and prevents valuable knowledge from spilling over to competing companies. As one interviewee reported:

A substantial part of my previous work may actually be a better fit for my current role. The concept of dynamic talent placement is about positioning people in roles that make the most sense. The experience and resources I've accumulated could provide greater value to the company's business. In this way, it really enhances the alignment between individuals and their roles.

Our survey indicated that 60.4 per cent of the respondents who had successfully achieved internal job transfer through Flowing Water believed that they brought new ideas, new product designs, or new technical solutions to their new team. A total of 58.5 per cent believed that their knowledge and skills had enhanced the performance of their new team. Similarly, survey-based research by Fu and Ding (2022) indicates that internal mobility significantly enhanced employee innovation at Tencent. Specifically, cross-department mobility had a more pronounced positive impact on innovation than mobility within the same department.

These talent flows played a crucial role in supporting and driving the development of key businesses and departments within the company. From 2012 to 2020, more than 12,000 employees successfully transitioned internally, with many joining critical projects and departments, particularly in emerging business sectors (Tencent, 2022). For the WeChat group, for instance, 60 per cent of experienced staff were recruited from other groups through Flowing Water. From 2018 to 2020 alone, individuals entering the WeChat group via the programme constituted 52 per cent of new talent. According to Allen Zhang, creator of WeChat, 'Flowing Water has fostered voluntary talent mobility within the organisation, supplied talent to the WeChat group, and mitigated talent attrition' (Tencent, 2022).

Following the 930 Reform in 2018, approximately 3,000 employees and 200 managers proactively pursued internal transfers based on their preferences. Figure 5.1 illustrates the success rate of applicants seeking transfers between 2012 and 2020. Despite a decline from 2012 to 2016, the success rate has been rising since 2017 and exceeded 20 per cent between 2018 and 2020. This upward trend is likely related to the 930 Reform that encouraged greater internal mobility within the organisation. Many of these individuals chose to contribute to pivotal projects or divisions such as Tencent Cloud, WeChat, video, and payment services. This voluntary mobility not only provided talent support for important projects but also gave more employees the opportunity to utilise their skills, providing motivation and encouraging engagement.

The continuous flow of talent strengthens organisational agility and adaptability, ensuring more preparedness for changes and fostering an environment of teamwork and innovation. In 2018, the HR department established a system within Flowing Water called

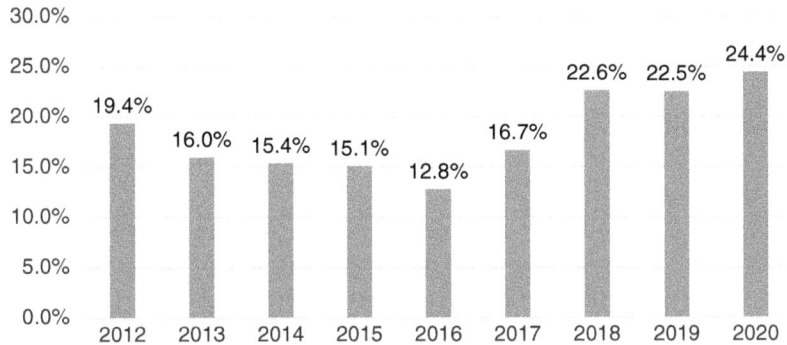

Figure 5.1 Success rate of Flowing Water applicants, 2012–2020.

Exigency Mobility that adjusted job transfer requirements for staff. When it came to strategically important products or urgent cases, employees could apply for internal transfers after working at the company for only three months (instead of one year), with a reduced transition period of just thirty days.

During the onset of the COVID-19 pandemic in early January 2020, many product teams at Tencent were able to swiftly offer services and support to both governments and citizens combating the epidemic. For instance, the WeChat teams played a pivotal role in designing and developing the health information code. The task of recruiting and allocating staff during such an emergency ordinarily involves significant challenges, but in response, the Flowing Water team promptly activated Exigency Mobility to mobilise volunteers. By 27 January 2020, over 1,000 staff members had applied through this system. A growing number of employees then joined projects and teams to provide vital assistance to governments and citizens during the pandemic.

5.3 Discussion and Conclusion

This chapter has examined how Tencent implemented internal mobility policies. The Tencent approach promoted dynamism, strengthened employee self-motivation, advanced organisational agility, and drove innovation at the company. It did so by fostering an open and distinctive 'flowing water' culture and developing an employee-centred digital product to better implement its internal mobility policies. In addition, the company enabled information sharing and transparency within the process to engage more employees with Flowing Water. The successful operation of the programme supported the development of employee skillsets and individual careers, cultivated more initiative and autonomy among employees, and provided more opportunities for employees' self-motivation in the organisation.

The Flowing Water programme not only provided a continuous and dynamic talent supply to the organisation and retained talent in a fiercely competitive environment but also advanced knowledge sharing and cooperation. This reduces organisational rigidity, which itself promotes innovation. Such free and dynamic talent flow also supported the development of key businesses and departments in the company, especially during periods of organisational transformation, and helped the organisation to become more agile and adaptive. As Jiménez-Jiménez and Sanz-Valle (2005) argue, the use of internal labour markets and practices that promote loyalty and participation is more likely to feed every type of innovation.

The Flowing Water programme served not only as a core mechanism for Tencent but also as a prominent and effective model of internal management. In this model, resources are mobilised and utilised within a competitive and open organisational environment. Such a management approach grants significant autonomy to employees, facilitating the efficient allocation, deployment, and development of resources that include human talent. Tencent's HR department places a strong focus on the effective allocation and development of internal talent through initiatives such as internal mobility programmes, incentive mechanisms, and comprehensive systems for training. These efforts are intended to optimise talent utilisation and development across the organisation. As Senior Vice President and Head of HR Dan Xi remarked, 'The Flowing Water programme provides a market mechanism for allocating talent effectively. When employees can pursue their passions and stay motivated, the organisation becomes more dynamic.'

While many companies around the world are increasingly prioritising internal mobility amid fierce talent competition, the task of implementing an effective internal mobility policy remains challenging. The story of Tencent's success with the Flowing Water programme offers valuable lessons for other organisations, particularly by highlighting its distinctive features. First, Tencent's internal mobility programme allowed human resources to flow freely within the organisation. This approach empowered employees to take an active role in deciding when and which positions to apply for, setting it apart from the approaches of other companies. In some companies, such as SAP China (HR Excellence Center, 2020), HR coordinators play a significant role by recommending and promoting internal opportunities to potential candidates. But information asymmetry means that employees may miss out on more suitable or favourable opportunities.

At Google, the Chameleon programme based on algorithm management acts as a matchmaker to determine staff assignment to different teams (Krapivin, 2018). However, despite its potential efficiency, there are concerns about the algorithm's accuracy and effectiveness. Moreover, the 'black box' nature of its operation can contribute to staff anxiety and distrust in the process. But at Tencent, mobility is driven by an employee's own initiative and judgement. This not only fosters personal career growth but also provides substantial autonomy and opportunities for self-motivation within the organisation. The approach has cultivated a dynamic internal market where employees are empowered to pursue opportunities aligned with their professional aspirations and interests.

At the organisational level, this approach aligns with the principle of 'survival of the fittest'. Teams with promising potential are more likely to attract internal talent, thereby bolstering their capabilities, while under-performing teams may experience talent outflow. This dynamic reflects and to some extent predicts the direction of business development or organisational priorities, fostering healthy competition among teams and innovation at the organisational level. This contrasts with Google, where the algorithm primarily relies on preference rankings from both jobseekers and roles. Under those conditions, the management must be deliberate in prioritising and balancing the market. Absent careful oversight, critical projects can remain understaffed, as noted by Cowgill and Koning (2018).

Second, effective internal mobility programmes require a commitment to transparency, communication, and engagement. Such a commitment must be strongly supported by top management. At Tencent, senior managers demonstrated a determination to carry out internal mobility policies and provided massive support. The HR department contributed greatly to the programme, as well. The internal mobility team fostered the organisational culture at Tencent by communicating the benefits of, procedures for, and information about the internal mobility programme to both staff and managers. Lacking a full understanding of the purpose and intent of Flowing Water, employees were once confused and less willing to engage with the programme. When managers had not fully understood how the internal mobility programme worked, along with its importance, they were reluctant to lose talent to other units and were unable to take full advantage of the programme. It was only when both employees and managers had sufficiently communicated or received transparent and open education that they were able to fully engage with the programme. This helped to foster an organisational culture of growth, support, and self-motivation.

Third, Tencent was able to develop a digital platform specifically for internal mobility thanks to advanced digital technologies and its rich experience with product development. As Chapter 4 suggested, digitalisation is key for the continuing success of HRM, and internal mobility is another avenue where an organisation can utilise digital tools or products. In practice, channels for posting internal opportunities vary among companies and can include e-mail, internal websites, and bulletins, among other things. However, an increasing number of organisations build their own internal mobility platforms. Such platforms help to connect employees to internal mobility opportunities through timely information delivered in an interactive way. More importantly, Flowing Water helped Tencent to establish related organisational policies and enhance the employee experience. The HR department not only continued to optimise internal mobility rules through product iteration but also collected and took into account staff feedback as end users of the product during the process of product development (Fu and Wei, 2023).

6 | Building an Open and Inclusive Ecosystem
WeChat's Rise to a Super App

With over 1.4 billion monthly active users (MAUs) in 2025 (Kharpal, 2025), WeChat is a prominent example of success within the Asian tech ecosystem that includes Kakao Talk in South Korea, Line in Japan, and Grab in Southeast Asia. These platform products are characterised by the so-called 'all-in-one' super app model. An all-in-one super app is a comprehensive application that integrates multiple services for daily personal or commercial use (Prud'homme, Chen and Tong, 2023). Leading global tech companies such as Meta, Snap, and Uber are introducing more functions and services into their existing all-in-one super apps. When Tesla and SpaceX founder Elon Musk bought Twitter, he stated his aspiration to turn Twitter into an everything app – a WeChat equivalent (Bleach, 2023). Similarly, Mark Zuckerberg has shown interest in replicating the model of the all-in-one super app within an integrated version of Facebook and WhatsApp (Morrison, 2022). This prompts the question: can existing super app models be successfully replicated?

To answer the question, this chapter explores the case of WeChat. The application is not only a superstar product developed by Tencent but also a typical example of an all-in-one super app. Combining the functionalities of Facebook, Twitter, WhatsApp, Instagram, Paypal, and YouTube into a single platform, WeChat is acclaimed for its multifunctionality and widespread use across various scenarios. This chapter examines WeChat's features, innovations, and ecosystem, all of which arguably contributed to its runaway success as an all-in-one super app. More specifically, the chapter analyses its development to reveal key factors behind the innovation of WeChat. It then explores how WeChat has built up an open and inclusive ecosystem wherein the WeChat team can interact with and empower other players (including individual consumers, business enterprises, and third-party service providers) to provide services, create value, and achieve co-growth within the ecosystem.

6.1 Becoming an All-in-One Super App: Evolution, Connection, and Reaction

In 2011, WeChat was launched as an instant messaging and social media app. By the first quarter of 2024, WeChat had attracted 1.359 billion MAUs worldwide while daily active users numbered over one billion. Figure 6.1 illustrates the growth of WeChat's MAUs alongside the release of new functions on the app. In addition to the app's original functions of instant messaging and social media, the following features were added over time: Voice Message, Moments, Official Account, WeChat Pay, WeCom, Mini Program, and Channels. In this section, we explain how WeChat evolved through the development of these features and examine the nature of connection as well as the 'chemical reactions' among features that ultimately enabled WeChat to become an 'all-in-one' super app.

6.1.1 The Evolution of WeChat

As the saying goes, Rome wasn't built in a day. One WeChat manager we interviewed recounted how WeChat was not originally or intentionally developed into an all-in-one super app. WeChat's journey began in 2010 when Allen Zhang, head of Tencent's R&D centre in Guangzhou, recognised the potential for mobile messaging apps such as WhatsApp and Kik Messenger. He foresaw the need for a dominant Chinese mobile messaging app to rival QQ's PC-based popularity and convinced Tencent's Pony Ma to prioritise it. In November

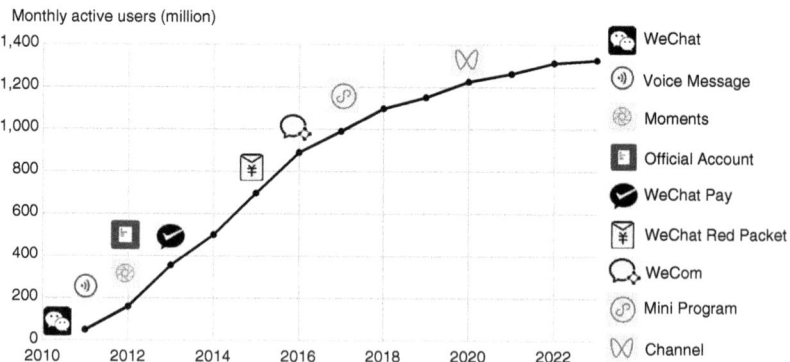

Figure 6.1 Development of an all-in-one super app: WeChat functions and MAUs, 2010–2022.

2010, the Guangzhou R&D centre began to undertake development of the WeChat project. After two months of relentless effort, the first version of WeChat was released on three operating systems (OSs) (Apple iOS, Google Android, and Symbian for Nokia) in January 2011. User growth was initially slow, and WeChat faced competition from apps such as MiTalk developed by Xiaomi. However, Allen was determined and kept exploring the unique spirit of WeChat.

Inspired by the popularity of Talkbox, WeChat introduced voice messaging in April 2011. Allen's team enhanced this feature to switch seamlessly between speaker and earpiece modes, adapting to user needs in various settings. This innovation helped WeChat stand out in the market. Later that year, WeChat launched the People Nearby, Drift Bottle, and Shake features to encourage social interactions among strangers. In April 2012, WeChat introduced Moments, a feature that allowed users to share photos and content from third-party apps with friends. These additions drove an explosion in user growth, expanding WeChat from a communication tool among friends into a broader social media platform.

In August 2012, WeChat launched the Official Account feature that enabled businesses and individuals to create content and engage subscribers, with options for subscription or service accounts tailored to different needs. This feature further allowed businesses to manage customer relations and a brand presence on the app. Official Accounts became a powerful tool for businesses, including small and medium-sized enterprises (SMEs), to reach and interact with a vast user base. At the same time, it enhanced user engagement and retention. Such an inclusive approach aligned with the original intention of Official Accounts: 'Even the smallest business can have its own brand.' As one manager explained: 'We hoped that small businesses could manage their brands like big companies such as Nike and Adidas. Through Official Accounts, users can follow [small business] accounts and connect with [their preferred] brands as if they were connecting with contacts or friends on WeChat. This was the earliest prototype and original intention for Official Accounts.'

WeChat entered China's online payment market in August 2013 with WeChat Pay, which allows users to connect their bank accounts with the app for seamless transactions. During the Lunar New Year of 2014, WeChat Pay's Red Packet feature, inspired by traditional red envelopes, became a hit as millions exchanged money through the app. According to the *2020 Mobile Payment User Survey Report* recently released by the China Payment and Clearing Association (People's Daily, 2021),[1] 74.0 per cent of users were using mobile payments on a daily basis in 2020 and WeChat Pay was one of the most frequently used mobile payment products. As the head of the WeChat Pay team, Ying Zhang recalled in the 2022 WeChat Open Class, 'WeChat Pay became a habit for users, an integral part of their lives.' WeChat Pay was simultaneously committed to digitising businesses, linking WeChat features with digital systems for business operations to distribute consumer vouchers.

In April 2016, Tencent launched WeCom to provide businesses with efficient communication and office automation tools similar to WeChat's interface. WeCom integrates with WeChat for chat, Mini Program, and WeChat Pay, allowing businesses to serve and retain customer relationships. Widely adopted across sectors, WeCom became essential to remote working, particularly during the COVID-19 pandemic. According to figures from the 2023 WeChat Open Class, WeCom has provided services to more than twelve million enterprises and organisations, with private domain transaction volumes reaching hundreds of billions of RMB.

In January 2017, WeChat introduced Mini Program, a sub-application that operates within the WeChat app. An original project created by the WeChat Group, this innovation allows users to access various services without the need to download or install separate mobile apps. When Allen Zhang first introduced Mini Program in the 2017 WeChat Open Class, he explained: 'It realises the dream of [applications] being within reach. Users can open an application simply by scanning a code or searching for it, embodying the "use it and leave" concept. This means that users do not need to install numerous applications, as apps can be accessed anytime without installation.'

Mini Program offered users instant access to a wide range of business services. As of March 2024, WeChat has amassed approximately 945 million MAUs of Mini Program in China (representing over 90 per cent of WeChat's total user base). In the third quarter of 2023, the transaction volume of Mini Program reached RMB 1.5 trillion, encompassing online and offline services such as food and beverage retail, transportation, and public utility payments.

---

[1] http://paper.people.com.cn/rmrbhwb/html/2021-01/19/content_2029778.htm

WeChat then launched Channels in January 2020, entering the short video market to compete with platforms such as TikTok. Channels allows users (both individuals and businesses) to create and discover multimedia content. In 2021, WeChat introduced live-streaming, enriching real-time interaction and engagement for users and content creators. This addition also boosted WeChat's e-commerce by enabling sellers to conduct live video broadcasts and directly engage with potential buyers.

As a result, the past few years have seen WeChat evolve into an all-in-one super app with multiple functions. Through the consolidation of services similar to Facebook, Skype, Slack, Amazon, and PayPal, WeChat became more than just a social app for Chinese consumers where they could communicate, shop, and play games. It also evolved into a super digital tool for businesses to provide various services (see Figure 6.2).

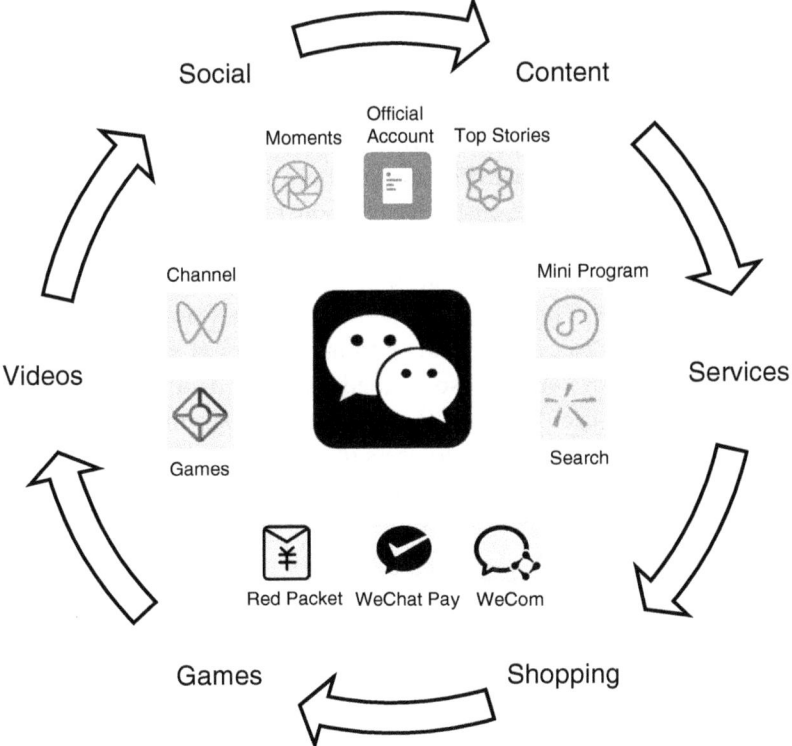

Figure 6.2 WeChat features and services.

6.1.2 Building Connections

The evolution of WeChat into an all-in-one super app was a natural progression rather than a predetermined goal. Throughout, WeChat consistently focused on *connection* as the core nature of the product. In addition, its multifunctionality developed in alignment with technological advancements and user (market) needs. As a result, the scope of the connection evolved continuously alongside the development of the product, technology, and market. WeChat began with the vision of using technology to facilitate interpersonal relationships in the form of a mobile internet communication tool. Features such as chat groups, Moments, and video calls expanded ways for users to stay connected. Building on these interpersonal connections, WeChat then naturally evolved to connect users with services and content. For example, creators and businesses can use Official Accounts to share their information and connect with users. As various connection scenarios emerged, the need for transactions was discovered and led to the introduction of WeChat Pay. WeChat Pay initially gained popularity through its Red Packet feature, which catered to the social networking desires of users; later, it evolved into a robust transaction platform for businesses and services. In addition, WeCom was designed to support both internal organisational connections and external customer relationships.

Mini Program provided a highly flexible means of connection that allowed users to access apps and information anytime, anywhere, at their convenience. The launch of Mini Program was driven by the need for WeChat to provide and support services in various scenarios within its ecosystem. It also aligned with trends in technological development and user habits at the time. Mini Program represented a pioneering solution that allowed users to access applications instantly without the traditional step of installation – an ambitious technical achievement by the WeChat team. Mini Program thus represented a new means of expression and connection. Its ultimate purpose extended beyond online games or service information to numerous offline scenarios. In museums, for example, users could scan QR codes to instantly access information about exhibit items or activities, making such details readily available. Channels enables connections through video creation and distribution, providing a new way for people to engage. Users can share their daily lives and also shop directly through the platform. As Allen Zhang mentioned in the 2021 WeChat Open Class, 'the era is shifting towards video-based expression, both in terms of personal expression and consumption habits'.

The nature of the connection embedded in WeChat is what determines its openness. With the development of connection-oriented functions, WeChat evolved into an open and inclusive platform that linked individuals and empowered content partners and service providers within its ecosystem to enhance their connections and offerings to users. Ultimately, its goal is to bring the world closer together through seamless and universal access in an all-in-one super app.

6.1.3 Chemical Reactions among Product Features

The all-in-one super app is not merely about stacking functionalities. In WeChat, features are designed to work together rather than function as separate standalone tools. A speaker from the Channels team explained in the 2022 WeChat Open Class that Channels is an atomised content component of WeChat. This is also an accurate metaphor that explains the functions of WeChat: all are atomised components of WeChat. As the user identification of these functions is the same, the different components can be interlinked easily within the WeChat infrastructure. More importantly, these functions interact synergistically with each other, naturally circulating within the WeChat ecosystem; their interactions can generate various incredible 'chemical reactions' in different scenarios for different needs. Such reactions allow each feature to complement and enhance the others, creating a seamless experience where users can effortlessly switch between chatting, shopping, paying, sharing, and accessing information – all within a single super app.

For example, the success of Channels is related to its integration with various features within the WeChat ecosystem, such as individual chats, group chats, Moments, Official Accounts, WeChat Pay, and Mini Program. This integration allows for the rapid sharing and dissemination of short videos, images, and live streams within the WeChat ecosystem. Moreover, the integration produced a 1+1 > 2 effect. Channels plus WeChat Pay can generate revenue from paid content for creators. Channels plus Official Accounts allows users to follow a creator's official account through videos, enabling the creator to gain more private domain traffic and engage fans more effectively.

In this way, Channels evolved into the optimal form for hosting content such as videos and live-streaming within WeChat.

The WeChat team has been continuously optimising the infrastructure to enable more extensive interactions between atomised components for more reactions. This not only enhances the product capabilities but also promotes the evolution of its ecosystem. As an interviewed manager from the Mini Program team commented: 'With these functions, we have released a lot of capabilities, and we will continue to release more in the future. More possibilities are expected.'

6.2 Key Sources of WeChat's Innovation Success

A senior WeChat product manager recounted how an all-in-one super app was not part of the initial design for WeChat, saying: 'We had no plan to make a super app at the beginning, not intentionally. Since the beginning, we have cared more about whether our product could address fundamental issues and user needs. I think it's this mindset that naturally fosters a super app, and perhaps also makes it truly super.'

It was thus the innovative nature of WeChat that drove its evolution into a super app. This section explores the factors that fuelled WeChat's innovation and distinctive characteristics.

6.2.1 'Deep Innovation': A First Principles-Orientation in Product Design

Drawing on extensive fieldwork at Tencent, we argue that a key distinguishing characteristic of WeChat's success is its deep innovation. *Deep innovation* refers to a form of innovation that involves an approach grounded in first principles, which allows designers/developers to explore fundamental concepts and uncover the core nature underlying the product, service, or even a single function. This goes beyond incremental improvements or superficial changes and often leads to breakthroughs that address core problems or limitations in a novel way.

'First principles' is a foundational proposition or assumption that stands alone and cannot be deduced from any other proposition or assumption. The philosopher Aristotle coined this concept, suggesting that: 'In every systematic enquiry (methods) where there are first principles, or causes, or elements, knowledge and science result from acquiring knowledge of these; for we think we know something just in case we acquire knowledge of the dry causes, the primary first principles, all the way to the elements.'

First principles serve as the fundamental building blocks for a system of thought or a domain of knowledge. Accordingly, the idea of first-principles thinking is to break down complicated problems into basic elements and then reassemble them from the ground up. It encourages ever-deeper exploration until the foundational truths of a situation are revealed.

Our interview data suggests that first-principles thinking is embedded in the product design of the WeChat team as it is able to identify the basic nature of a product or function. This is related to the mindset of the leader, Allen Zhang, who is seen as the soul of the WeChat group. Allen holds the view that innovation comes from continuous independent thinking, constant questioning, and relentless creation. For that reason, he likes to ask questions about the nature of things. When developing the function of online documents for WeCom, for example, Allen asked the team what a document was and what it was for WeCom. Such questions confused the team as most of the staff thought of a document as simply a document that users can edit. However, Allen inspired the team by explaining that a document is essentially a space for collaboration and exchange through which WeCom can bring people together. Based on this understanding, the WeCom team placed greater emphasis on the core element of collaboration within WeCom functions.

Allen was thus constantly thinking about the nature of products and their functions. More importantly, he encouraged the WeChat group to think in the same way. As several managers commented in interviews:

What is the nature of a product? What is the nature of communication? What is the nature of Moments? Allen is always thinking about the nature of things, and he likes to ask us about the nature of things as well.

In meetings, we often ask ourselves why we do something. If we have a new idea for a function for a product, for example, we'll ask why we may or may not need this function before we implement the idea. We know Allen likes to get to the root of a matter. In fact, many product managers in the WeChat group are often asked a soul-stirring question: What is the essence of this thing? So, we developed a habit of thinking this way.

In developing this way of thinking, the WeChat group not only formed a habitual way of thinking but also developed a first principles-oriented product design. Within this approach, the WeChat team placed great emphasis on the process of first principles-oriented thinking well before the design stage of a product or even taking concrete actions. This thinking centres on clarifying and defining the essence or core element of the product or project. Then, the WeChat group broke down a problem into its fundamental elements and built solutions from scratch based on the foundational principles rather than relying solely on existing solutions or conventions. In other words, they were committed to delving deep into the essence of a problem to grasp its fundamentals while remaining unbiased by existing solutions.

This approach entails a thorough understanding of both the underlying principles governing the problem as well as the essential requirements and limitations of the context in which the product will operate. By shedding preconceived notions and conventional approaches, this approach empowers WeChat teams to explore innovative solutions that effectively tackle the root challenges rather than simply replicating the approach used by competitors. 'We never care about what competitors are doing. We only care about what we need to do next', one interviewed manager commented. Another explained: 'The product team prioritises emphasising the essence of the matter rather than reacting hastily to competitors' actions or implementing every user suggestion. This approach prevents the product from becoming unnecessarily cumbersome and overly complex.'

6.2.2 Understanding Users Better Than They Understand Themselves

Based on a first principles-oriented process for product design, the WeChat team develops a deep understanding of the essential needs of users. It has long been recognised that Tencent adheres to the principle of putting users first and letting user value guide decision-making. The company developed a so-called 10/100/1,000 rule, which means that product managers are required to conduct ten user surveys, follow 100 user blogs, and collect feedback from 1,000 user experiences each month. The WeChat group also applied this rule to collect user feedback.

However, responding to user feedback is a challenge for the WeChat team as it has a massive base of over one billion users per day. User feedback can be scattered and disorganised. It is impossible to accept and implement all feedback from users and specific feedback simply does not represent users in general. As a result, understanding user needs can involve more than just blindly responding to user requests. Product designers and developers must grasp the essence of their products, then extract essential insights from the massive volume of complex user information to identify what users genuinely need. A manager at WeCom provided the following explanation on how to deal with the relationship between the essence of a product and user feedback: 'You need to understand the essence of the product, which is the tree trunk. You need to identify which user feedback addresses issues with the trunk of your tree, and which addresses issues with the leaves. You should prioritise fixing the trunk to make sure it is straight and strong, then trim the leaves.'

For example, online discussion on WeChat thought that the company should introduce a read feature for its messaging, which many social software applications have. The read feature indicates whether the receiver has received and viewed the message by displaying the word 'read' on the message. Users had various reactions and opinions. One group of users suggested introducing a read feature and asked why WeChat hadn't done so yet. However, the WeChat team had a good understanding of users' communication and social needs as well as their privacy concerns. They felt that a read feature would increase the psychological burden and social pressure on the receiver, who might feel an obligation to reply because the sender would know the message had been read. From the very beginning, the WeChat team had firmly decided not to display this feature. The team has stated that it will not do so in the future, nor will they add it as an adaptation for overseas customers because they believe that the foundation of social needs and user experience is the same worldwide, despite cultural differences. A manager explained why the team did not simply respond to the demands of some users: 'If we just simply adopted the typical user feedback (regarding "read"), [we] would go wrong. In fact, we had thought about this matter thoroughly for ourselves. We heard user feedback and observed user behaviour. However, we know what the core logic of WeChat is and have a clear idea of user needs.'

In fact, the WeChat group creates needs for users based on a deep understanding of users, the market, and products. A senior manager of the WeChat group reported that:

As product managers, we need to understand users and their needs. But the biggest problem with users is that they won't tell you what they need. For example, a user won't tell you they need a WeChat as they don't have a specific idea. They just need a tool on their phone to communicate with others anytime and anywhere. So we need to create it for users.

The WeChat team thus understands users better than users understand themselves as the team assumed users may not actually know what they want within the product. In addition to observing and analysing user needs and use of a product, the team thinks independently about the core nature and logic of the product so that they can create new functions within products to meet those needs. A product manager commented: 'We believe that users don't necessarily know what they want. We need to create something, and only when they see it will they realise it's what they really wanted.'

A good example is Red Packet, an innovation developed by the WeChat team. This feature was inspired by Chinese culture, successfully merging traditional customs with a digital social network. In Chinese tradition, gift-giving is vital for maintaining relationships with family, friends, and business partners, especially during holidays, festivals, and special occasions such as the Chinese New Year, weddings, or birthdays. WeChat Red Packet preserves this tradition by allowing friends to send money – often in small amounts – digitally. This can be done in individual chats or group chats. For group chats, users can choose either an equal red packet (everyone receives the same amount) or a random red packet (the total amount is split randomly). The random distribution algorithm adds an element of fun, playfulness, and friendly competition that traditional gift-giving rarely offers. The popularity of Red Packet demonstrates the WeChat team's deep understanding of Chinese culture and user psychology as well as their ability to leverage it to create user needs and gain user acceptance. Allen Zhang once said, 'After working for so many years, I feel that understanding human nature is the most important.' This is precisely the foundation of WeChat Red Packet's success.

6.2.3 Long-Term Perspectives and Rapid Mini-Upgrades

WeChat's evolution from a social messaging tool to an all-in-one super app over the past decade is a result of the team's long-term perspective. The long-term perspective establishes the core values and principles for WeChat, enabling it to grow in a healthy and sustainable manner free from the constraints of short-term returns and rigid performance indicators. It also provides ample time and space for innovation.

To begin, the WeChat team paid a great deal of attention to the sustainable and healthy development of a product as they believed that this would promote innovation in the long term. By 2012 and 2013, WeChat had gained a large user base but remained unprofitable. Concerns were raised about WeChat's business model and lack of profitability. However, WeChat adhered to the unique philosophy behind its business approach. The team did not seek instant success or quick profits, believing instead that a successful product would naturally lead to a viable business model. Rather than focusing on profit or traffic, the team emphasised the product itself and innovation. This approach reflects their belief that the so-called business model is a byproduct of a successful product, not the primary goal. As a senior manager at WeChat commented:

The core thing is to have enough patience. I think patience is especially important. We don't create products to make a profit. As long as a product is successful [at what it aims to do], it will naturally be profitable. This is something WeChat has adhered to as our goal since the beginning, and it's actually very important for a product's innovation. If the goal is incorrect, or if the initial definition of the product is incorrect, then your subsequent innovations will be off track.

Next, the WeChat team refrains from using key performance indicators (KPIs) for performance management – a departure from common practice in most IT companies. While many IT companies focus their KPIs on generating traffic to achieve business goals such as monetisation, WeChat avoids this approach. This is because KPIs often emphasise short-term measurable outcomes. They tend to neglect long-term development, which is usually unmeasurable but crucial for fostering innovation. Allen Zhang argued that setting KPIs leads product managers to prioritise short-term traffic acquisition over creating the best product for users in the long term. By not setting KPIs, the WeChat team can focus more on developing excellent products and fostering user engagement.

Furthermore, it is not feasible to set suitable KPIs for a team focused on an innovative project. As a manager from Mini Program explained:

To be honest, since the establishment of the WeChat team, we have never aimed to achieve KPIs. Yet this has not hindered our ability to improve continuously. At the Mini Program team, for instance, focusing on KPIs would have been challenging because there isn't a predefined framework for setting them. If we had focused on KPIs, the team might not have undertaken this project at all.

Another senior manager at WeChat similarly explained that free from the constraints of KPIs, the teams can focus more on understanding the essence of things and how to solve problems instead of chasing after a KPI figure:

WeChat believes that all data [for KPIs] is a result. We shouldn't take action just to chase after numbers. Instead, the data emerges naturally as a consequence of your actions. This result is then used to validate your ideas. For innovation teams such as ours, not having KPIs is beneficial [as they would] restrict us. Therefore, our approach is not about achieving a specific number but about how we can achieve it.

WeChat's focus on long-term development rather than immediate profits, and its freedom from rigid KPIs, is closely tied to Tencent's supportive organisational environment. Tencent provides WeChat with the space to grow and innovate, and empowers its teams with significant autonomy.

Furthermore, the WeChat team invests significant effort in improving foundational infrastructure, such as underlying architecture, product capabilities, and ecosystem design. This is because the foundational infrastructure will directly determine the overall stability of the product's technical platform in the long term. As more functions are developed, more modules will be integrated into the product architecture. It is crucial to ensure that the integration of these modules does not affect the user experience while maintaining the stability of the platform. The task of continuously improving infrastructure and architecture requires patience, but WeChat believes that it is worthwhile for long-term development:

We have spent the most time and effort on foundational infrastructure, and we have enough patience for it – perhaps more patience than third parties. That's because for some foundational infrastructure aimed at the future, we cannot expect immediate success just by designing features well and having users immediately engage with it. On the contrary, I think we need a lengthier period to lay the groundwork and let [the product] grow gradually.

We hope to see it grow step by step and do not want it to suddenly become something that is forcefully inflated. So I hope everyone can be as patient as we are in observing its development.

Finally, WeChat focuses on long-term impacts and closely monitors industrial trends over extended periods. Their product development approach goes beyond meeting current user or market needs; they consider the potential 'butterfly effect' of their actions and their far-reaching impacts. The group proactively anticipates future market and industry trends; it has a dedicated team for product planning and operations, specialising in forecasting trends for the next six months to a year, which aids in making decisions for long-term development.

However, this long-term vision is not at odds with rapid mini upgrades. During the product development process, the WeChat team conducts rapid iterations and incremental upgrades to improve the user experience and ensure technological advancement. Although the foundational product design and long-term perspective establish the vision and direction for WeChat's development, there are no fixed steps for product optimisation – especially when it comes to enhancing the user experience. With the rapid evolution of the internet industry, user needs, market demands, and technology have developed swiftly. Therefore, rapid mini-upgrades that encourage repeated trials and refinements allow the WeChat team to better and more quickly capture user needs, implement them, and enhance the user experience. As a staff member at Mini Program commented: 'We undertake continuous adjustments. If one feature doesn't work today, we try another tomorrow and if that doesn't work, we add a different one the next day. This is our approach to innovation.'

6.2.4 Invisible, Compound, and Continuous Innovation: A Combination of Technological, Process, Product, and Business Model Innovations

We argue that the success of WeChat as an all-in-one super app also benefits from the invisible, compound, and continuous innovation that integrates product, process, and business model innovations. *Invisible innovation* refers to innovations that are not immediately obvious or visible to the general public but have a significant impact on processes, systems, and outcomes (Djellal and Gallouj, 2010; Hastings and Finch, 2007). *Compound innovation* refers to the development of multiple innovations within a single platform, where each innovation not only introduces new products or services to users but also generates additional value through their interactions. These interconnected innovations work synergistically, enhancing and supporting one another, ultimately amplifying the overall value of the product or organisation.

In the case of WeChat, the stability, security, and ability to protect user privacy rely on technological capabilities and innovation. The seamless integration of various functions and services with excellent user experience is supported by continuous high-level process innovation that tends to be invisible to users. This also hinges on product innovation and the evolution of business models tailored to diverse application scenarios. These innovations do not exist in isolation; they are interrelated, interconnected, and interactive. Through invisible, compound, and continuous innovation, WeChat not only offers multi-applicability across various scenarios and industries but also supports and ensures the safety and stability of large-scale usage.

WeChat has strong in-house R&D capabilities that allow it to develop its technology independently without relying on any third-party solutions. The WeChat Group firmly believes that, regardless of the type of technology, they must start from scratch and follow the learning path others have taken – but they must learn faster and acquire the technology in a shorter time frame. Only then will they have the chance to establish their own solid technological capabilities. The technological capabilities and innovation ensure the product's long-term stability, confidentiality, security, and reliability, even with a large user base and under various conditions. During every Spring Festival period in China, for example, WeChat experiences an exceptionally high volume of messages and Red Packet exchanges all at once. However, WeChat has consistently managed to withstand the pressure of massive spikes in usage without any disruptions during these peak periods.

The Mini Program function created by the WeChat Group introduced innovative solutions to mark a significant technological breakthrough, primarily by eliminating the burden of downloading an app for users. Although managing applications on smartphones has become lighter and easier, allowing those not familiar with computers to use them effortlessly, it still involves a tedious process in which all applications must be downloaded and installed before they can be used. Mini Program eliminates the need for downloads as in effect, external applications can be used directly through the WeChat platform. Users can swipe down on WeChat to access a list of saved or recently used mini-programs. Users can also access a mini-program via other channels, such as through the WeChat Official Account menu, by scanning a mini-program QR code, or by sharing a mini-program card in chat groups. Several interviewed staff members from the Mini Program team explained the innovation as follows:

All applications require you to download [the application] and install it before you can use it. This is a very cumbersome process. The first feature of the mini-program is that it eliminates the download process and can be used directly, so there is no need to install it. It is the most basic feature of the mini-program.

I believe that mini-programs and apps are two different ways of organising applications. We do not think that mini-programs are meant to replace apps. On the contrary, mini-programs are meant to enrich many scenarios of apps. In many situations, downloading an app might be too cumbersome and inconvenient.

Once you have accessed a mini program, you do not need a program manager to manage it. It appears in a completely different format from past apps and has a more flexible form of organisation. It is more flexible and more accessible than all our existing apps.

In addition, Mini Program lowers barriers for app developers. In the past, software development required developers to consider different programming languages, device compatibility, and costs associated with various development environments. But as Mini Program provides a solution to the global challenge of cross-system development, developers can create applications within a development system that overcomes the limitations of traditional development environments. This initiative considers not only technical implementation within WeChat but also adaptability across various programming languages.

Mini Program has already established a complete development environment and developer ecosystem. By 2018, over 1.5 million developers had joined the Mini Program ecosystem, creating 1.04 million jobs in 2017. The subject of a mini program entered university computer science classrooms, giving rise to the new profession of 'mini programmer'. At the Fifth World Internet Conference held in Wuzhen, China, the mini-program was selected for the first time as a leading technological achievement in the world. This recognition was part of the World Leading Internet Scientific and Technological Achievements event, highlighting mini-program as a brand new technological and application innovation. As Pony Ma commented at the conference: 'Mini Program is an innovation for developers in the IT sector as it creates an "unlimited" environment for developers and provides Chinese solutions to the challenge of "cross-system" development.'

Next, WeChat transcended previous conceptual boundaries to introduce an innovative model that established a unique relationship dynamic distinct from those of other social media platforms. X (formerly Twitter) is clearly a many-to-many platform, as is Facebook. WhatsApp primarily supports one-to-one, and in some cases many-to-many communication through group chat. In contrast, WeChat has become exceptionally complex by incorporating multiple relationship models simultaneously and seamlessly.

To illustrate, WeChat employs the one-to-one relationship model through private chat, the many-to-many relationship model through group chat, and the one-to-many relationship model through Official Accounts. Meanwhile, Moments is built on a one-to-many relationship model, but limited to interactions between a user and his/her friends, since only WeChat contacts are permitted to view Moments content published by the user. This diversity in relationship models appearing across a single app is remarkable because it integrates various modes into one application. Such a comprehensive approach has rarely been seen in other applications to date and is grounded in the fact that the WeChat team has a profound understanding of human relationships.

WeChat's process innovation is demonstrated through its integration of various functions and services into a single application, alongside its functional applicability across diverse scenarios and industries. The innovative application of its functionalities to real-world scenarios is challenging. As noted by a staff member in an interview:

Many of the challenges we encounter are not at the technical level but lie in how to apply and promote these technologies across different industries, truly integrating them into industry-specific application scenarios.

Therefore, we believe that real challenge and innovation lie in finding ways to couple our product and service with the industry ecosystem when we engage with an industry.

The WeChat team has thus dedicated significant effort to refining product functionality and adapting it to real-world scenarios. Relying solely on individual efforts is insufficient; the creation of an open ecosystem is needed to foster collaboration with other entities and promote collective growth. Consequently, Tencent adopted an approach of fostering an open ecosystem, recognising that innovative applications require collaboration among all stakeholders. The user experience was also prioritised in the process of innovation, successfully attracting users and facilitating growth for both businesses and consumers on the platform. As a manager explained:

Innovation is a continuous process. We aim to improve user experience and do not introduce new functions arbitrarily. We adopt a user-centric perspective, putting ourselves in the user's shoes, considering real-life scenarios, and ensuring they use these features naturally. We assist businesses in enhancing their operational efficiency while maintaining a set of guidelines; for example, businesses are prohibited from disturbing their users on WeChat. Users have the right and freedom to enable or disable certain WeChat features or services offered by businesses.

Leveraging the integration of its functions, WeChat showcases rich business model innovation (including social e-commerce) in the form of Official Accounts, Mini Program, social network finance based on WeChat Red Packet, community group-buying via Mini Program, and the online–offline integrated model demonstrated by WeCom. To illustrate, WeCom provides an effective tool for digitalisation in the manufacturing sector and broader real economy. This, in turn, represents the in-depth integration of digital and physical realms.

In recent years, over 80 per cent of the top automobile manufacturers in China, particularly new energy vehicle manufacturers, have adopted WeCom. With their large employee base, these manufacturers need an easy, efficient communication and management tool for internal use. WeCom ensures the continuous flow of business data, swift approval, and rapid operation of business processes. Externally, WeCom connects enterprises with individual customers. During vehicle sales and delivery, manufacturers can use WeCom to communicate directly with customers. As many new energy vehicles are bespoke, customers' specific preferences can be sent directly to manufacturers via WeCom, allowing for the swift transmission of data and preferences from the sales phase to the production phase.

6.3 Building an Open, Decentralised, and Inclusive Ecosystem for Co-growth

The unique nature of WeChat is reflected not only in its status as an all-in-one super app but also in its ecosystem (Bai and Liu, 2023). WeChat has embraced an open ecosystem approach since its inception. Originally, the primary reason for this strategy was related to constraints on resources and personnel. As it adheres to small team management and avoids significant team expansion, WeChat had to leverage openness as a strategic solution to these internal constraints in order to achieve long-term development. For instance, the WeChat Pay team collaborated with more than 1,800 banks and payment institutions to collectively foster the growth of mobile payments; every month, approximately 23,000 service providers catered to millions of merchants. However, there were only 1,000 employees on the internal team. This meant that WeChat had to rely on the one million professionals operating in the ecosystem and these external stakeholders were actively involved in promoting mobile payments, advancing WeChat Pay, and aiding merchants in digitalisation efforts. That is the power of an open ecosystem. As a senior manager of WeChat elaborated:

Whether a product chooses to be open or self-contained depends on organisational and manpower costs as well as internal resource constraints. If internal resources aren't sufficient, we must find ways to optimise our entire ecosystem. WeChat initially chose openness because it needed a method to rapidly strengthen its ecosystem. Since it couldn't achieve this alone, it had to open up and share these opportunities with everyone.

As the application of the functionalities to various scenarios and different industries requires collaboration among all relevant stakeholders, an open ecosystem can mobilise the enthusiasm of all parties involved and encourage them to participate in co-creation and symbiosis. The Deputy General Manager of WeChat Open Platform commented: 'Our goal is to collaborate with our partners to promote the healthy and vigorous growth of the ecosystem, collectively addressing challenges and opportunities in the industrial Internet and digital era.'

This not only helps WeChat to enhance and explore new capabilities in various scenarios but also enables other stakeholders to realise their value, fostering mutual growth. Over time, openness has become more than just a strategy for WeChat; it is now an integral part of its core values. WeChat aims to cultivate a forest rather than construct a palace solely for itself. This forest offers a healthy and sustainable environment for growth and development, allowing all entities to flourish independently rather than having WeChat build and control every aspect.

By building an open and inclusive ecosystem, WeChat interacts with, empowers, and supports various players – including individual consumers, businesses, and third-party service providers – to deliver services, create value, and achieve mutual growth. Drawing on the field data, we identified the three main approaches used by WeChat to develop its ecosystem.

6.3.1 Providing an Excellent Tool by Enhancing Product Capabilities

Within the ecosystem, WeChat positions itself as a tool – not as the centre of the ecosystem. As Allen Zhang explained in the 2018 WeChat Open Class, the core of WeChat is to be a reliable tool that users can rely on for years, earning their trust and recognition: 'In the eyes of users, this tool should be like an old friend. We cannot accept adding a lousy feature that would burden users.' In addition, WeChat aims to improve user efficiency by becoming a use-and-go tool. According to Allen, 'The essence of the use-and-go tool is that it helps users complete a task efficiently. After completing a task, we want users to move on to other things rather than spending unnecessary time within the tool.' For this reason, WeChat focuses on helping users to complete tasks efficiently rather than overwhelming them with endless options. Despite frequent updates, it maintains a clean and simple interface, carefully evaluating each new feature to ensure that it does not disrupt the user experience. This approach allows users to enjoy a streamlined, intuitive product.

WeChat offers users a tool that is not only efficient but also cost-effective. This is evident in the low-cost development and operation of Mini Program for businesses. Traditional app development cycles take at least two to three months, with development costs running to millions. Mini programs can be developed by just two or three software engineers in three to four days, achieving the same functionality as traditional apps. This significantly lowers barriers and costs, making mini-programs accessible to a wide range of businesses, including SMEs and startups. A good example is Baiyun, a local locksmith in Hunan Province, who developed his own mini-program for his business. Before the advent of WeChat Mini Program, advertising was challenging for him and other locksmiths. He had to shuttle between neighbourhoods daily, posting adhesive advertisements door-to-door and stuffing business cards at every entrance. By chance, he discovered WeChat Mini Programs and thought, 'Can I create a locksmith mini-program so users can find my service by searching "locksmith" on WeChat and contacting me directly?'

With this idea, Baiyun immediately registered the mini-program name Locksmith Headquarters. He enlisted a developer friend on WeChat to build a locksmith platform within the mini-program. He shared it in hundreds of WeChat groups, gathering the first batch of locksmiths to join. He also promoted Locksmith Headquarters in his Moments, informing all his WeChat friends about it. After six months of relentless effort and continuous promotion in WeChat groups and Moments, his mini-program ranked first in search results for 'locksmith' on WeChat, attracting free traffic. It drew in 15,000 locksmiths and accumulated thirty million visits. Eventually, he began charging a verification entry fee of RMB 98 per year, earning RMB 220,000 in four months.

In keeping with the Chinese saying 'better to teach a man to fish than to give him fish', WeChat provides tools for external partners to grow rather than simply completing tasks for them. This ensures the health and sustainable development of the ecosystem. As Pony Ma explained, 'What we can do is provide tools and components for all industries, allowing them to rise higher and navigate more safely through the wave of mobile internet integration.' While WeChat offers a toolbox for partners, it is up to the businesses and users to decide when and how to use WeChat. This approach not only equips them with capabilities but also grants them autonomy for growth within the ecosystem.

To support the growth of an ecosystem with a large user and player base, WeChat must enhance its product capabilities to provide a reliable, safe, and affordable product. The primary challenge lies in balancing the compliance, compatibility, and flexibility of the functions in the product. For example, Mini Program must find a balance between having sufficiently foundational technology and providing partners with enough space to innovate. This balance involves ensuring compatibility that empowers future users on the WeChat platform while giving them enough room to implement their own solutions. On the one hand, WeChat aims to find the most suitable and likely industry-standard solutions to provide the fundamental infrastructure for ecosystem development. This requires not only achieving technical implementation but also ensuring language compatibility for developers. On the other hand, maintaining product flexibility is crucial as WeChat recognises that the more they handle, the less room there is for developer creativity. During one period, WeChat released a new version almost every week, continuously adding interface capabilities to ensure developers had ample exploration space to grow alongside them. One Mini Program manager commented: 'We need to ensure their flexibility while also keeping them on the intended usage track. So we not only improve the technical capacities, but also refine the product and rules design.'

6.3.2 Empowering Players in the Ecosystem: Fairness, Decentralisation, and Inclusivity

'Make the product the best it can be, then respect the user's choice', said one interviewed manager who illustrated WeChat's position and attitude towards users in the ecosystem. Whether individual users or different types and sizes of businesses, WeChat aims to empower players in the ecosystem by providing excellent tools. More importantly, WeChat established principles that respect users by focusing on fairness, decentralisation, and inclusivity. In fact, the fundamental logic of WeChat's ecosystem rules is fairness and inclusivity. SMEs can thrive, evolve, and grow stronger on the platform as much as large companies and brands can.

WeChat advocated for a decentralised structure without controlling traffic entry. One manager reported: 'WeChat has always followed the principle that we should not affect the existence of each service. What we should do is to try our best to allow more valuable services to emerge and be found by users rather than us influencing them. [The principle] is a manifestation of our respect for users.'

In a centralised entry model, small businesses often struggle to grow owing to limited resources for acquiring traffic and gaining exposure. WeChat took a different approach by relinquishing advantages to users and third-party providers, notably eliminating categorisation, rankings, or recommendations for Official Accounts. In the PC internet era, traffic entry typically occurred through search boxes but in the mobile internet era, QR codes have become decentralised entry points that facilitate direct user–service connections. WeChat has actively promoted QR code adoption in China, making it essential for enterprises offering official accounts or mini-programs to distribute their QR codes widely.

This shift means that the entry point for these services lies outside WeChat, specifically within QR codes. Traffic is now sourced directly from users and operators, promoting fairness across enterprises of varying sizes. This decentralised approach levels the playing field, allowing small businesses – even those in remote areas or operated by the elderly – to use QR codes for transactions at street stalls. Such convenience reduces concerns about counterfeit currency and change, thereby supporting the growth of small vendors. Empowering SMEs in this manner ensures that they can thrive regardless of their size, marking a significant step towards inclusive growth on the platform. As one interviewed manager commented: 'SMEs make up a vast part of the market. As long as your tool is fair enough and not centralised, they can use it without any pressure or burden. That is the best way to help them.'

Allen Zhang explained that WeChat adopted a decentralised structure to reflect WeChat's long-term perspective:

> If decentralisation does not occur and Tencent monopolises the mini programs, there would be no opportunities for external developers. While Tencent might profit in the short term, the ecosystem would cease to exist. Even companies invested in by Tencent should follow the platform's rules; otherwise, the platform's fairness would be undermined. We place greater importance on the platform's health.

6.3.3 *Supporting Third-Party Service Providers*

The term 'third-party service providers' usually refers to companies or developers that offer various services and solutions that integrate with or extend the functionality of WeChat. These providers contribute to the ecosystem by developing mini programs, creating official accounts, or offering mobile payment solutions, advertising services, and other applications within the WeChat platform. Mini Program, WeCom, WeChat Pay, and other functions have formed a sizeable and well-developed ecosystem, bringing together tens of thousands of third-party service providers. These providers play a vital role in enriching the WeChat ecosystem, catering to the diverse needs of users and businesses while leveraging WeChat's extensive user base and infrastructure. In 2021, service providers related to WeChat Mini Program, WeCom, and other functions created over six million job opportunities and income streams (China Academy of Labour and Social Security, 2022).[2]

WeChat not only provided the fundamental infrastructure for third-party service providers but also supported them and provided sufficient space for them to innovate and grow. This is partly because WeChat offers unlimited possibilities for third-party service providers to develop. A WeCom manager explained using a metaphor: 'WeChat provides a roughcast house, leaving the detailed decoration work to more service providers. Every user can choose their own style of décor, whether Japanese or Italian, and find their own team of decorators. This approach makes decorator teams very motivated and active. As our products serve millions or even billions of users, they must be very versatile.'

WeChat teams encourage third-party service providers to work with WeChat to build the ecosystem, giving providers a high level of autonomy. They believe that by working together, the ecosystem will become a dynamic and self-improving one rather than remaining relatively rigid.

WeChat has always been very attentive to the provision of training to third-party service providers. WeChat's biggest annual event is not a product launch but rather the WeChat Open Class. When WeChat first started Official Accounts, many users were confused about how to operate them effectively and beneficially. Various courses were available on the market, so WeChat thought, 'Why don't we provide some official guidance?' The WeChat team discussed this idea with Allen Zhang, who insisted that if the event were to boast about WeChat, he would definitely not participate, but if they were to hold

[2] www.tisi.org/24430

open-ended courses where everyone could share ideas, thoughts, and methods on the platform, he would be willing to participate. Instead of teaching users exactly what to do, WeChat Open Class showcases successful examples to inspire users.

Since its inception, WeChat has paid special attention to market training and cultivation and there have been ongoing programmes to nurture development and third-party service provision. Some initiatives are conducted internally while others involve collaboration with other partners. Such training and nurturing programmes foster knowledge accumulation and promote positive collaborative relationships within the ecosystem.

6.4 Discussion and Conclusion

In recent years, several super apps have emerged across Asia, by integrating a wide range of services into a single digital platform. Notable examples include KakaoTalk in South Korea, Grab in Southeast Asia, and Line in Japan and Taiwan. These platforms have sought to expand beyond messaging into areas such as payments, shopping, and transport. Simultaneously, several Western tech companies have made efforts to build similar integrated ecosystems. For instance, Facebook (now Meta) has attempted to incorporate messaging, payments, shopping, and gaming into its suite of apps. However, despite these integrations, it lacks offline service integration and does not offer the same seamless in-app experience found in its Asian counterparts. Apple and Google, on the other hand, provide integration at the OS level, offering services such as Apple Wallet, Google Wallet, voice assistants, app integrations, and smart home control. However, their ecosystems remain fragmented across multiple apps, lacking a unified, all-in-one interface that serves as a singular portal for daily digital life. Meanwhile, Elon Musk's X (formerly Twitter) has publicly declared its ambition to evolve into a super app, offering services that go far beyond social media. However, this vision remains in its early stages, with an uncertain roadmap and limited execution thus far. In contrast, WeChat stands as arguably the world's most advanced and deeply integrated super app. Originating in China, WeChat has evolved far beyond its roots as a messaging platform. It now combines instant messaging, mobile payments, e-commerce, media, government services, and a vast ecosystem of mini-programs – all within a single app interface. This unparalleled breadth and depth of services have led to WeChat being referred to as a 'platform-as-life infrastructure', offering users a seamless and centralised digital experience for both online and offline life.

Through analysing the case of WeChat, one of the most successful products in the digital platform world, this chapter has revealed the development of an all-in-one super app, examined the innovation behind it, and explored how WeChat established an open and inclusive ecosystem. Based on our fieldwork research, we argue that an all-in-one super app was a natural outcome of the evolution of WeChat and its functions, which focus on providing connections between individuals, businesses, and society. The all-in-one super app is not merely about stacking functionalities; like atomised components, all of these functions interact synergistically within the WeChat ecosystem. Their interactions can generate incredible reactions in various scenarios to meet diverse user needs. The distinctive feature of WeChat's approach to innovation is *deep innovation* with a first-principles orientation in product design. The WeChat team is able to identify the nature of the product or function in question and has a deep understanding of the essential needs of its users.

On the one hand, the WeChat team designs products and explores functions from a long-term perspective, establishing core values and principles that guide WeChat's development. Rather than pursuing instant profit or being confined by KPIs, they prioritise health, sustainable development, and long-term impact. They continually improve foundational infrastructure and anticipate industry and market trends. On the other hand, they conduct rapid iterations and incremental upgrades for product optimisation.

The success of WeChat as an all-in-one super app also arguably benefits from *invisible, compound,* and *continuous innovation* that promotes the interaction of multiple innovations and amplifies the overall value created. WeChat further establishes an open, decentralised, and inclusive ecosystem for co-growth in three main ways:

(1) enhancing product capabilities internally;
(2) empowering players in the ecosystem, including individual consumers and business enterprises, to provide services and create value for them based on the principle of fairness and decentralisation; and
(3) supporting third-party service providers and giving them space for growth.

We not only contribute to the debate on all-in-one super apps and open ecosystems but also reveal findings that distinguish our research from previous studies on WeChat's innovation. WeChat's success raises an important question: can an all-in-one super app, such as WeChat, be replicated? The answer is not as simple as either yes or no. To address this, we must first understand WeChat's distinctive features. WeChat was not initially built as an all-in-one app; its evolution into one was a natural progression. This transformation was more of a journey than a predetermined goal. The evolution was rooted in WeChat's core feature of connection, meaning that it gradually connected people, services, and goods. In addition, the app's multifunctionality was developed in response to technological advancements and market needs. However, being an all-in-one app is not just about combining functionalities. The WeChat team continuously optimises the infrastructure, enabling extensive interactions between its functions, creating more reactive features. The growth of an all-in-one app depends not only on its core values and internal product capabilities but also on an ecosystem that is supported and enhanced by external players.

External contextual factors also contribute significantly to the success of an all-in-one super app. WeChat emerged at an opportune time, leveraging the rapid development of the mobile internet in China over the past decade. The relatively saturated PC internet, combined with the advancements in 4G and 5G technologies, provided the innovative environment necessary for WeChat's success. Another driving factor is the payment system. Unlike in Western countries, many businesses (and especially SMEs) in China have been hesitant to use debit or credit cards owing to transaction fees and infrastructure requirements. WeChat Pay offers a low-cost solution with minimal infrastructure needs, attracting a significant number of SMEs. Such external market contexts are crucial factors in WeChat's development. Cultural factors further play a role. For instance, WeChat Pay's growth benefited from the ubiquitous culture of monetary gift-giving.

Previous studies (Birkinshaw et al., 2019; Luo et al., 2015; Yang et al., 2016) have examined the reasons behind WeChat's innovation. For example, Luo et al. (2015) and Yang et al. (2016) suggest that WeChat's success is related to micro-innovation characterised by the rapid, repetitive, and precise iteration of innovations based on technical knowledge and user information. However, our research reveals that micro-innovation does not sufficiently capture the characteristics of WeChat's innovation. In addition to micro-innovation, we place more emphasis on *deep innovation*. The WeChat team prioritises user needs but declines to merely iterate based on every user request. For the WeChat team, it is particularly important to avoid allowing the opinions of a specific user group to disproportionately influence decisions regarding the product's future development.

With a first-principles orientation in product design, the WeChat team maintains independent thinking and possesses a deep understanding of product fundamentals. This allows them to distil essential insights from complex user information and identify genuine user needs. The team understands users better than users understand themselves, enabling them to thoughtfully consider the core nature and logic of the product and create new features that truly meet user needs. They are not motivated to act by short-term profit making but instead employ long-term thinking. They align with industry developments, envision where the product will be in three or five years, and incorporate mid- to long-term thinking into their plans. However, the long-term vision is not at odds with rapid iteration and upgrades. The WeChat team conducts rapid iterations and incremental upgrades to improve the user experience and ensure technological advancement. Such an approach combines the independent thinking and visionary style of companies such as Apple and Tesla with the close user needs-following approach of companies such as Xiaomi.

In addition, Birkinshaw et al. (2019) argue that WeChat's success and innovation were achieved through the grand design of its creator, Allen Zhang. The grand design approach suggests that a new product or service emerges fully formed in the innovator's mind before it is developed and commercialised. They propose that this approach to innovation can be particularly effective in a market's early formative stages when user needs are fluid and malleable. Allen Zhang's grand design for WeChat succeeded because he was able to shape the emerging market space. But as WeChat has evolved into a different stage of development with multiple functions and a mature ecosystem, the grand design approach may not fully capture the ongoing innovation of WeChat. We argue that WeChat's continuous innovation is now driven by first principles-oriented product design and a long-term perspective.

First principles-oriented product design focuses on the essence of the product and user needs, while a long-term perspective establishes core values and principles guiding the WeChat team's development. A deep understanding of the essence of the product and a long-term vision enables designers to envision new products or functions and support their healthy and sustainable growth. Only in this way can they create innovative and pioneering products. We find that Birkinshaw et al. (2019) place too much emphasis on the role of leader Allen Zhang while neglecting the contributions of WeChat's small, creative, and agile teams that operate with a high degree of autonomy. WeChat's success has arguably benefited from the supportive environment at Tencent that encourages innovation and provides autonomy on both the team and individual levels. As a senior manager of WeChat commented: 'I think WeChat is very fortunate to be in an environment like [that of] Tencent, which allows WeChat to develop steadily, to stick to its principles, and to grow slowly without any pressure. This is very rare.'

In the early days of WeChat, it was seen as copying the features of existing products and was often thought to excel only in business model innovation. We argue that while WeChat initially developed similar basic functions to other social products, it continued to develop its own unique features and technologies, such as miniprograms, on the path to becoming an all-in-one app. One distinctive feature that sets WeChat apart from other social platforms is its open, decentralised, and inclusive ecosystem that not only enhances the product itself but also empowers a wide range of participants within the ecosystem. WeChat has undoubtedly created various business models, such as social e-commerce via Official Accounts and Mini Program, social network finance through Red Packet, community group-buying via Mini Program, and the online–offline integrated model utilising WeCom. But beyond business model innovation, WeChat also showcases compound innovation, integrating process, product, and business model advancements.

More importantly, these combined innovations interact seamlessly to amplify the product's overall value. Behind the more visible business model innovation are other innovations that may not be immediately noticeable to users. For instance, WeChat's technological advancements ensure the product's long-term stability, confidentiality, security, and reliability, even with a large user base and under various conditions. Process innovation is evident in WeChat's integration of various functions and services into a single app and its versatility across diverse scenarios and industries.

In addition, our research offers deep insights into the design of an open ecosystem by analysing the key strategies employed by WeChat. In fact, other companies have explored concepts similar to Mini Program, such as the Instant Apps proposal from Google. But unlike Mini Program, these initiatives lacked the comprehensive ecosystem that WeChat offers. WeChat not only provides a robust set of functions and services but also has established an open and inclusive ecosystem for co-growth. This constitutes its unique advantage: openness is not just a strategic choice for WeChat owing to limited internal resources but also a core value of WeChat's ecosystem. The WeChat team established key principles in its ecosystem design. First, they positioned WeChat as a powerful tool rather than as the centre of the ecosystem. This approach equips WeChat with capabilities while granting partners autonomy for growth within the ecosystem. Second, in empowering external players for co-growth, WeChat emphasises fairness and decentralisation. Third, WeChat provides the fundamental infrastructure for third-party service providers, supporting and giving them ample space to innovate and grow. Such ecosystem design not only promotes the development of WeChat but also fosters the growth and prosperity of the entire ecosystem.

As Bai and Liu (2023) suggest, the WeChat ecosystem played a crucial role in Tencent's broader strategy. It was launched with the mission of advancing Tencent's new vision of openness, symbolising the company's commitment to change following accusations of monopolistic behaviour surrounding its former flagship product, QQ (Bai and Liu, 2023). To a large extent, WeChat's ecosystem strategy reflected Tencent's overall approach-emphasising openness, inclusiveness, and partnership.

While both Tencent and Alibaba have built vast and complex ecosystems as two of China's most influential technology giants, their ecosystem strategies differ significantly. First, Tencent's ecosystem is primarily centred around its dominant social networking platforms, especially WeChat. This social foundation allows Tencent to 'connect everything' by embedding a wide range of services – such as payments, content, and mini-programs – within these highly engaging applications. In contrast, Alibaba's ecosystem is rooted in e-commerce and logistics, aiming to facilitate seamless commerce for both businesses and consumers. Its flagship platforms, Taobao (C2C) and Tmall (B2C), dominate online retail in China, supported by an extensive logistics network through Cainiao. Second, Tencent uses WeChat as a gateway for third-party services, enabling external developers and companies to integrate mini-programs, payments, and other functionalities. This approach fosters partnerships rather than direct competition. Alibaba, on the other hand, favours vertical integration-building or acquiring majority control over key components of its ecosystem, including marketplaces (Taobao, Tmall), payments (Alipay), logistics (Cainiao), and cloud infrastructure (Alibaba Cloud). This difference is also evident in each company's investment strategies in its ecosystem. Tencent often invests in promising startups and tech companies by taking minority stakes, encouraging innovation, and maintaining the independence and entrepreneurial spirit of its partners. This model allows Tencent to expand its ecosystem through collaboration. Conversely, Alibaba typically seeks controlling stakes in companies that align with its core commerce strategy, integrating them tightly into its operations, and often installing its own executives to ensure strategic alignment.

The case of WeChat provides valuable insights into what it takes to build and sustain a successful super app. Four key lessons stand out: first, user-centric design requires strategic interpretation. User-centric product design does not mean blindly implementing every user request. While a deep understanding of user behaviour is foundational to good product design, it must be balanced with a clear vision of the product's core value and purpose. Users often articulate their needs in fragmented, inconsistent, or even contradictory ways. Not all feedback is actionable or aligned with long-term goals. Successful product teams go beyond reacting to input – they interpret it. This requires a solid grasp of the product's fundamental principles and strategic objectives, allowing teams to distil meaningful insights from complex and noisy user data. The key is to identify which needs are both genuine and broadly shared, and then to address them in a way that supports long-term product coherence and sustainability. By maintaining this balance, product teams can avoid feature bloat, preserve a seamless user experience, and make deliberate design choices that support strategic growth. Ultimately, mature user-centricity is not about doing everything users ask, but about understanding why they ask, and delivering solutions that are both user-friendly and strategically sound.

Second, super apps require integrated, not accumulated, features. A super app is not created by simply piling multiple features – messaging, payments, shopping, ride-hailing, gaming – into a single interface. Functionality alone does not make a platform 'super'. What distinguishes a true super app is the creation of a deeply integrated digital infrastructure, where features are not only co-located but interconnected and mutually reinforcing. In WeChat's case, services are built on a shared foundation of identity, data, and workflows, allowing users to move fluidly between social communication, financial transactions, government services, and more. This seamless integration enables personalisation, trust, and operational efficiency at scale. Such synergy creates a compounding effect: as users rely on one function, they derive increasing value from others. In essence, a super app is not defined by the quantity of features, but by how effectively those features are architected to work together, forming a coherent ecosystem that supports a wide range of interrelated daily activities.

Third, co-growth with partners is the foundation of a healthy ecosystem. A truly sustainable digital ecosystem is not built through dominance, but through co-growth with partners. Rather than positioning itself as the sole focal point or monopolistic controller of its ecosystem, WeChat has adopted a model that emphasises openness, fairness, decentralisation, and shared opportunity-a strategy that has proven vital to its long-term health and resilience. Through tools such as Mini Programs, APIs, and public accounts, WeChat empowers third-party developers, businesses, and service providers to build and deliver their own services directly within the platform. In this model, WeChat provides the foundational infrastructure – identity, payments, communication, and distribution – while partners contribute innovation, domain expertise, and specialised offerings. This mutually reinforcing dynamic not only accelerates the growth of ecosystem participants but also enhances the overall value of the platform, making it more indispensable to users. The result is a virtuous cycle, where the success of one actor strengthens the whole. The key takeaway is that ecosystem health thrives on collaboration, not competition. A platform should act as an enabler rather than a competitor – providing the tools, accessibility, and infrastructure that allow partners to innovate, scale, and lead in their respective spaces.

By doing so, the platform cultivates trust, diversity, inclusiveness, and long-term ecosystem sustainability.

Fourth, the success of a super app is deeply influenced by its external institutional environment. Internal product excellence – while essential – is not sufficient on its own. The surrounding context, including government policy, technological infrastructure, cultural norms, and market readiness, plays a crucial role in enabling or constraining growth. WeChat's rise to a super app in China was not simply the result of strong product design or innovation, but also of strategic alignment with China's digital development priorities. The Chinese government actively promoted digital payments, e-governance, and mobile internet access, creating fertile ground for WeChat to integrate services like WeChat Pay and government mini-programs. In parallel, China's population, increasingly reliant on smartphones, was primed for a mobile-native super app experience. Furthermore, WeChat succeeded by fitting seamlessly into local cultural behaviours. Chinese users were already accustomed to group-based communication, Red Packet gifting, and QR code usage, making it easier to adopt integrated features like group chats, peer-to-peer payments, and QR-based offline services. Therefore, a key lesson is that external factors are not fixed constraints – they can be leveraged as strategic advantages. For aspiring super app builders, understanding and aligning with the local institutional environment is essential. Success depends not only on what you build, but on how well it fits into the broader socio-technical system in which it operates.

7 | *Developing Leading Products through Continuous Innovation*
The Case of QQ and Tencent Docs

A persistent theme in the business world is that new products and technologies emerge continuously, destroying and replacing the old ones in the market. With economic globalisation, technological advancements, the rise of the open innovation framework, and rapid market changes, this phenomenon may be even more common nowadays than it once was. Scholars typically depict market incumbents as declining because they have great difficulty crossing the abyss created by the creative destruction of startups or entrants from other industries (Hill and Rothaermel, 2003). Incumbents usually find it difficult to respond to the innovations of new entrants.

This is because either they have experienced market power and monopoly rents that encourage them to invest in incremental innovations to enhance their existing knowledge base (Reinganum, 1983), or they are reluctant to act and adapt to the changing environment owing to organisational inertia and core rigidities (Leonard-Barton, 1992). The existing value network is also considered a barrier to incumbents as they tend to satisfy their established customers and suppliers (Christensen, 1997). For their part, new entrants are trying to introduce more radical innovations to replace those of the incumbents. We have seen many examples in history; for example, when Nokia was disrupted by Apple's iPhone and Google's Android, Google overtook Yahoo, and MySpace was disrupted by Facebook.

In the rapidly evolving digital economy, staying competitive requires incumbents to not only maintain the vitality of existing products but also consistently pursue breakthrough innovations. Different products and market scenarios necessitate a variety of strategies and approaches. It is essential for companies to prioritise user stickiness and to uphold the reputation of traditional products; an exclusive focus on monetisation should be avoided as it could compromise the user experience. At the same time, companies must develop effective strategies for new product launches to ensure successful market penetration and growth. These strategic considerations are vital for companies aiming to sustain and expand their market presence.

The internet is a realm where novelty quickly captivates and the old is swiftly discarded. In the internet industry, Tencent stands out for its ability to create leading products serving hundreds of millions of users, some of which have endured for a considerable period in this space of rapid innovation and technological upgrades. So far, Tencent has developed an extensive array of offerings across diverse business sectors catering to both business-to-business (B2B) and business-to-consumer (B2C) markets. Whether for old or new products, Tencent has continued to build product innovation over the past two decades despite its extensive product portfolio.

In fact, it is a bit of a miracle that twenty-five-year-old QQ still has hundreds of millions of MAUs. The popularity of the product has endured despite a number of challenges, especially after the internal invention and global spread of WeChat. However, QQ played a key role in many moments that decided Tencent's fate. It is also difficult for a company as large as Tencent, which rose to prominence in the social media and entertainment domains, to enter a new industry. The office work tool field is particularly difficult to enter as there are already a number of incumbents in the market. However, as a new product, Tencent Docs has gained rapid user growth within a competitive market and achieved technological catch-up since its release in 2018.

In this chapter, we have selected QQ and Tencent Docs as representative examples of Tencent products. Developed in 1999, QQ is an instant messaging software service, web portal product, and one of the company's oldest offerings. Tencent Docs, a document-sharing product similar to Google Docs, is an example of a new product developed in 2017. It has become one of the most popular document-collaboration products in China.

This chapter broadly examines how Tencent achieved continuous innovation for both old and new products. We analyse the approaches Tencent adopted to maintain the vitality of its original products and investigate how it was able to keep new products competitive in the market at the same time. The first section introduces the case of QQ and explains its iterative innovation and rejuvenation. The second section then introduces the case of Tencent Docs, examining its strategic innovation and rapid technological development. The third and final section discusses the findings and explores some implications.

7.1 Self-Transformation and Differentiation of Old Products

Tencent has famously developed two social apps that each have over 500 million active users: WeChat and QQ. In Chapter 6, we introduced how WeChat developed into an all-in-one app. This section will introduce the development of QQ, one of the company's oldest products, including how it came to be and what was done to innovate, differentiate, and transform QQ to maintain its competitive advantage even after the popularity of WeChat grew and despite rapid changes in the market.

7.1.1 Introduction of QQ

Launched on 10 February 1999, QQ was initially called OICQ in a nod to the Israeli-developed ICQ. Also known as an 'internet pager' or 'buddy list', the instant messenger enabled real-time communication and online status tracking. When Tencent was founded in 1998, its primary business focused on selling paging systems. OICQ was created as a free add-on to enhance these systems with real-time communication. But once mobile phone prices dropped around 2000, paging systems became obsolete and many of Tencent's clients went out of business. Despite these challenges, QQ's user base grew rapidly and became Tencent's lifeline.

In 2000, OICQ was officially renamed QQ and at times, QQ was more recognisable than Tencent itself. Tencent went public relatively early, listing in Hong Kong in 2004 – before Alibaba (2014 in New York, 2019 in Hong Kong) and Baidu (2005 on NASDAQ). As Tencent's number three employee Gangwu Xu once noted: 'Few knew Tencent before it went public, but everyone knew QQ.' During the PC internet era, QQ outperformed competitors such as Microsoft's MSN, China Telecom's Feixin, Xiaomi's MiTalk, and South Korea's Line by catering to local needs and responding swiftly. QQ became not only the foundation of Tencent's growth but also the first 'national application' at the infrastructure level, serving millions and shaping the company's future.

As of 2024, QQ has a twenty-five-year history that witnessed the evolution from the PC to the mobile internet era in China. For a social software product, twenty-five years is considered old. However, QQ remains a lasting success in the fast-paced mobile internet era. QQ is the oldest of China's super products that still retains hundreds of millions of users and is the only social platform to span the 2G to 5G eras – it is even older than most of its current users. While its earliest users have married and advanced in their careers, QQ has stayed young, continuously innovating with new features, business models, and value-added services to adapt to the needs of new generations of users. As a cross-platform instant messaging and social app, QQ now offers a wide range of features that include online chat, video and voice calls, file transfers, and QQ Mail. Over time, it has grown into a diverse product ecosystem, as shown in Figure 7.1, with services such as Qzone, QQ VIP, QQ Kandian, QQ Wallet, CM Show, and QQ Sports, among others.

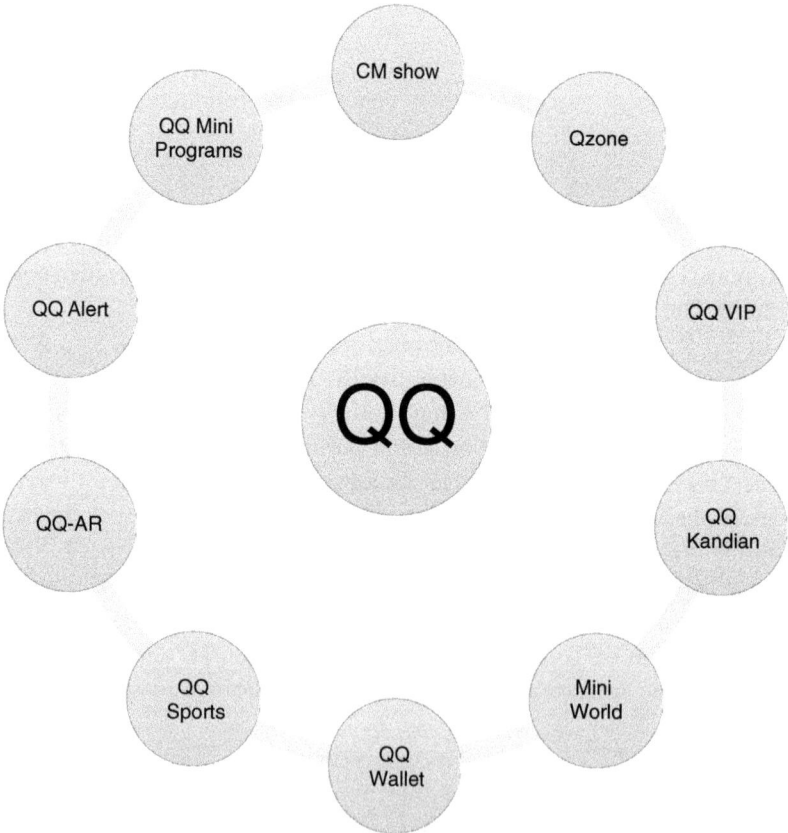

Figure 7.1 Services provided in the QQ product ecosystem.

When QQ launched, co-founder Tony Zhang set a five-year goal of reaching 10,000 simultaneous online users. In reality, QQ hit one million users within two years. By February of 2001, QQ had 20 million registered users; by 2003, that number had surpassed 200 million. The founding team never anticipated such rapid internet growth in China. Although it took QQ eleven years to surpass 100 million simultaneous online users, which occurred in March of 2010, with the rise of mobile internet, it took only four years to reach the next 100 million.

QQ saw rapid growth from late 2013 to 2014, but the social media landscape soon changed with the emergence of WeChat, Douyin, and Kuaishou, which divided the market. Beginning in 2011, QQ users began shifting to Tencent's new app, WeChat. In 2015, WeChat's MAUs surpassed those of QQ for the first time. By Q3 2020, WeChat had over 1.2 billion MAUs while QQ had a mere 600 million (Tencent, 2020). However, despite the decline in users, Tencent's 2022 annual report showed that QQ still had nearly 580 million MAUs, making it China's second most popular social platform. Figure 7.2 illustrates the growth and decline in QQ's MAUs over the past twenty years.[1]

7.1.2 Iterative Innovation and Transformation for Dynamic Competitiveness

Originally a web-based instant messaging tool, over time QQ expanded its features to become a personalised social platform. QQ has consistently innovated, adapting to China's evolving internet

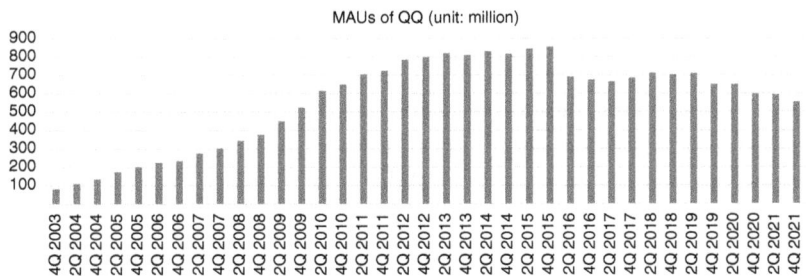

Figure 7.2 QQ MAUs, Q3 2003–Q4 2021.

[1] Note: Since Q1 2016, MAU data are sourced from smart devices (restated).

infrastructure and user preferences. The platform has transformed its longstanding features and embraced new developments. As QQ Head Hao Zhang noted, 'We are always anticipating changes; [our] product designers continuously explore new technologies and models to enhance user value.'

As one of the first Chinese instant communication products, QQ focused on independent R&D and technological innovation to address China's unique needs. Early on, Tencent introduced Q coin to establish its own payment system and diverge from American platforms that relied heavily on advertising. QQ instead monetised through in-app purchases and memberships. Qzone, which was built on the Q coin system, further innovated by offering features such as diaries, photo albums, and graffiti boards, creating a virtual space where users could customise their zones through purchases. QQ also pioneered mobile screen-sharing, overcoming technical challenges to bring this PC feature to the mobile internet.

The QQ team prioritises rapid product iteration; in 2019, for instance, the platform was updated roughly every two weeks. In 2020, updates were sometimes occurring four times a month. In Table 7.1, we summarise QQ's major updates and innovations of its features from 1999 to 2021 and give a detailed description accordingly. These updates were crucial for user retention and generated significant revenue, solidifying Tencent's status as a leading empire in social media.

Aside from the innovations shown in Table 7.1, QQ also conducted several micro-innovations during the COVID-19 pandemic. QQ's vast user base positioned it as a key platform during the pandemic, where it demonstrated both responsibility and adaptability by launching timely innovations to meet the needs of students, teachers, and users seeking social interaction. In a span of just two weeks, QQ built an online classroom feature that enabled teachers and students to communicate efficiently through homework submission, file uploading, and video replay capabilities. These features were accessible across PC, iOS, and Android systems, providing flexibility and ease of use when in-person learning was halted. QQ's educational enhancements included unique functions such as group homework and the red-pen correction tool, setting industry benchmarks. The platform also provided teachers with mini-programs for class management, attendance, and assignment grading, enhancing the user

Table 7.1 *Innovation of QQ's major features*

Year	Primary features	Detailed description
1999	Personalised avatar	Enabled users to design personalised avatars for use online
	Design network protocol	Adoption of UDP technology to save server costs
	Miniaturised software installation package	First version of the OICQ installation package is only 200KB
2000	Invisibility function	Enabled users to independently set online statuses (invisible, busy, etc.)
	Video communication	Forefront of domestic instant messaging software in terms of audiovisual technology
	File transfer function	Enabled HTTP (resume transfer from break point), folder transfer, and other optimisation functions
	QQ membership	Earliest monthly value-added service for the internet in China
2001	Mobile QQ	Successful development of a business model for mobile value-added services Winner of the China Patent Excellence award
	Instant messaging software banner advertising	Predecessor of the early client-side advertising model
2002	QQ Group	World's first instant messaging group Pioneer of the 1vN communication model
2003	QQ Show	Red diamond aristocrat, which originated the diamond system for different levels of membership with different benefits
	QQ Xuanling	Enabled users to set personalised prompt tones, patented in South Korea
	QQ Game	Tencent's first self-developed game product and the world's largest leisure game community platform with over 100 categories of games
2004	Remote assistance	Enabled QQ friends to establish remote connections with one click and quickly obtain assistance from each other
	QQ Level	User upgrade based on daily accumulated online time or other accelerated services
	QQ Screenshot	An indispensable tool in work and life for millions of internet users

Table 7.1 (*cont.*)

Year	Primary features	Detailed description
2005	Qzone	One of the largest social networking websites in China
		Online home for QQ users to write blogs, keep diaries, send photos, listen to music, and watch videos
	Offline messages	Provided a server to ensure user reception of offline messages
	QQ Music	A freemium music streaming service
	QQ Pets	A virtual community feeding game involving pet care throughout the lifespan of a pet
2006	Mobile QQ	QQ software for mobile phone use
	Super QQ	Wireless VIP service with online and offline privileges
2007	Offline file transfer	Supported file transfers when the other party is offline
	Window shake	Shake the chat window of users' friends by clicking the button
	QQ Password Protection Card	A solution for account security problems
2009	Friend impressions	Evaluate friends by tagging them
	Message box	A convenient display of a centralised collection of messages
2010	QQ Lock	Enabled hiding a session window to protect user privacy
	QQ Reading	A depository of reading resources
2011	Colourful fonts	A tool for changing font colours
	Nearby People and Groups	LBS-based friendship chain extension
2013	QQ personalisation	Theme skins, emoticons, chat boxes, background avatars, pendants, etc.
2014	QQ phone	Provided voice calls to mobile QQ users
	QQ roaming	Offered file, expression, and detached roaming
	Interest Tribe (兴趣部落)	An interest-based public community
2015	QQ Red Packets	Featured enabling the exchange of red envelopes (through video calls and games, by geolocation, and for groups)
2016	CM Show	Enabled interaction with friends through the use of avatars in chat

Table 7.1 (*cont.*)

Year	Primary features	Detailed description
2017	DIY emojis	Enabled users to create animated emojis from multiple pictures
	Chat voice to barrage	Converted speech into text through voice recognition
	Fun videos and widgets	Provided users with special effects while video chatting
2018	QQ Tanbaishuo	Enabled anonymous interaction with friends
2019	Progress control of voice message	Supported pause and progress dragging in voice messaging
2020	QQ Small World	A new feature section for user discovery of interests and other users
	Group classroom (群课堂)	Live teaching mode available in QQ group
2021	3D Super QQ Show	All-around upgrade that transformed QQ Show from 2D static to 3D dynamic. Users can make DIY facial expressions based on an avatar, and automatically establish avatars and other functions based on facial recognition
	QQ self-learning room	An online self-study room featuring learning. Includes a companion multi-person live broadcast product based on the mobile phone QQ platform

Source: Provided by Tencent and organised by the authors

experience through homework statistics and streamlined communication tools for announcements and teacher–student interactions.

Beyond education, QQ also capitalised on its entertainment and social capabilities by providing features to enable users to listen to music, play games, watch movies, and even host virtual parties together, helping them stay connected with friends while social distancing. These interactive functions fostered a sense of community. With the Together feature series gaining over 10 million users and QQ's emoticon recommendation feature serving over 100 million daily users, the product created a social lifeline for many during the pandemic.

The QQ team continuously and carefully tracks user preferences and behaviours, and has eliminated over 100 low-use functions in

2023. They then completed a major overhaul in early 2024, rebuilding the framework they had developed over twenty-five years. This project aimed to improve stability, the user experience, and security while mitigating user decline and security risks. The team rewrote the code of tens of thousands of feature points while ensuring seamless daily operations. Migrating user data between old and new databases without loss was a significant technical challenge that took over a year to accomplish. Tencent's extensive product offerings were supported by cutting-edge technologies developed in-house over the years. As of April 2019, for instance, Tencent QQ had applied for over 3,000 patents globally and received more than 1,500. Three of these patents went on to win gold medals at the China Patent Awards (Tencent QQ, 2019).

7.1.3 Focusing on Diversified Needs and User Feedback

From the inception of OICQ, the small entrepreneurial team prioritised user experience. Tencent established the company's first design department, the Customer Research and User Experience Design Centre (CDC) in 2003. Formally established in 2006, the CDC aimed to become a world-class internet design team dedicated to enhancing the user experience across Tencent products. It significantly influenced the design of key products such as QQ, Qzone, QQ Games, QQ Computer Manager, QQ Browser, and QQ Music. In addition, the customer research team regularly identified pain points through the analysis of function usage and user feedback to optimise features.

QQ's growth was fuelled by its commitment to customer feedback and small, rapid innovations to ensure ongoing competitiveness. Its rejuvenation strategy focused on making the product feel youthful, albeit not just for young users. The QQ team actively conducted micro-innovations, identifying and addressing young users' feedback to enhance their experience and boost user engagement. For instance, QQ's unique approach to clearing red dots (unread message indicators) differed from that of other platforms because it aimed at directly solving a common user pain point and increasing satisfaction. As General Manager of Tencent's Social Platform Department Junhong Huang emphasised:

In order to improve the user experience and address pain points faced by special groups of people, we established a dedicated team to actively collaborate with the Information Accessibility Association. We also created an Accessibility Leaders Group to offer expert advice on feature improvements. Involving visually impaired users in testing during the internal phase, we continuously optimised our accessibility versions. Today, QQ and Qzone are major social platforms for visually impaired users in China. We aim to build a bridge for these individuals to communicate with the outside world and enhance their quality of life through technology.

Born in the PC era, QQ gained popularity through features such as QQ Show, QQ Groups, and Qzone. In the mobile internet era, it expanded further with features such as QQ Kandian, QQ Channel, Super QQ Show, and Interest Tribes. These developments reflect its diverse and trend-driven nature. QQ continues to innovate for young users through features such as the Expanding that helps users build connections based on their needs and interests, or the Kandian that matches users by interests. QQ has evolved from a simple communication tool into a multifunctional platform that integrates information, social interactions, and entertainment. The comprehensive and diversified functions characteristic of QQ provide it with a market advantage. It offers voice and video calls, music, games, communities, and more, allowing users to share life moments, connect with friends, and seek entertainment all within one versatile platform.

7.1.4 Competing with WeChat: Internal Differentiation

WeChat and QQ are both instant messaging platforms with similar core features. However, they were initially developed in different eras. Launched in 2011, WeChat quickly rose to become China's predominant social media platform by 2014. However, despite WeChat's success, QQ has remained the second-largest social media platform in China – an impressive feat for a twenty-five-year-old product.

QQ differentiates itself by focusing on openness and personalisation, whereas WeChat has become more of an all-encompassing lifestyle app that integrates personal and professional interactions. Many users feel that WeChat blends their private and work lives while QQ offers more virtual interactions with strangers, allowing users to connect with others who share similar interests. Targeting over a billion users, WeChat prioritises versatility. In contrast, QQ strives to be fun and youthful, offering features such as bubbles, decorations, and interactive logos that cater to personalisation. While QQ has adopted some features from WeChat, it continues to innovate with more playful elements, distinguishing itself as a more personalised platform in a manner akin to how Snapchat contrasts with Facebook by staying relevant to younger audiences even though the latter has a market penetration of over 90 per cent worldwide.

Compared with WeChat, QQ also offers more robust file-related features such as permanent file storage, easier management, and seamless synchronisation across devices. For instance, QQ files do not expire and chat history is always accessible even when switching devices (unlike WeChat files). QQ also caters to hobbyists by offering a platform for merchandise and interest-based groups, with large group chats accommodating up to 2,000 members (far exceeding WeChat's 500-member limit). Its multi-device login and message synchronisation make for smoother transitions, adding to its appeal as a communication tool for active users.

QQ's longstanding membership recharge system allows users to enjoy special features and a sense of status, fostering community loyalty. Interactive elements, such as 'sparks' mark for continuous communication (users who send messages to friends on QQ for over three consecutive days earn the 'sparks' mark), while interest-based group activities keep QQ vibrant and engaging. Some interest-based QQ groups remain highly active, with chat bubbles popping up one after another from time to time. Designed for broader, more formal communication, WeChat lacks such dynamic features. Despite facing technological challenges, such as limits on mobile screen-sharing, the QQ team overcame technical obstacles and pioneered screen-sharing for mobile users – a function that is not available on WeChat. However, the innovation naturally increases the learning costs for QQ users. For this reason, QQ continues to attract younger audiences who are more willing to adopt new and more complex features.

This focus on youth is key to QQ's growth strategy as Tencent aims to secure the next generation of users in a rapidly changing digital landscape. There will always be some social needs that WeChat cannot meet in this world. As Zhu Liang, the fifth-generation director of QQ, noted, 'The world will always need a second communication tool.' His vision is for QQ to embody a youthful, iconic lifestyle, capturing young users as traditional internet growth slows. For instance, China's two-child policy has created a large and special market demand, and QQ intends to capture this segment of users. As Zhu emphasised, 'We hope QQ represents a young lifestyle, embodies young people, thus, should have some iconic features' (Zhang, 2021)

7.1.5 Creating More User Value via Internal Collaboration

To deliver better services and innovative products, the QQ team collaborates deeply with Tencent's technological platforms. This cross-team synergy has led to groundbreaking contributions in digital accessibility that have received global recognition. In 2018, Tencent received the UNESCO Emir Jaber Al Ahmad Al Jaber Al Sabah Prize for Digital Empowerment of Persons with Disabilities, becoming the first organisation in Asia and the first company globally to receive this award (Tencent, 2018). The recognition underscored Tencent's efforts to promote inclusiveness and enhance the lives of people with disabilities through digital technologies.

Since 2009, Tencent has focused on improving product accessibility, particularly for users with visual impairments. Mobile QQ has introduced over 2,425 accessibility features, including innovations such as Add a Friend by Voice, Sticker Reader, and Send a Red Packet by Voice that are used by over sixty million people annually. Qzone has also been optimised with accessibility features that include the Voice Description of Image function powered by the Tencent AI Lab's image description generation technology. This feature allows visually impaired users to hear descriptions of images, significantly improving their social experience.

Qzone continued to optimise the accessibility experience of its major functions, such as Friend Update, Messages, and Personal Page. Accessibility features on Qzone alone were used over 1.6 billion times in 2018, and over 100 million people currently benefit from these features. QQ's collaboration with Tencent's AI Lab and Audio and Video Lab also resulted in innovations such as the AR traversal function and the industry-first gesture AI recognition and tracking technology. Such technological advancements highlight QQ's commitment to offering diverse and engaging experiences to its users.

The QQ team also collaborates with other departments such as Tencent Games, inviting experienced teams to co-create and realise new functionalities. In recent years, QQ and WeChat have increased their cooperation. In 2018, the WeChat mini-program version of QQ was launched, allowing users to check QQ messages through WeChat. This collaborative approach enables QQ to explore new possibilities while maintaining its own distinctive features. In addition, QQ benefits from shared technologies across Tencent, such as noise reduction for calls and AI voice capabilities from Tencent Meeting. The interconnectedness fosters continual improvement and innovation, ensuring QQ remains a dynamic platform that meets diverse user needs.

7.1.6 *Rejuvenation of QQ in a New and Youthful World*

Despite being considered an 'old' instant messaging platform, QQ has shown resilience and a clear strategy for staying youthful and relevant – especially among users born after 2005. The emergence of WeChat posed a significant challenge for QQ. In response, Pony Ma set a goal in 2013 to ensure that QQ stayed relevant to young people. This gave rise to QQ's rejuvenation strategy in 2014, which initially sparked internal debate. Despite the debate, the team implemented the strategy wholeheartedly to yield several innovations targeting younger users.

The rejuvenation strategy is centred on understanding the psychological needs and social behaviour of young people. QQ introduced new features such as QQ Kuolie (expanding friend lists), Nuanshuoshuo (liking, commenting, and sharing posts), and Yanghuohua (sparks from continued interactions). Alongside personalisation (avatars, bubbles, fonts, pendants), such features allowed users to express their individuality and creativity. Seemingly impractical from the perspective of older users, the features proved highly attractive to young users who value self-expression, attention, and recognition.

Based on semi-open relationship chains and semi-anonymous social networking, this youth-centric approach has been instrumental to QQ's success. Today, QQ's user base thrives in an ecosystem where young people connect in groups based on shared interests using the platform's unique language and group dynamics. QQ's strategy of constant adaptation to meet young users' needs through innovation in social functions and gameplay has allowed it to remain a cultural hub for youths. The QQ team understands that vitality can be sustained only through continuous adaptation. The R&D team diligently studies the needs of younger generations and strives to meet these needs through innovative solutions. QQ is also exploring future market opportunities that will be shaped by China's second-child policy, which is expected to bring a new wave of users onto the platform. By identifying and responding to emerging trends, QQ positions itself to sustain its relevance and growth.

In April 2020, Tencent launched Small World, a content-sharing platform where users can post videos and graphics beyond their QQ friend network. This feature resembles WeChat's video accounts. Designed to create a more open social experience, QQ now offers both closed and open modes, allowing users to reveal different sides of themselves. The R&D team sees Small World as a key step in QQ's future, reflecting their broader vision for its evolution.

QQ has become a key platform for fans of niche cultures, such as anime, comics, games (ACG), and two-dimensional culture. These subcultures thrive in unique communication ecosystems with Qzone serving as a hub for information sharing. Through QQ groups and Interest Tribes, users easily connect with like-minded individuals. In June 2020, QQ launched the QQ Argot mini-program to engage young people with the latest slang and trending search terms, attracting over twenty million active users by the year's end. Many young users, especially those of the post-1995 and post-2000 generations, participate in large QQ groups that often exceed 2,000 members, and even in offline gatherings. QQ understands their pursuit of cultural self-expression, quality, and a balance between celebration and solitude. This understanding further reflects a deeper grasp of their psychological needs.

For young people, QQ offers a social space that resonates with their age group. This is in contrast to WeChat, where users navigate complex social circles involving parents, teachers, and colleagues. To remain popular with younger audiences, QQ must align with social trends and position itself as a desirable platform. Initiatives such as QQJOY and QQ Trendy Toys are aimed at creating a vibrant cultural ecosystem both online and offline, with QQ at the centre. The goal was to attract not just existing users but also non-QQ users by offering engaging, trendy content. At the same time, QQ aspires to be seen as a youthful app rather than just an app for the young. There will always be young people in the market and each generation forms its own identity. In addition to keeping up with the preferences of young users, QQ is re-evaluating its approach to youth. While QQ caters to a predominantly young user base, its aim is broader: to support anyone, regardless of their age, who craves youthful expression. Rather than categorising users based on age, QQ enables anyone to express themselves in a youthful manner.

A media outlet once asked Zhidong Zhang, one of Tencent's founders and the former CTO, about QQ's future. He replied, 'If QQ wants to maintain its vitality, it must continue to pursue differentiated innovation while also addressing the historical baggage it has accumulated.' This highlights the challenge QQ faces as Tencent's 'eldest son': balancing its legacy while remaining innovative. Despite its crucial role in supporting new ventures, QQ must foster open-mindedness within its management to avoid being weighed down by its past. To adapt to a changing landscape and appeal to younger users, QQ has rolled out regular updates – about one major update per year over the past decade. The team itself has also evolved and now consists of around 700 members made up of a dynamic mix of experienced professionals and younger talent, including post-1995s and even interns born after 2000. Dan Li, General Manager of Tencent Social Platform Marketing Centre, commented on this rejuvenation: 'We don't want to push out older employees and we also welcome them in particular, but we are really afraid that we ourselves don't know young people. So we choose to recruit the younger generation as the new blood.'

Around 2022, the number of QQ's MAUs began to grow again. This is because a substantial part of the so-called post-2000s generation began to use QQ, and this became the primary driver of growth in QQ users. According to statistics from third-party organisations published in March 2023, the most popular app out of the top five most commonly used among the post-2000s generation is still QQ (Questmobile, 2023). Tencent's performance report also stated that QQ has high user stickiness among young users.

Among QQ users, those aged twenty-six to thirty-five years are the second-largest user group according to the 2023 Mobile Traffic White Paper survey, indicating that older generations also continue to use QQ. Reasons why the post-1995 and post-1990 generations use QQ mainly fall into two categories: (1) to work more efficiently, leveraging QQ's advantages in file transfer, screen-sharing, and similar functions; and (2) to escape from work, using QQ to stay connected with gaming friends as well as for relaxation and entertainment. As a product of the late 1990s, QQ holds a special place for users born in the 1980s and 1990s as it represents more than just a social platform – it is a nostalgic part of their youth. Despite numerous updates, many users still keep QQ installed and a trend of earlier users returning to the platform has recently emerged. This resurgence is driven by nostalgia, practical needs, and QQ's unique functionalities. The platform offers significant advantages in specific operations and functions that continue to attract users for social interaction. Some early users even use QQ for work purposes. Teachers, for example, rely on QQ for communicating with students and sharing files. With features such as remote assistance and temporary sessions, QQ remains appealing, especially among professionals and educators born after the 1980s. Looking at the global social media landscape, few platforms have seen a user return phenomenon like QQ's.

Tencent's 2024 report shows that QQ's MAUs still hover around 554 million, far surpassing platforms such as Weibo and Zhihu. Despite competition from newer apps such as WeChat, Douyin, Xiaohongshu, and Kuaishou, QQ maintains a large, loyal user base. This highlights its longstanding influence in the social media landscape. QQ's sustained relevance is driven by the team's deep understanding of user needs, a bold willingness to challenge norms, and proactive innovations. Each minor improvement was designed to bring significant user satisfaction, keeping the team focused on answering the core question: what is QQ's greatest value to its users?

7.2 Strategic Innovation and Technological Catch-Up in New Products

With a focus on Tencent Docs, this section examines how a new product came to stand out in the market. We first introduce this product, then describe how the product development team engaged in strategic innovation and technological catch-up. We argue that these are the primary factors contributing to the success of Tencent Docs in the field of online document editing.

7.2.1 *Introduction of Tencent Docs*

Tencent Docs is a collaborative tool for editing documents in real time; documents can be shared, opened, and edited by multiple users simultaneously. The original team responsible for developing Tencent Docs came from the QQ team. In 2015, the QQ team began to design a product for use in office scenarios. In 2016, a version of QQ called TIM was developed. Users began to demand more advanced features from TIM (e.g. office e-mail, online document editing, and cloud storage). TIM opted to cooperate with two mature internal products, QQ Mail and Weiyun[2] for cloud storage, to add more functions to the product. At that time, it was difficult to find a mature product for online documents in either the company or the Chinese market in general. The QQ team approached Microsoft, but the service threshold and integration costs for Microsoft Office Online were high, and it would have taken over a year to implement (Xiaoxi, 2024). In light of the growing user demand for cooperative document editing, the QQ team decided to design a product for online documents on their own.

In April of 2018, Tencent launched Tencent Docs as a new product and the Tencent Docs team was established independently of the QQ team. The Tencent Docs team provided multiple access points for users, whether through a mini-program in WeChat or QQ, TIM, and the Tencent Docs app. In addition to accessibility, Tencent Docs offered a range of new functions to users that included watermarks, a time limit for access permission, notifications of editing, and more. The 2018 version of Tencent Docs included over 2,600 new functions based on over 30,000 instances of user feedback (Tencent Docs, 2022).

Since the launch of Tencent Docs, its number of MAUs has grown rapidly. By August 2018, its MAUs numbered over sixteen million. By April 2019, that number had almost doubled to over thirty million. The company received 38,552 instances of user feedback and continued updating the app in real time (Tencent Docs, 2022). It also added the e-commerce company Vipshop and online music provider Kugoo to its corporate clients. By the end of 2020, the number of MAUs

---

[2] Tencent Weiyun is one of the products that provides the personal cloud storage service for users.

reached 200 million and users had created over 300 million documents (Tencent Docs, 2022). As a collaborative tool for editing documents, Tencent Docs was being used outside the office in areas that included online education, emergency rescue, e-commerce livestreaming, and online mental health services.

7.2.2 Strategic Innovation: Gaining Competitive Advantage

The rapid growth in MAUs and the use of Tencent Docs in a variety of environments was strongly connected to the strategic innovation of the Tencent Docs team. Aside from Tencent Docs, other online document editors in the market range from Google Docs and Microsoft Office Online to 360 Docs, ShiMo, and WPS Office. These products have been in the market for a long time; the initial release date for Google Docs was 2006, for example, while ShiMo was released in 2015 in China. However, all of these products mainly target the business market. In comparison, Tencent Docs entered the market as a latecomer. In order to achieve a competitive advantage, Tencent Docs adopted a different business strategy. Rather than focusing solely on the business market, Tencent Docs initially targeted individual customers to drive user growth. It then leveraged this growth to expand its business customer market share, strategically following a development pathway that moved from a B2C to a B2B approach.

7.2.2.1 Starting from a B2C Approach: Positioning for Market Opportunities

There are three main reasons why Tencent Docs chose to adopt a B2C approach at an early stage. First, the Tencent Docs team had extensive experience developing B2C products as it had spun off from the QQ team. Most companies developing online document editors have more experience designing office products and focus primarily on office document functions, such as formatting and compatibility. In contrast, the latecomer Tencent Docs team had little experience in office products for the business customer market. However, they had inherited valuable knowledge from the QQ team that included rich experience in developing social media products with a strong focus on user-centric design principles.

The Tencent Docs team thus excelled in developing products for social interaction and collaboration, and possessed deep expertise in various related scenarios. They were also highly adept at capturing user needs and solving user problems. For this reason, they oriented Tencent Docs' product design towards social collaboration, aiming to strike a balance between social media platforms (such as QQ), and standardised office productivity tools. Tencent Docs placed a strong emphasis on social collaboration within its product design and value proposition, establishing a key competitive advantage. On the one hand, information can be efficiently produced, edited, and organised within online documents. On the other hand, these tasks can be achieved simultaneously and flexibly by a large number of users far beyond the confines of a business organisation.

Second, this development pathway leveraged the unique characteristics of the Chinese internet industry, showcasing the team's acute market sense and sound judgement. In China, the individual customer market is more developed than the business market. It offers lower customer acquisition costs and a larger customer base. Other online document editors such as ShiMo and WPS Office have successfully captured a significant share of the business customer segment. If Tencent Docs had initially entered the business market, it would have encountered fierce competition from existing online document products and faced higher customer acquisition costs.

Third, the strategy leveraged Tencent's platform network effect. Tencent Docs is integrated with Tencent's existing platform products (e.g. WeChat and QQ), each of which boasts a vast user base across China. This integration ensures that WeChat and QQ users can easily access Tencent Docs when needed. By harnessing Tencent's substantial user traffic, Tencent Docs capitalised on the growing demand for its products. Thus, Tencent Docs opted to focus on the individual customer market early on and placed a strong emphasis on social collaboration within its product functions. This strategic approach positioned Tencent Docs favourably to capitalise on market opportunities, attracting a larger base of individual users, and gaining a competitive edge.

7.2.2.2 Social Events as Catalysts

Regardless, building user awareness of social collaboration was challenging during the initial stages of Tencent Docs' entry into the individual customer market. Tencent Docs conducted various tests to explore social collaboration concepts and features in its product design and promotion. The team introduced their products to differ-ent online groups and encouraged users to test them. For example, they introduced the product to a gaming guild where thousands of members collected, updated, and shared information about games, which proved to be successful. But alongside these successes, the Tencent Docs team also encountered some failures. From these experiences, they identified two key factors for promoting social collaboration within the product: (1) well-organised events or activ-ities to foster networking among participants; and (2) clear objec-tives for these activities.

Social events engaging the public with specific objectives acted as catalysts in the rapid user growth of Tencent Docs. In 2020, the COVID-19 pandemic normalised remote work and increased demand for online office tools. As an online document editing tool, Tencent Docs began to be used not only for office work but also for infor-mation gathering. For instance, Tencent Docs facilitated information collection for community members in need of food or assistance dur-ing the pandemic. The Tencent Docs team ensured that information could be communicated efficiently to relevant organisations that could facilitate medical support. At the same time, it also implemented spe-cific functions to protect personal data.

Another significant social event that contributed to the user growth of Tencent Docs was the flood in Henan province in 2021. In July of 2021, heavy rainfall caused widespread flooding that trapped many people who then sought assistance through online social media plat-forms such as WeChat and Weibo. However, the scattered nature of their posts made it difficult for local authorities and rescue teams to gather and respond to critical information. Drawing from their expe-rience during previous anti-epidemic efforts, the Tencent Docs team responded swiftly by establishing a dedicated group. This group coordinated the collection of assistance information from various social media platforms, organised it into spreadsheets on Tencent Docs, and shared these files in WeChat groups.

The collaborative effort enabled more individuals in need to update their information directly. During this crisis, the Tencent Docs team observed that a document titled 'People to be rescued' created by a university student had garnered a large number of page views. This document became a crucial resource shared among flood victims. However, the team noted that some information in the document lacked clarity and structure. Information updates, too, were not maintained consistently and the disorganisation posed challenges to rescue teams. To enhance the document's utility, additional Tencent Docs staff edited and verified rescue information as well as collaborated with local rescue teams.

On the first night of the flood, approximately 2.5 million people accessed the document. By the following day, it had been updated over 270 times. The initiative successfully connected flood victims with first responders, showcasing the document's pivotal role in facilitating aid during the crisis (Tencent, 2021). As staff from the Tencent Docs team commented:

The rescue document is a good example of social collaboration within our product. During the flooding, the objective was very obvious: to rescue people. Rescue activities were organised by a group of people that included volunteers and rescue teams. Thanks to the document, people were able to exchange rescue information easily and efficiently.

During the flooding, Tencent Docs was easy, open, and stable to operate. On Tencent Docs, people could coordinate and information could be exchanged, shared, and integrated. This is why Tencent Docs was widely used in such a social event.

After the flood, the team enhanced their emergency response and organisational capabilities. They focused on improving the product's stability to accommodate a large number of users, ensuring that Tencent Docs could better support similar social events in the future. As demand had grown, the Tencent Docs team had designed over fifty assistance and rescue information templates for different needs and actors, such as government, rescue teams, and NGOs. Using the templates, people trapped in the flood could fill out a form with detailed information, such as their location, the number of people trapped, the primary issues, and telephone numbers.

Additional forms of social collaboration within Tencent Docs emerged in other scenarios. For example, graduates of one high school used Tencent Docs to record their high school memories. Tencent Docs also enabled e-commerce livestreaming companies to share and update sales information for customers. Some documents on Tencent Docs have been called 'temporary crying stations', offering psychologically reciprocal support wherein people can share their inner thoughts or moods to access social support and improve their social integration. As staff at the Tencent Docs team explained: 'We thought about how to respond to the social events and how to deal with different scenarios. So, more people are using our product in different scenarios. Tencent Docs can be a productivity tool for public use in a wide range of scenarios.'

7.2.2.3 Switching to a B2B Approach: Increasing Business Value

Thanks to outstanding performance in response to social events, Tencent Docs significantly enhanced its brand awareness and attracted a substantial user base in the individual customer market within its first three years. After that, the Tencent Docs team switched to a B2B approach and placed greater emphasis on the business customer market to increase its business value. In 2022, the Tencent team collaborated with the WeCom and Tencent Meeting teams to integrate Tencent Docs into their products. This integration resulted in a comprehensive suite of digital services for businesses. For example, business customers could easily access Tencent Docs and Tencent Meeting through WeCom, thereby improving office efficiency. The integration not only enhanced collaboration and productivity for businesses via WeCom but also drove significant user growth and deepened Tencent Docs' penetration into key verticals.

In addition to internal collaboration to unlock more business value, Tencent Docs established an open ecosystem to connect with a broader range of business partners. For example, Tencent Docs offers a library of templates, APIs, and mini-programs for other developers. It also supports a variety of plug-ins, allowing partners to add functionalities such as digital signatures, emojis, custom figures, and even music. This approach enabled Tencent Docs to provide more creative, flexible, and customised services to its business partners.

In this way, Tencent Docs not only provided its services independently but also integrated seamlessly with other products and collaborators within Tencent's ecosystem of partners. It excelled in focused efforts and modular integration to serve enterprises, integrating productivity at the front end and connectivity at the back end – a rare combination in the SaaS domain. Wherever WeCom's user base expands, for instance, Tencent Docs can extend its services accordingly. As of 2024, Tencent Docs is used by 1.2 million enterprises and organisations. It has accumulated 20,000 paying businesses since 2022, accelerating its growth.

7.2.3 *Technological Catch-Up*

The development of Tencent Docs benefited from strategic choices and innovation that leveraged Tencent's extensive experience in social media product development and its platform network advantages alongside a keen understanding of the Chinese market. Most importantly, these achievements were underpinned by Tencent's robust technological capabilities.

An online document-editing tool enables a large number of users to simultaneously edit a single document – for instance by inserting or deleting text – or applying styles to text. The more people there are editing one document, the more likely it is that some editors are working in the same place at the same time. Such real-time collaborative editing will cause conflicts, and the level of difficulty and complications grows with the number of editors. Solutions to this challenge rely on complicated technology and algorithms.

During the early stages of development, Tencent used open-source code to establish a prototype of the product. With the early version, Tencent Docs started to attract more users in the individual market owing to the network effect and good user experience. However, the app's capabilities for real-time collaboration were insufficient to support larger-scale use. This meant that the Tencent Docs team faced a dilemma regarding further development. Their first option was to build a simple underlying framework for product design with simple algorithms. This was the approach taken by several other online-document products, such as ShiMo. The option can speed up product iteration and ensure rapid gains in user growth in the short term but yields a lower capability to resolve conflicts in large-scale online editing.

The second option was to develop a more complex framework with sophisticated algorithms for real-time collaboration conflicts. This was the approach used by Google Docs. It was more challenging and would require more time and resources for R&D as well as carry more uncertainty. After all, the team itself could not guarantee whether this option would succeed. But the Tencent Docs team placed more emphasis on social collaboration within the product, which demanded high-level capabilities to resolve real-time collaboration conflicts (especially if Tencent Docs were to be used again during larger-scale social events).

If the team went with the simpler framework, they would likely gain user growth in the short term but fail to be able to respond to major social events. This would lead to system breakdowns following a surge in users. For this reason, the Tencent Docs team decided to choose the second option for long-term development, despite limited resources and a lack of experience. Three staff members and several interns spent several months rewriting the code for the system while developing the product based on user feedback in real time. As a staff member at Tencent Docs explained, they received over 150 reports of bugs on a single day in 2018 when the app was initially released and the team had to learn how to code while dealing with the feedback. In the end, they built up an advanced underlying framework to resolve conflicts in real-time online editing.

Leveraging its robust product capabilities, Tencent Docs embodies the essence of collaborative documents: it is lightweight, fast, and stable. The team thus managed to host a large volume of users without the app crashing as well as enable rapid response to emergency situations, as was seen during the pandemic. Today, Tencent Docs boasts the largest user capacity among all online collaborative document tools, enabling over one million users to open and work on documents simultaneously. Beyond its stability and extensive usage, Tencent Docs operates efficiently. The speed of opening and editing an online document in Tencent Docs is nearly as fast as working with an offline document.

During the B2B phase and alongside enhancing its collaborative capabilities, Tencent Docs focused on elevating product professionalism, gradually combining the features of collaborative and professional documents. By 2024, they had closed the loop on the foundational editing engine by including full support and compatibility with Microsoft Office formats. This meant that Tencent Docs was able to achieve collaborative functions on professional Office documents. They continued to support lightweight document types, such as intelligent documents, spreadsheets, and whiteboards, within a new generation of document-table graphics. These functions are designed for lighter scenarios using elegant layouts and a structured tree hierarchy for content management. In this way, Tencent Docs provided a complete solution for 'collaborative + professional documents', achieving such integration through data interoperability.

The integration of 'collaborative + professional documents' required technological expertise and innovation, both of which Tencent Docs achieved through in-house development capabilities. By January 2023, Tencent Docs had more than seventy patents. For example, their self-developed Kaiwu Engine supported atomic increment mechanisms, significantly reducing cloud storage consumption for users. It was considered a pioneer in both technical solutions and mindset. As a result, Tencent became one of the few domestic vendors with full-stack, self-developed professional document capabilities. Even Tencent CEO Pony Ma commended the release of the Tencent Docs in 2018, reporting that: 'The team gave me a big surprise. Eight years ago, the R&D team in Guangzhou was developing the product. However, they successfully developed WeChat instead. Now, the QQ team has made it!'

As a latecomer to the market, why was Tencent Docs able to achieve such technological catch-up in a few years? The Tencent Docs team attributed their success to the culture of intrapreneurship in the organisation, which allows employees to use entrepreneurial skills and approaches. One staff member noted that: 'Our culture at Tencent is very open and inclusive. From the first idea to the end product, the development process is one of intrapreneurship. We have the autonomy and space to explore technological innovation and tackle technological challenges, although it is not easy at all and we encounter many problems.'

It is the inclusive and intrapreneurship culture that allows and encourages staff to take risks and explore new fields even with limited resources and experience. Driven by enthusiasm and self-motivation, employees prioritise long-term technological challenges over short-term interests such as immediate user growth. As a senior manager of Tencent Docs commented (Xiaoxi, 2024): 'Throughout its six years of development, Tencent Docs has maintained an intrapreneurship model with a particular focus on sustainable positive value within manageable resource allocation. This approach enables us to adopt a long-term, pragmatic mindset and rhythm to create superior products.'

7.3 Discussion and Conclusion

This chapter has explored how Tencent has developed leading products and maintained its leadership in relevant fields through

Table 7.2 *Key factors driving successful product development at Tencent*

	QQ	Tencent Docs
Differences	• product differentiation and transformation • iterative innovation and radical innovation	• strategic innovation • technological catch-up
Similarities	• user-oriented product value, actively capturing user needs • strong technological capabilities (both in-house and internal collaboration) • inclusive and intrapreneurial culture	

Source: Authors' elaboration

continuous innovation over the past two decades. We selected an old product (QQ) and a new product (Tencent Docs) as our two case studies. Through comparison, we have examined the approaches Tencent adopted to maintain the vitality of its original products while also keeping new products competitive in the market. We identified both similarities and differences in the development of the two products. In Table 7.2, we highlight the key factors behind the success of Tencent's leading products and will elaborate on this in detail in the following sections.

QQ's enduring popularity is nothing short of remarkable. What began as a fledgling chat tool has grown, evolved, and reinvented itself through bold innovation and relentless iteration. While many early internet messaging platforms have faded into digital history, QQ has stood firm-retaining hundreds of millions of active users more than two decades after its birth. Consider the fate of ICQ, the pioneering messaging app launched in 1996, which QQ initially modelled itself after. Once a household name, ICQ's daily users dwindled from forty-two million in 2010 to just eleven million by 2022. After changing hands several times, the service was finally shut down in June 2024, ending a twenty-eight-year run. MSN Messenger – another major player launched in 1999 and once seen as QQ's global rival – was discontinued in 2013, its legacy absorbed by Skype. Even Skype, which once boasted over 300 million monthly users and dominated global communications in the 2010s, could not escape the tide of change. It was officially shuttered by Microsoft in

May 2025, overtaken by rising stars like WhatsApp and Zoom – and by Microsoft's own pivot to Teams. Meanwhile, Twitter, born in 2006, is undergoing an identity transformation. Rebranded as 'X' under Elon Musk, it is attempting to become an 'everything app', incorporating payments and messaging.

A recent survey report published by the Pew Research Centre shows that Facebook's market share of young Americans on social media has been decreasing, with the share of teens who use Facebook falling sharply from 71 per cent between 2014 and 2015 to 32 per cent in 2022 (Pew Research Center, 2022). Despite Facebook's many initiatives aimed at young people, these numbers have yet to improve. In contrast, QQ still plays an important role in social networks and shows an unstoppable vitality. Amid all this flux, Tencent QQ has pulled off what many would consider a miracle. Twenty years ago, it was Tencent's only real asset. Ten years ago, it remained the crown jewel of the company. Having witnessed Tencent's growth, QQ embodies the company's DNA and values. Now, it stands as an emblem of youth, vitality, and innovation. QQ innovates iteratively and quickly based on user feedback and learns from both internal challengers and global competitors.

Over the past two decades, instead of resting on its early success, QQ has maintained frequent updates that have strengthened user stickiness and attracted more users. The QQ team introduced a number of radical innovations to the product as well as differentiating itself from WeChat and other products. Today, QQ still has many distinctive functions that other communication software can learn from, such as file management and group chat. But undeniably, QQ's innovation motivation also comes from the internal competition from WeChat, which is stimulated by Tencent which creates a dynamic, decentralised innovation culture within the company. QQ's self-transformation experience provides a point of reference for many other existing popular products and products that come after in the internet era. Despite a strong legacy, QQ knows how to leverage its legacy and remains open-minded. QQ managed to maintain its relevance not by clinging to the past, but by refreshing its brand while retaining its emotional identity. The product became a nostalgic icon for older users and a playful space for newer ones. Companies can thrive by honouring their legacy but staying culturally and technologically fresh. Listening to the users is important. From customising avatars to adding educational tools, QQ evolved with its users' habits. This agility gave it a lasting emotional connection with younger generations. QQ's growth over time reveals how an old product can maintain its competitiveness over a lengthy period by focusing on user experience, exploring new possibilities and differentiations, and engaging in continuous technological innovation. Longevity in the high-speed digital age comes not from avoiding change, but from embracing it – again and again. So far, QQ has also helped with a great deal of internal product development, making major contributions to Tencent and bringing much joy to China's internet users.

As a newly launched product, the success of Tencent Docs can be attributed to a combination of strategic innovation and rapid technological advancement. Rather than following a conventional path, Tencent Docs took a differentiated approach by leveraging the company's existing strengths – specifically, Tencent's vast and well-established user base in the individual (B2C) customer segment and its deep experience in designing and delivering consumer-facing digital products. This strong foundation enabled the team to act with agility and foresight in a highly competitive and rapidly evolving market.

The product team at Tencent Docs implemented a forward-looking strategy that initially focused on gaining traction in the individual user market before gradually transitioning toward serving business clients (B2B). This B2C-to-B2B evolution marked a significant departure from the strategies of many other online office platforms, which often prioritised enterprise users from the outset. By concentrating first on individual users, Tencent Docs was able to quickly attract a broad user base, generate early user engagement, and foster strong brand recognition. This approach also created a solid platform from which the product could later expand into more complex enterprise use cases with an already loyal user community. Moreover, this strategic emphasis on the B2C market allowed Tencent Docs to tap into widespread market opportunities – such as remote work, online learning, and document-collaboration trends – enabling the product to scale quickly in both usage and visibility. This early traction provided a key competitive advantage, positioning Tencent Docs as a credible and innovative alternative in the online productivity space.

On the technological front, the Tencent Docs team demonstrated strong execution by overcoming significant technical barriers and achieving rapid catch-up with more established players. Through internal R&D and innovation, the team developed and refined core features necessary for a modern online office suite, including real-time collaboration, cross-platform compatibility, and robust document editing tools. This technical progress was achieved using Tencent's in-house capabilities, allowing the team to retain control over critical components of the product.

One of the defining aspects of Tencent Docs' technological edge was its comprehensive solution tailored for both 'collaborative' and 'professional' document needs. This dual focus addressed the varying expectations of casual users as well as more demanding enterprise clients, thereby widening its appeal across customer segments. The platform's ability to support seamless cooperation among multiple users – while also maintaining professional-grade document formatting and functionality – was a testament to the team's ability to balance user experience with technical sophistication.

In summary, Tencent Docs's rise in the online office tools market was not incidental, but rather the result of a deliberate and well-executed strategy that combined market-driven innovation with technological excellence. By capitalising on Tencent's B2C legacy and strategically transitioning to a B2B model, the product carved out a unique trajectory that allowed it to grow rapidly, adapt to user needs, and stand out in a crowded digital landscape.

By analysing similarities in the development of QQ and Tencent Docs, we uncovered key factors behind the success of Tencent's leading products. These successes offer several lessons for other companies especially those in fast-evolving tech sectors. First, we argue that the cases of QQ and Tencent Docs both reflect Tencent's user-oriented product value. Tencent has consistently emphasised capturing user needs as they are seen as the cornerstone of product development and iteration. Regardless of whether a product is new or old, this is the only way it can keep up with user and market needs and accurately locate its position in the market.

In addition to actively understanding user needs, Tencent is dedicated to providing services that are deeply integrated into its application scenarios. The company believes that delivering core value to users occurs when product functionalities are tailored and applied within specific user scenarios. For example, the vitality of QQ is related to iterative innovation based primarily on user feedback. The rejuvenation of QQ benefits from this feedback as the end product then fits well with the tastes and needs of younger generations. Similarly, the Tencent Docs team was able to grasp unique opportunities in the individual customer market by responding to user needs during social events and a range of scenarios.

The development of a strategy for differentiation and the adoption of an innovative approach are both essential to sustaining the vitality of legacy products and keeping new ones competitive in the market, despite the challenges with executing such strategies. The key to successful differentiation lies in the ability to accurately capture user needs. For QQ, its focus on the preferences of the younger generation has driven its rejuvenation while the success of Tencent Docs stems from a deep understanding of the Chinese market and extensive experience with B2C products.

Next, ongoing product innovation and leadership in the digital product arena at Tencent are intricately linked to the company's strong technological capabilities. Tencent has invested significantly in developing a cutting-edge technological infrastructure that includes advanced R&D facilities, a skilled workforce, and a commitment to embracing emerging technologies. This strong foundation enables Tencent to rapidly adapt to changing market demands and user preferences. Tencent not only has robust in-house technological capabilities at the team level (such as the Tencent Docs team), but also emphasises collaboration and knowledge-sharing among its teams. This fosters an environment where technological advancements can be integrated into product development seamlessly, contributing to continuous product innovation.

Tencent can keep abreast of competitors as a result, launching new features and products that resonate with users and address their evolving needs. The company's strong technological capabilities serve as the backbone of its product innovation strategy, empowering it to maintain its leadership position in the competitive digital landscape and ensuring it continues to deliver impactful products to users and markets.

Finally, Tencent's inclusive and intrapreneurial culture has been the cornerstone of its successful development of leading products. This culture fosters an environment where employees feel empowered to innovate and take ownership of their projects regardless of their position in the company's organisational hierarchy. By promoting a sense of responsibility and entrepreneurial spirit within the company, Tencent encourages its teams to continuously improve and enhance existing products to achieve their transformation and even rejuvenation.

At the same time, this culture inspires employees to push beyond their comfort zones and explore new, uncharted territories. Even when facing resource constraints or limited experience in new areas, teams are motivated to tackle complex technological challenges with creativity and resilience. The flexibility to experiment and support for intrapreneurial initiatives allow employees to take risks and think outside the box, driving the development of new products. This approach not only fuels product innovation but also creates a dynamic work environment where talent thrives, contributing to Tencent's sustained market leadership and its ability to create leading products.

8 | Maximising the Value of Platforms
Social Innovation and Social Value Creation

The rise of digital platforms has had a transformative influence on organisations, businesses, and society. Existing studies have acknowledged that digital platforms play a crucial role in generating economic value for businesses and organisations. While the private returns, competitiveness, and redistributional outcomes generated by digital platforms have been studied (see, e.g. Constantinides et al., 2018; Sutherland and Jarrahi, 2018), recent research has increasingly begun to explore the impact of digital platforms on society.

In the extant literature, many studies have shed light on the positive impact of various forms of digital platforms on players (e.g. users, local communities, marginalised groups) in various sectors (e.g. healthcare, finance, transportation, the circular economy), including those by Bonina et al. (2021), Chamakiotis et al. (2021), and Meijer and Boon (2021). Among these studies, some emerging research focuses on the social innovation facilitated by various platforms and the social value they create.

Social innovation refers to the creation and implementation of novel, scalable, and sustainable ideas and solutions to solve systemic societal problems (Caridà et al., 2022; van Wijk et al., 2019). By addressing societal problems, social innovations contribute to both human life and social development and thereby create social value for various stakeholders by fulfilling their needs (Van Der Have and Rubalcaba, 2016). However, current studies mainly focus on the social innovation or social value creation of a particular platform. This means that they overlook how and why platform companies leverage multiple digital platforms or technologies to engage in solving societal problems, driving social innovation, and generating social value.

This chapter focuses on Tencent as a leading internet-based platform company, examining how it achieves social innovation and creates social value to maximise the value of its platforms. More specifically, this chapter explores the motivation, manifestations, forms, and mechanisms of social innovation achieved by Tencent, highlighting key approaches that have contributed to the successful creation of social value. It begins by detailing the strategic upgrade that emphasises sustainable social value in Tencent's corporate development. We discuss how social value creation was integrated into the company's business operations and explain the relationship between social and economic value at Tencent. The chapter also presents the multidimensional and multi-scenario social value that Tencent creates for the benefit of customers, businesses, and society. Our findings indicate that Tencent promotes co-creation within its ecosystem for social innovation by leveraging platform technologies. Based on these insights, we reveal the mechanisms that Tencent employs to generate social value. Finally, the chapter details the implications for other companies when it comes to using digital platforms and technologies to generate social value for various stakeholders within the platform ecosystem and society at large.

8.1 Social Value Creation as a Corporate Strategy at Tencent

In 2020, as part of its fourth strategic evolution, Tencent placed 'sustainable innovation for social value' at the core of its corporate strategy and business. This was a strategic upgrade from 'nurturing the consumer internet and embracing the industrial internet'. Following this, Tencent took a big step forward as 'promoting sustainable innovations for social value' became a new foundation for Tencent's development, driving its core businesses. The upgrade was also guided by and aligned with Tencent's mission, Tech for Good. In doing so, the concept of creating social value was deeply embodied in the company's corporate strategy, which underscored its dedication to addressing key societal challenges within the context of the new development paradigm. Tencent endeavoured to pioneer high-quality and sustainable initiatives through innovations in technology as well as product and business models, with the overall aim of creating social value and enhancing overall societal well-being.

This strategic upgrade was accompanied by organisational change. Tencent merged its Tencent Foundation and corporate social responsibility (CSR) activities into a new Sustainable Social Value (SSV) unit within its CDG. Specifically, the SSV unit set up a Goodwill Lab Cluster, employing a dynamic internal entrepreneurial approach.

This cluster served as an incubator for projects that spanned domains as diverse as technological innovation, education reform, rural development, and environmental sustainability, especially in terms of achieving carbon neutrality. The projects were then developed into independent studios within their respective sectors.

The Lab Cluster operates under a mission-oriented business evaluation framework, promoting an open and collaborative operational environment. Its objective is to act as a catalyst for significant strategic initiatives, encouraging innovative collaboration across cross-sectoral teams and all stakeholders. By 2022, ten labs (for digital teaching, inclusive healthcare, public emergency response, culture digitalisation, gerontechnology, rural revitalisation, carbon neutrality, technology ecology, education innovation, and digital ecology, along with an experimental products centre) were formed and developed in the SSV unit.

In addition, Tencent has committed substantial investment to foster social value creation, ensuring ample space for trial and error and allowing for significant growth potential. With an initial funding of RMB 50 billion, these investments are considered as vital as R&D input. Despite potential costs, Tencent views social value creation as strategically imperative to fortifying the foundation of its corporate sustainability. As Pony Ma commented: 'Like a banyan tree growing out to become a forest over time, the deeper the roots of sustainable social value penetrate the soil of the society, the lusher the leaves of user and industry value grow.'

8.2 Creating Social Value through Business Operations

As the achievement of sustainability for social value at scale exclusively through conventional donations is unlikely, Tencent believes that the optimal approach involves leveraging both technological and business capabilities for social innovation. In addition to a strategic upgrade, the process of creating social value has been integrated into the company's business operations to cover its technologies products, and services.

First, social value creation is operated in the manner of professional business operations at Tencent. The SSV unit adopts a systematic approach to project management, utilising a structured principle and workflow of 'approve (before), track (during), evaluate (after)' to monitor the life cycle of projects associated with SSV's core areas (Tencent, 2024). This process spans from the initial evaluation and scrutiny to implementation and large-scale deployment, ensuring that SSV's initiatives are grounded in an in-depth understanding of societal needs. At the preliminary stage of project evaluation, for example, the SSV unit evaluates whether projects are aligned with the corporate innovation strategy – a stage that also considers internal and external stakeholder expectations. Then, the SSV unit assesses the project plan itself to ensure that it focuses on the SSV's ten core areas ahead of approval. Approval itself is based on a professional decision-making mechanism. Once the project is executed, the SSV unit establishes a performance measurement framework, tracking the progress of the project so the company can identify and address any potential risks promptly. Relevant teams seek to continuously refine the process of the operating model as the business evolves. As one member of the SSV unit states: 'We would like to contribute to social value creation and address social problems through professional and sophisticated operations, not just in the form of donations, because [the former] will be more sustainable and have long-term effects.'

Second, the SSV unit is not the only entity that creates social value. Tencent SSV unit has strengthened its collaboration with business units, linking SSV projects with the company's internal product and business departments. This creates a mutually supportive, collaborative, and deeply embedded framework for social value creation. The creation of social value has become a way of thinking and a key consideration in the company's core strategies for business development. In this way, social value creation is integrated into Tencent's core business, and various business departments have proactively involved themselves in it. After all, it is only by doing so that the overall amount of social value creation can achieve scalable growth.

Tencent's focus on deploying its products and technologies to find innovative pathways to solve societal pain points further encourages business departments to enhance the social value of their products. As frontline interfaces with customers and business partners, business departments are uniquely positioned to swiftly detect and address emerging social needs and issues. They can sense and respond to opportunities quickly, helping or collaborating with external actors in society and supporting or empowering these partners to create value for themselves and for society. For example, during the pandemic, the WeChat product team approached shops and restaurants to provide printed QR codes for payment when they discovered that some shop owners did not know how to create or print them. This initiative helped more small businesses adopt and use the digital payment system WeChat Pay provided.

In addition to sensing and responding to social problems triggered by social events, business departments took the initiative to apply advanced technologies and promote product optimisation for social needs, leveraging their technological and product capabilities. In doing so, social innovation was interlinked with technological and product innovation, all of which is led or participated in by business departments. To illustrate, the Tencent Meeting team extended their noise reduction technology to improve cochlear implants and hearing aids for children and the elderly. In a similar vein, the gaming department utilised gaming-related technologies for the construction of highly simulated internet-based factories. Elsewhere, AI technologies were harnessed to assist the cosmic exploration of pulsars through the FAST telescope.

Third, in pursuit of promoting SSV creation, Tencent explored the use of professional methods to measure the social impact, sustainability, and long-term benefits of these practical projects in a quantifiable manner. The company's goal is to provide a scientifically precise assessment of the outcomes generated by goodwill, ensuring investments in goodwill yield optimal returns. Drawing from the experience of numerous social value innovation projects and integrating various evaluation methods from global and local contexts, the Tencent SSV unit initially developed an SQI (scale, quality, impact) evaluation system comprised of three indices. This system aimed to establish a tangible benchmark for social value innovation and was distinguished by its interdisciplinary approach (Tencent, 2024).

The first index assesses scale (S). It measures the scale of the audience that social value innovation projects can reach, the extent of facility and ecosystem coverage, whether the project's problem-solving model carries universal significance, and whether it could be promoted and replicated as a benchmark. For example, the largest traditional volunteer teaching organisation can support only about 200 rural schools each year. A project in the field of digital volunteer teaching not only provides remote dual-teacher classrooms but also deeply understands the actual needs of rural education. It broadly engages volunteers, education experts, and other committed individuals to contribute their positive attitudes and efforts, driving the digitalisation of the volunteer teaching industry.

The second index assesses quality (Q). It focuses on evaluating whether the methods of social value innovation projects are sufficiently efficient, whether the impact on the audience was greater, and the extent to which improvement could be achieved. For example, a health economist estimated that for every RMB 1 invested in the SSV pilot project 'A Comprehensive Network for Screening and Treating Congenital Heart Disease in Newborns' in Ningxia province, RMB 31.4 in health costs related to congenital heart disease could be averted (Tencent, 2024). The averted expenses can then be translated into future social benefits. Compared with the traditional charity clinic method, this project can yield an input–output ratio of over 1:20 and can be replicated in other low-resource healthcare areas, achieving significant improvements for the target audience as well as efficient problem-solving.

The third index assesses impact (I). Tencent evaluates projects based on their key contributions to industry development and capacity to drive industry progress. The company measures the recognised value achieved not only through the project itself but also through extending and adapting the model to expand and evolve the project's social value impact. For example, Tencent's SSV Village CEO Training programme seeks to cultivate entrepreneurial talent for rural revitalisation. Like an EMBA programme for entrepreneurs, it systematically designs courses and compiles case studies for this group, creating a training system that integrates corporate management skills with rural conditions. Through marketing, it became one of the primary models for rural talent revitalisation nationwide and achieved sustainable operation.

8.3 The Interplay between Social and Economic Value

As social innovation became integrated into business operations, Tencent gained a clearer understanding of the interplay between social and economic value. Tencent believes that the creation of economic and social value should neither be strictly separate nor necessarily in conflict with one another. Social and economic value can each reinforce the other through creation, conversion, overflow, and propulsion, thereby achieving integration.

Social value creation can simultaneously happen within the framework of business operations aimed at generating economic value. For example, Tencent Docs is mainly positioned as a B2B online document product. But when triggered by relevant social events, the platform can be used by the public and rescue organisations to transmit information and engage in knowledge exchange through social collaboration. The case of WeChat further suggests that relevant product offerings and functions can not only help micro-, small, and medium-sized enterprises (MSMEs) develop their businesses but also facilitate financial inclusion within the open ecosystem of WeChat to create value for those enterprises.

Tencent creates social value within other industries through support for their digitisation or upgrade by acting as a digital assistant, which in turn allows Tencent to share economic value in the process. Moreover, some projects or initiatives targeting specific social issues could bring about new opportunities to create economic value. The low-carbon industry is a good example: solutions to address climate change hinge on both technical advancements and models for efficient business operations. Initially, efforts to address relevant issues may rely heavily on the application and development of advanced technology. But to achieve scalability, effective business operational models become essential within the industry. In 2021, a team led by Pony Ma conducted in-depth research on the low-carbon industry. The team's findings suggested that the low-carbon industry could cultivate a sustainable and self-sufficient model that did not depend on subsidies. As one senior manager noted:

If a project can create massive social value, this will generate business or commercial value in the long term. We focus on looking for solutions to climate change, which is urgent, in the short term. In the longer term, however, we hope to explore new directions for a company's business development once there are mature business models in the industry.

Tencent's motives for involvement in social value creation by addressing social problems went beyond the pressures of legitimacy from a CSR perspective. They were also about anticipating potential economic value in a long-term perspective. Still, this does not mean Tencent was seeking quick success and instant benefits. As Pony Ma suggested: 'Good R&D programmes do not aim for instant success and benefits, and the same holds for investment in social value creation. The R&D of social value and scientific innovation can lay a solid foundation for the long-term development of the company.'

Tencent does not necessarily need to prioritise returns across different sectors in the short term and can instead progressively establish sustainable development models wherein revenues are reinvested in new initiatives. This approach fosters long-term expansion and development. As Tencent President Martin Lau commented, 'Social value creation requires us to hold a long-term view and strengthen our resolve to execute gradual but lasting outcomes.'

Nonetheless, the company is acutely aware that the pursuit of economic value is not the primary objective in areas such as the philanthropy sector. Tencent is very cautious about monetising social platforms positioned as open ecosystems where individuals or organisations with diverse capabilities, resources, and skillsets can access their respective user bases and generate commercial returns. Tencent only receives a modest share of these returns for providing user traffic, technological support, and infrastructure, despite the significance of the company's contributions.

8.4 Multifaceted Social Value across Diverse Scenarios

As social value creation was integrated into Tencent's business operations and various business groups became involved in social innovation, the company's social innovation grew to cover various groups of customers, businesses, and industries alongside society at large. It thus created multifaceted social value across a range of diverse scenarios, such as social inclusion and the advancement of industry digitalisation, and in the service of the public interest, rural revitalisation, disaster response and relief, and carbon neutrality.

8.4.1 Social Inclusion

Tencent strives to provide solutions to address social issues for various groups of users, especially disadvantaged, socially excluded, or marginalised groups (e.g. the elderly, persons with disabilities). Through the innovative use of technology, Tencent has aimed at overcoming the challenges of an ageing population in China. For instance, the company improved barrier-free technologies to enable seniors to adapt more easily to digital tools and the digital world. Tencent's products typically include a senior mode and barrier-free accessibility features. For example, WeChat's senior mode offers larger text, a simplified interface, and clearer icons, while its accessibility options include voice-to-text input and screen reader support. Tencent also provides a dedicated service hotline for senior users. In an effort to mitigate the health risks posed to seniors – particularly those living alone – of accidental falls, Tencent introduced a smart home guardian system called the Invisible Caregiver.

Leveraging advancements in cloud computing and IoT technology, this innovative system employs more than 100 detectors to accurately identify the occurrence of a fall or other accident. It can promptly send automated alerts to caregivers, ensuring the timely provision of assistance. The product was later upgraded with a multimodal recognition mode that enabled it to comprehend and autonomously respond to a senior's call for assistance by identifying keywords. With improved security monitoring and protective features, it effectively safeguards the health and safety of seniors. By the end of 2022, the Invisible Caregiver system had been operational at the Shenzhen Pension Nursing Hospital for three years while the household version of the product had been embraced by over 1,000 senior households (Tencent, 2023).

Tencent has also leveraged technological innovation to address the social issue of hearing impairment. With the 'Tianlai' initiative, Tencent innovatively applied relevant technologies that originated from Tencent Meeting teams to improve and upgrade hearing aid devices. In doing so, the company facilitated the development of the hearing assistance industry. Through collaborative innovation, Tencent ultimately developed a systematic integrated solution to address hearing impairment. This solution not only provided cost-effective hearing aids for people with impairment and raised public awareness of hearing health but also assisted disadvantaged groups in obtaining free hearing aids to create comprehensive social value.

8.4.2 Promoting Industry Digitalisation

In the digital era, leveraging digital technologies to enhance industrial efficiency and strengthen the core competitiveness of enterprises is crucial for driving economic growth and social development. Tencent continues to make breakthroughs in smart tools for fields ranging from healthcare, education, cultural tourism, and transport to retail, energy, and finance, injecting new momentum into the ecosystem of smart technologies.

To begin, Tencent actively invests in the R&D of smart industry tools, continuously developing new industry tools and functions. Tencent's three key SaaS products – WeCom, Tencent Docs, and Tencent Meeting – are typical examples. With online communication and virtual offices now commonplace, enterprises are increasingly demanding new applications for SaaS products. In response, Tencent has integrated and connected WeCom, Tencent Docs, and Tencent Meeting for business needs and optimised the functions of industry tools. The integration offers a new experience for collaborative office work – one created from internal system connections to external human connections. The innovation significantly improved efficiency for users of these three major tools, as reflected in the improved efficacy of enterprise management, production, and industrial development. On the whole, the effort created social value that is efficient, carbon-reducing, and resource-saving.

Tencent further provides bespoke services and solutions for specific industries. In the healthcare sector, for instance, Tencent's health mini-program offers a comprehensive online and offline service platform that caters to individual users, seamlessly connecting them with vital public health services offered at hospitals and vaccination centres. The programme serves as a reliable source for authoritative medical information, empowering users with essential knowledge of various healthcare matters. In addition, Tencent offers tools to facilitate the digitalisation of medical institutions and associations, bolster municipal health platforms, enhance public health management (partly through early warning systems), and implement intelligent solutions for medical insurance management and decision-making processes.

In the education sector, Tencent Education applies cutting-edge AI, audio, and video technologies to introduce digital 'education toolboxes' that cater to the diverse needs of education authorities, school administrators, teachers, and students. These comprehensive toolsets encompass functions for teaching, learning, management, evaluation, and testing, with the overarching aim of enhancing the efficiency and effectiveness of educational processes. In the field of urban transportation, Tencent developed a cloud platform that merges cloud computing technology with digital mapping resources. The integration enables the platform to facilitate smart transport applications, offer a nuanced analysis of regional traffic patterns, and ultimately enhance the efficiency of traffic management operations.

Tencent is further attuned to the digitalisation of MSMEs; this was particularly evident during the pandemic. For example, WeChat provided easy-to-learn digital solutions in business management to MSMEs. WeChat Pay has a team dedicated to MSME services that is responsible for marketing new products and collecting customer feedback through in-store visits. During the pandemic, the team introduced a free SaaS project for MSMEs and guided them on how to use WeChat Pay to receive and manage payments. Street vendors and mom-and-pop shops, which typically struggle with sophisticated business management as well as with finding employees, benefitted greatly from the digital payment system. The digital system enabled them to save time when dealing with cash payments and sidestep the risk of receiving counterfeit bills. It also automatically generated daily operation reports for restaurants, enabling them to have a basic understanding of their income and expenditures for better business management. Vendors no longer needed to spend hours going through transactions one by one to prepare financial reports at the end of each business day.

Finally, WeChat helped establish a digital purchase-sell-stock management system for retail stores and restaurants, especially those that sold fast-moving consumer goods. For example, some micro- and small retail shops, as well as street restaurants, could now order products – such as beverages – directly from suppliers via WeChat's B2B mini-programs, bypassing local dealers. This not only enabled retailers to receive goods faster and at lower cost but also allowed suppliers to access real-time market data.

8.4.3 Rural Revitalisation

In 2017, the Chinese government introduced a national strategy for rural revitalisation aimed at improving the economic, social, and environmental conditions of rural areas. In line with national development goals, Tencent leveraged its digital capabilities to drive continuous improvements in rural governance, modernise the agricultural sector, and provide training in rural governance and agricultural business management for professional and vocational talent. This was carried out through a special programme called the Cultivator Revitalisation Plan initiated by Tencent to help 'cultivators' in a variety of ways.

For example, the company developed an AI-powered crop protection tool with the capacity to swiftly and accurately identify crop diseases and pests (Tencent, 2023). This tool provided an innovative solution to help prevent crop yield losses and mitigate the overuse of pesticides. The company also launched a knowledge-sharing platform tailored to rural communities that enabled the dissemination of rural revitalisation policies, agricultural business management strategies, farming techniques, and offline educational resources. A dedicated channel, 'FAQs on Rural Revitalisation', on the platform streamlined communication and fostered knowledge exchange among over 600,000 grassroots leaders (Tencent, 2023). Tencent thus not only helped advance the digitisation of agriculture but also fostered sustainable development in rural communities.

8.4.4 *Disaster and Emergency Response*

On 20 July 2021, massive flooding struck the city of Zhengzhou and other areas in Henan province. Many people were trapped in the devastating floods and tried to guide rescuers to their location via online social media platforms such as Weibo. However, the information was dispersed and disorganised. As an online document platform that enabled collaborative multi-user editing, Tencent Docs played an important role in the disaster response and rescue. A spreadsheet titled 'People to be Rescued' on Tencent Docs, originally created by a university student, quickly went viral among WeChat groups. On the spreadsheet, those who needed help and rescue could edit and input key information, such as location, number of people, and required materials. At the same time, local government and rescue teams could gather, identify, and classify the timely information. The Tencent Docs team responded promptly and became actively involved as well. Once Tencent staff noticed that the online spreadsheet had a growing number of page views, they organised a volunteer group within the company to gather and verify information from various sources, then contact relevant rescue teams to support other partners.

Within the first twenty-four hours of its creation, around two and a half million people accessed the document. By the following day, it had already been updated more than 270 times as it successfully linked flood victims with first responders. One week into the flood, the document was still playing a critical role in saving lives and providing other important information. It thus grew from a spreadsheet to a multilayered information hub for people affected by the flood, particularly once professional rescue groups and volunteers connected with the spreadsheet to manage and update the documents together on the platform. New sub-tables and functions continued to be generated, including a sheet on medical information and psychological counselling. After the flood, the Tencent team developed emergency response capabilities, such as enhancing the product's stability while subject to heavy use, so Tencent Docs could function better for disaster response and rescue in the future.

Tencent Docs has been used as a tool not just to disseminate and exchange information but also to categorise and organise key information during other disasters aside from the Henan flood. On the whole, this function enhances the efficiency and accuracy of disaster rescue teams. More importantly, the company gained rich experience in disaster and emergency response, both in establishing and developing modes of emergency disaster relief. In response to the need for disaster relief, Tencent made information channels accessible to the public and served municipal authorities to provide survival guidelines and popularise safety science.

8.4.5 Digital Philanthropy

Tencent Charity is the first, largest, and most established internet-based charity fundraising platform in China. By 2021, over 20,000 partner charity organisations and over 440 million donors joined the Tencent Charity platform, raising more than RMB 11.8 billion in support of roughly 90,000 projects (Tencent, 2023). As the first online charity platform in China, Tencent Charity not only operates its self-developed online donation platform to assist philanthropy organisations in reaching out to hundreds of millions of users in China, facilitating matching and donation across a number of projects, but also promotes digitalisation to drive more efficient collaborations in the field of philanthropy. Collectively, these efforts improve social well-being.

More specifically, Tencent Charity has pioneered new means to inspire more public participation and establish a convenient and transparent platform. It provides low-barrier access for potential donors to participate in public welfare activities by linking to the widely used smartphone application—WeChat. At the same time, it also encourages more informed decision-making by providing potential donors with information to help them decide which projects to fund and support on the platform. Tencent Charity itself supports regular donors by matching larger donations to encourage greater involvement from netizens. Tencent Charity further helps charity organisations strengthen accountability by providing digital support for transparency, compliance training, and third-party evaluations. For example, the Tencent Charity team has not only applied digital technologies such as blockchain technology to increase the transparency of project operations and ensure projects are both traceable and verifiable, but it has also helped charity organisations achieve better project management by providing a systematic template on the digital platform.

At the same time, Tencent Charity also focuses on building long-term and sustainable partnerships between donors, charity organisations, and recipients. In 2015, Tencent Charity identified 9 September as China's annual Charity Day. Employees were actively engaged in charity events through donations and designing activities. Netizens, businesses, and charitable organisations were also able to participate in public welfare through a variety of interactive initiatives. In 2022, Tencent pioneered the initiative of donor general meetings in collaboration with charitable organisations. These meetings are designed to engage donors directly, inviting participation through platforms such as Tencent Meeting or Video Accounts at WeChat. The objective is to provide transparent insights into project progress and the use of donated funds. Throughout 2022, Tencent hosted a total of 118 donor general meetings, garnering a remarkable online viewership of 37.3 million (Tencent, 2023).

8.4.6 Carbon Neutrality

Tencent has been committed to carbon neutrality. Through its technological and platform advantages, the company is helping to achieve carbon neutrality goals in various fields. First, Tencent is dedicated to promoting low-carbon lifestyles within society through various digital tools. For example, it launched a Carbon Neutrality Quiz mini-program to promote awareness and build knowledge about how to live a low-carbon lifestyle. It also developed the Carbon Island mini-game to guide the public towards carbon neutrality.

Next, Tencent leveraged its digital capabilities to facilitate a low-carbon transformation within various industrial sectors. For example, Tencent Cloud offers sustainable computing power to businesses to help build a low-carbon digital infrastructure.

Leveraging the network effect, Tencent also developed digital platforms to facilitate information sharing and collaboration. Stakeholders of low-carbon technologies (e.g. entrepreneurs, investors, and research institutions) have been struggling to identify and access resources and partners to drive real change. In response, Tencent launched a platform called TanLIVE to bring together technical tools and insights to accelerate the implementation of climate solutions. Designed to connect and empower organisations working towards carbon neutrality, TanLIVE functions as a digital hub to offer collaborative tools that include community networking, project listings, and an ecosystem of technological and financing solutions for entrepreneurs, investors, and research institutions in the sector. Entrepreneurs can showcase innovative technologies on the platform and find investors. Companies can source low-carbon products and technologies as well as learn about low-carbon transition pathways.

In 2023, Tencent also launched the Carbon Quest Plan aimed at jointly building a CCUS (carbon capture, utilisation, and storage) ecosystem to promote the large-scale application of advanced CCUS technologies. The company introduced Carbon BASE, a carbon neutralisation computing platform that promotes the digitalisation, visualisation, and creditisation of individual and corporate carbon reduction behaviours. Carbon BASE supports enterprises and government departments in flexibly developing customised carbon-inclusive platforms through open APIs, enabling rapid integration and deployment. The Carbon BASE platform provides standardised templates for organisations and companies undertaking low-carbon activities, saving time on development as well as reducing costs for companies. The initiative thus offers reliable computing and technical support to promote a green, low-carbon lifestyle across society.

Finally, Tencent has been dedicated to developing and exploring new low-carbon technologies based on its Carbon Neutrality Lab. It provides a range of resources to support the efforts of other parties, including universities and research institutes, to accelerate the deployment and application of low-carbon technologies through scientific research, pilot demonstrations, and innovative business models.

8.5 Social Value Co-creation in the Ecosystem

Social problems often involve complex and deeply entrenched challenges, which means that they cannot be solved by simplistic technological fixes alone. Tencent is aware of the difficulty in realising the goal of creating social value on its own as effective solutions require collaborative efforts from multiple stakeholders. While the company can lead the initial stages of progress, ongoing participation from other players is crucial to achieving lasting social value. Tencent leverages its technological capabilities and innovative spirit to cultivate platform ecosystems. By fostering connections and collaborations among diverse stakeholders, the company actively co-creates greater social value with the other players in its ecosystem, catalysing positive outcomes for society at large.

The issue of carbon neutrality offers an illustration. The electricity consumed by data centres is the main source of carbon emissions for Tencent's operations. For Tencent, the key challenge is reducing carbon emissions to achieve carbon neutrality while meeting the company's demand for electricity. To increase the proportion of renewables in the energy it consumed, Tencent explored the use of distributed new energy sources and energy storage technologies as well as actively participated in green electricity trading. While Tencent has made major efforts to reduce carbon emissions from its data centres, the primary target of the company's carbon neutrality plan was helping both industry and society with the transition to low-carbon energy consumption. Tencent provides partners with a platform to connect the innovators and research institutions that own advanced technologies as well as investment companies with financial resources.

However, Tencent also launches projects for technical alliances between IT giants in China and globally, collaborating with Microsoft and Alibaba to work on open-source technological applications and innovation in carbon neutrality. As one manager responsible for carbon neutrality at Tencent commented: 'We are trying to not only identify decarbonisation solutions for our own endeavours, but also explore how we can apply the insights gained from our experiences to other industries, amplifying our impact on a larger scale.'

More importantly, Tencent formulates its principles around stakeholder access to the platform ecosystem and their involvement in co-creation for social value: openness, fairness, and decentralisation. Openness and fairness mean these platforms are equally open to and inclusive of stakeholders and partners, no matter how small or societally marginalised they may be. Decentralisation means each user functions independently in the network or ecosystem generated by platforms where no single entity has absolute authority. In contrast to some platforms that distribute public traffic based on their preferences, the WeChat platform does not control traffic in the public domain and the right to generate traffic is handed over to each user. Whether individual users or MSMEs, they can engage the ecosystem, build partnerships, and create value. Similarly, Tencent Charity demonstrates how small-sized charity organisations in rural areas were not left behind once Tencent Charity provided funding and technical support that enabled them to use the platform to promote their projects.

These principles were emphasised by a senior manager of the WeChat group, who stated: 'The reason why SMEs can live and develop on our platforms is that we have set our principles. Decentralisation can guarantee it is fair for any organisation, whether an SME or a big company. Because of our principles, we are able to build a friendly environment for SMEs and create sustainable social value.'

Likewise, Tencent Charity is not simply open to charity organisations of different sizes and in different locations; it also welcomes other organisations, even competitor companies, to contribute to internet-based charity activities. A manager at Tencent Charity commented:

We created Chinese Charity Day not for Tencent itself, but for all of the stakeholders in this sector and in society. Although we are the first to do so, we don't want to be the dominant actor. We welcome and encourage more platforms to join us and work together. We also open up our resources to our partners as much as possible in order to promote the development of the sector for societal well-being.

Tencent further extends legitimacy and credibility to the involvement of other players in the ecosystem. For example, WeChat Pay was legally required to perform know-your-customer checks on its users to prevent identity theft, combat money laundering, and prevent financial fraud. To register as commercial customers, MSMEs were required to submit documents that included a business licence and payment verification to WeChat Pay. Because a wide range of non-profit organisations were involved in online charity activities, the Tencent Charity team made a significant effort to ensure the organisations complied with relevant regulations. As one member of the Tencent Charity team suggested: 'Tencent Charity needs to guarantee legal compliance when providing their platform [to the public]. In other words, we need to make sure that charity organisations follow the rules for disclosure and procedures for raising money.'

8.6 Mechanisms for Social Innovation and Social Value Creation at Tencent

Tencent has established a mechanism for social innovation and social value creation (see Figure 8.1). First, social innovation serves as the foundation for Tencent's strategy to create SSV. Social innovation itself is grounded in three key dimensions: technological, product, and business model innovation. Technological innovation underpins social innovation as it allows the company to undertake original technological breakthroughs in response to specific user needs or societal issues as well as apply existing technologies to new scenarios. Product innovation provides the pathway for social innovation. Through analysis of specific societal issues, Tencent can leverage its capacity to develop and deliver various products that meet user needs and offer more efficient solutions. Business model innovation involves exploring innovative business models that enable Tencent to create social value through business operations.

The three dimensions are interrelated: business model innovation builds on technological and product innovations. As its focus falls on expanding and sustaining social value in various scenarios, the innovative business model can stimulate additional advances in technology and products. By integrating product, technological, and business model innovation, Tencent can generate social value through its business operations in a sustainable way.

Second, by combining the 'user-oriented' value in business operations with 'tech for good' in its corporate mission, the integration

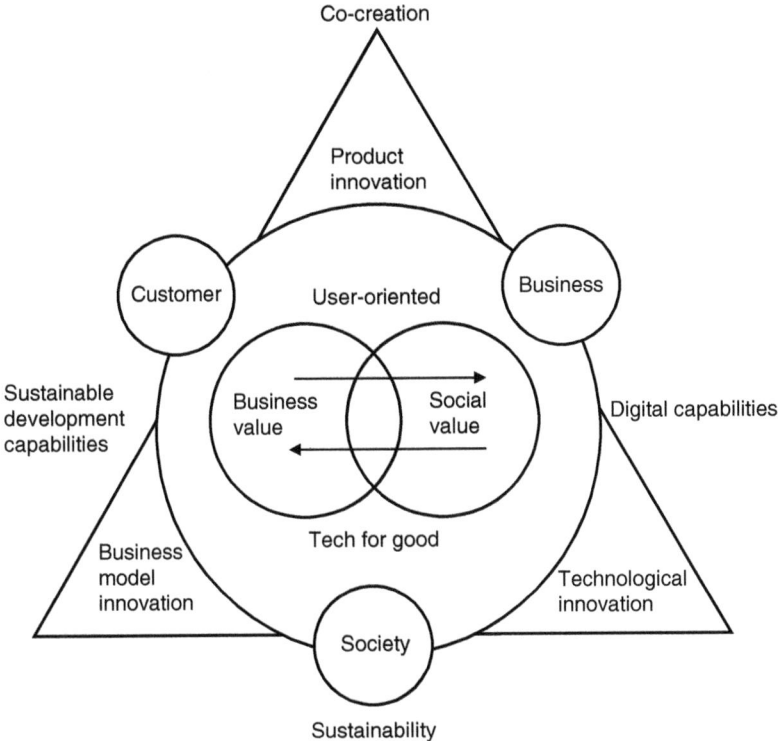

Figure 8.1 The Tencent mechanism for social value creation.
(Source: Tencent)

of social and economic value became the ultimate goal in the strategy for SSV innovation at Tencent. Tencent believed that through mutual promotion and transformation of the other, social and economic value would achieve organic integration. In this process, the integration of social and economic value is driven by both social needs and commercial logic. At the same time, Tencent leverages and develops digital and sustainable development capabilities. This not only conveys and incentivises technological, product, and business model innovation but also continuously increases economic value and amplifies social value. Ultimately, the end result is sustainable social innovation.

Third, multifaceted social value creation across various diverse scenarios benefits from the idea of a 'CBS trinity', which emphasises the importance of simultaneously serving customers (C), businesses (B), and society (S). This approach drives broader value creation and maximises positive impact. Through the CBS trinity, Tencent creates multiple social values for various groups in different sectors and areas. It also integrates value creation for society (S) into meeting the needs of and providing services for industries/businesses (B) and users/customers (C). For example, the digital tools for social inclusion and disaster response were originally based on an understanding of user needs and later evolved into fulfilling societal needs. The provision of digital solutions to industries has enhanced efficiency for users and businesses as well as contributed to addressing social challenges, particularly when it comes to reducing carbon emissions.

Fourth, the analysis suggests that building an ecosystem for co-creation was a crucial method for achieving sustainable social innovation at Tencent. Tencent encourages collaboration among partners within its ecosystem to achieve shared value and address social challenges. This approach enhances integration and cooperation, leading to deeper, higher-level co-creation. The result is improvements to the efficiency and quality of value creation, as well as the promotion of scalability and amplification of social impact, which ultimately drives sustainability for both Tencent and society as a whole.

8.7 Discussion and Conclusion

This chapter has examined how Tencent, a leading internet-based platform company, creates social value and fosters social innovation to maximise the value of platforms. It highlights key aspects of Tencent's social innovation and social value creation, including its motivation, manifestations, approaches to, and mechanisms for doing so. Social innovation at Tencent is driven by strategic upgrades that emphasise social value creation at a strategic level. Tencent recognises the crucial role of social value in its corporate development and understands the interplay between social and economic value. Unlike traditional CSR practices, which often serve as window dressing to maintain market competitiveness, Tencent's approach integrates social and economic value creation. The company demonstrates that these values can coexist and complement each other within business operations (Van Der Have and Rubalcaba, 2016).

Some of Tencent's platforms are specifically designed to generate social value while others do so indirectly while pursuing profit. In addition, Tencent's digital capabilities (which include advantaged technologies and innovative products) are an important enabler of its achievement of social innovation. As a leading platform company, it could be argued that Tencent has strong enough capabilities in technological and product development to provide effective digital solutions for social problems. In contrast, SMEs have fewer resources and capabilities and face more pressure from daily business operations. This makes it challenging for SMEs to devise mechanisms or muster the willpower to address social issues. With abundant resources and capabilities, Tencent is able to tackle social problems by leveraging its own business and technologies and integrating them into social value creation.

Within the process of social innovation itself, Tencent embraces a long-term mindset that looks beyond immediate business concerns to focus on long-term growth. Tencent is seeking neither quick success nor instant benefits, and the company does not eagerly pursue exclusively short-term economic gains. Tencent is also acutely aware that the pursuit of economic value should not be the primary objective within certain areas or sectors, such as the philanthropy sector.

Tencent has established a mechanism for social innovation to create social value. This mechanism highlights three distinctive approaches to doing so, which collectively carry implications for how Tencent leverages digital platforms to generate social value for various stakeholders within the platform ecosystem and society at large. For one, various business departments are involved in social value creation that has itself been integrated into the company's daily operations. In this way, social innovation benefits from the technological, product, and business model innovation by business departments and teams. Technological innovation serves as the foundation for social innovation while product innovation provides the pathway for it. Business model innovation drives the development of business models and the ecosystem to create SSV. Business departments actively sense and respond to social pain points and scenarios, seeking out solutions to meet social needs or address social problems. More importantly, Tencent's social innovation also benefits from internal collaboration driven by shared goals and corporate strategy. Different business departments contribute their technological or product capabilities to social innovation initiatives and projects.

Another key approach to social value creation at Tencent is co-creation within its ecosystem. The company leverages its digital capabilities to build platform ecosystems, facilitating connections and collaborations across a wide range of external stakeholders. Tencent not only empowers external players to get involved in social value creation but also establishes principles for stakeholder access and involvement in co-creation. This approach emphasises openness, fairness, and decentralisation, ensuring legitimacy and credibility within the process of co-creation. It also allows stakeholders of all sizes and from all sectors to engage in co-creating greater and more sustainable social value.

Likewise, the CBS trinity approach is crucial to social innovation. Tencent aims at creating value for users (C), industries/businesses (B), and society (S) through technological, product, and business model innovation. The aim not only helps meet the needs of users and businesses but also addresses social challenges. More importantly, it integrates the creation of value for society (S) and the provision of services for industries/businesses (B) and users (C), fostering a holistic and sustainable approach to social innovation and social value creation.

Because social value creation has been integrated into daily operations and various groups (CBS) have involved themselves in social innovation for social value co-creation, Tencent is able to create multifaceted social value across a range of scenarios, whether in terms of social inclusion, the promotion of digitalisation for industries, service of the public interest, rural revitalisation, disaster response and relief, or carbon neutrality. Social innovation thus extends across different groups of users, different businesses and industries, and society at large.

Furthermore, Tencent offers several insightful lessons on how companies can effectively create social value while achieving business success in the digital age. First is integrating social value creation into core business strategy and activities. Tencent embeds its social value creation into its corporate strategy and the very fabric of the company's business model and operations – rather than treating it as an afterthought or a separate CSR initiative. Tencent's commitment to addressing societal challenges, such as digital inclusion, public health, and environmental sustainability, is not confined to philanthropy; instead, these goals are tightly interwoven into its products, platforms, businesses, and services. These actions not only provide immediate societal benefits but also enhance the relevance and trustworthiness of Tencent's ecosystem. This alignment between social value and business operations illustrates a strategic approach where doing good and doing well are not mutually exclusive but mutually reinforcing.

Secondly, Tencent's approach is based on a sophisticated understanding of the dynamic relationship between social value and economic value. The company does not view these two dimensions as inherently separate or in conflict; instead, it recognises that they can be mutually reinforcing. This perspective allows Tencent to identify and harness opportunities where social and economic outcomes align and support each other. Crucially, Tencent understands that the balance between social and economic value is not fixed but varies across different products, services, and business models. Some offerings may be primarily commercially driven but still generate meaningful social impact during their development or application. For example, digital tools designed for commercial use may also improve access to education or healthcare. Conversely, certain initiatives may be rooted in the pursuit of social value, such as carbon neutrality, yet hold the potential to create long-term economic gain. At the same time, Tencent is careful to differentiate between profit-driven goals and public interest objectives, particularly in areas such as philanthropy. In these contexts, economic gain should not be the primary focus. Tencent's approach offers important insights for other companies seeking to navigate the intersection of social and economic value. By recognising this relationship and adapting strategies to different contexts, businesses can create more holistic, sustainable value across both societal and commercial dimensions.

Thirdly, a key factor in Tencent's success in generating social value lies in its strategic use of digital platforms to foster multi-stakeholder partnerships. The Tencent case illustrates how platform companies are uniquely positioned to deliver innovative solutions to complex social challenges across diverse contexts and populations – particularly among disadvantaged, marginalised, or socially excluded groups. Tencent's platforms function not only as digital infrastructure but also as catalysts for collaborative innovation to create social value. This further underscores the developmental potential of digital platforms, especially in the Global South (Bonina et al., 2021; Fu et al., 2021; Qureshi et al., 2021). When thoughtfully designed and deployed, digital platforms can serve as powerful tools for addressing social grand challenges such as poverty, inequality, and limited access to healthcare and education. In doing so, they can make a direct contribution to the advancement of the United Nations Sustainable Development Goals (SDGs). More significantly, Tencent leverages its expansive digital ecosystem to act as an enabler and connector among diverse actors – including government agencies, non-governmental organisations (NGOs), academic institutions, and private enterprises. By facilitating multi-stakeholder partnerships, Tencent helps to mobilise shared resources, knowledge, and capabilities towards common goals. These partnerships not only enhance the scale and scope of social initiatives but are also essential for addressing complex, systemic problems that a single entity cannot resolve independently.

9 | Conclusions
Tencent's Innovation Model

Historically, Chinese companies have often been characterised as merely imitative, with growth driven by minor innovations, business model innovation, and a perceived lack of original innovation (Abrami et al., 2014). However, after thirty years of rapid development, some Chinese companies have not only achieved global standards but also set new benchmarks for innovation and technology in both traditional sectors, such as major appliance manufacture and retail (Greeven et al., 2021), as well as in emerging sectors, such as ICT, and in their management methods (Greeven et al., 2023). These companies also represent important examples and inspiration for other companies worldwide. China has also evolved into an R&D laboratory for Western companies, initially supporting innovation for the Chinese market and now contributing to innovation efforts on a global scale (McKern et al., 2022; *The Economist*, 2024).

Among these companies, Tencent, which has developed a global reputation as a gaming and social media empire, is often discussed owing to its strategy of imitating the successful ideas and business models of Western companies. This approach was evident in its early days, with QQ compared to ICQ and WeChat mirroring aspects of WhatsApp and Facebook. However, Tencent has also excelled in creating an expansive digital ecosystem, integrating social media, gaming, fintech, cloud computing, and AI, and producing numerous outstanding products supported by superior technology. Tencent's trajectory demonstrates a more comprehensive and dynamic approach to innovation and growth, and its ability to lead in the global technology market.

Based on our detailed four-year mixed-methods study, which included a survey of almost 2,000 employees and interviews with more than 100 stakeholders, we found that Tencent's innovation mechanisms reflect a market-type organisation with an OCEAN ecosystem, focusing on *openness, coopetition, empowerment, autonomy*, and *needs*. Applying this approach, Tencent has developed numerous high-quality products and has created value in many areas, supported by its workforce of tens of thousands of high-calibre, creative employees. We also found that Tencent was unique in its sequoia-like innovation featured by 'DDIC' innovations – that is, its *deep, directed, invisible,* and *compound* approaches to innovation – helping Tencent refine its user experience, maintain customer engagement, create value, and sustain a competitive advantage in the digital era. In this chapter, we shall summarise these research findings in detail.

9.1 Tencent's Uniqueness: Sequoia-Like Innovations

Moving beyond imitation, Tencent has been recognised for its micro-innovations – its small, incremental improvements and adaptations to existing technologies and platforms (Luo et al., 2015). Tencent has also pioneered the integration of social and financial services into its platforms, exemplified by its seamless incorporation of WeChat Pay into its WeChat app, transforming how Chinese consumers manage transactions. This blend of social connectivity and financial services has not only driven user engagement but also created a robust ecosystem sustaining long-term growth; moreover, it is considered a new-to-the-world innovation (Murmann and Zhu, 2021). However, these examples do not reflect the breadth of Tencent's innovation achievements and mechanisms.

Our research reveals that Tencent's uniqueness and enduring competitiveness stem from what we call its 'sequoia-like innovation' – a distinctive type of innovation marked by depth, directionality, resilience, and ecosystemic impact. Much like a towering sequoia tree, Tencent's innovation is anchored in deep and expansive roots, guided by a strong sense of direction. These roots represent a profound understanding of the fundamentals of products and services, along with sustained investments in core technologies, organisational capabilities, and cultural foundations – elements that often remain invisible on the surface. Importantly, these roots are not isolated; they are interconnected and mutually reinforcing, forming a robust internal structure that enables Tencent to adapt and thrive amid constant change. This tightly integrated innovation system gives Tencent exceptional resilience, allowing it to withstand regulatory shifts, market volatility, and technological disruption – just as a sequoia endures the storms of nature. At the same time, this foundational strength extends

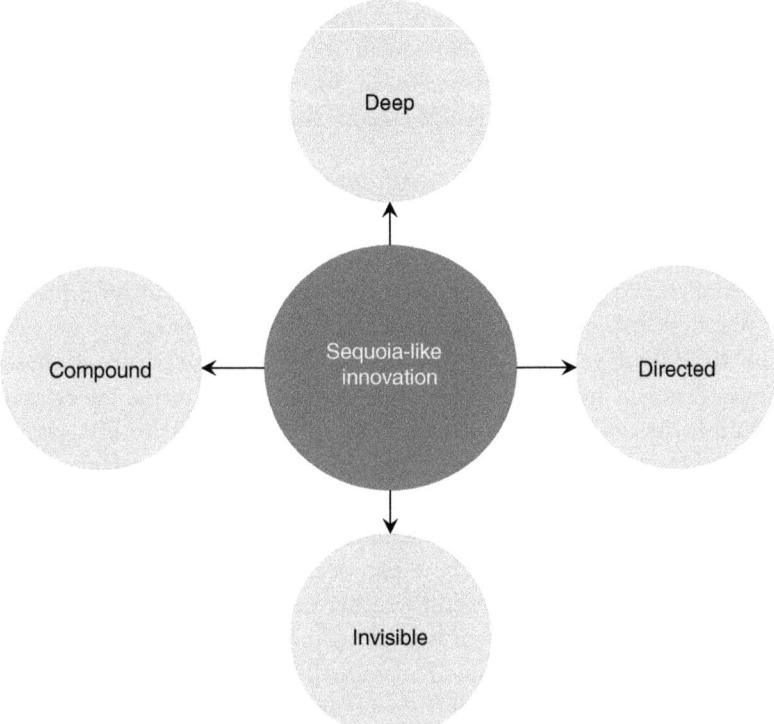

Figure 9.1 Features of Tencent's sequoia-like innovations.

outward, supporting the growth of a broader ecosystem. In this eco-system, Tencent acts not as a dominant controller, but as an enabler and connector, cultivating the vitality of partners, developers, and col-laborators who grow alongside the platform. More specifically, the features of Tencent's innovation include *deep*, *directed*, *invisible*, and *compound* innovation (see Figure 9.1).

9.1.1 Deep Innovation

Tencent's strength is its deep innovation, which we have defined as innovation based on 'first principles' thinking, enabling designers and developers to explore fundamental concepts and identify the core char-acteristics inherent to a product, service, or function. Product design-ers and developers at Tencent do not simply respond to user needs; they determine the essence of its products and services and extract key insights from its massive volume of complex user information to identify what users fundamentally require. As such, this innovation goes beyond incremental improvements or superficial changes and often produces developmental breakthroughs that address core issues or limitations in novel ways.

The concept of first principles thinking breaks down complicated problems into their basic elements, which are then reassembled from the ground up. Such a thinking and working style focuses on fundamental human needs. Tencent's approach to innovation adheres to the first principles approach in which user needs are always prioritised by developing a deep understanding of the nature of these needs. Tencent applies this principle to both its external users and its employees, who are considered internal users of its HR products. When designing products, Tencent's R&D teams always consider the essential needs of its users, prioritising health, sustainable development, and long-term impacts rather than pursuing short-term profits and benefits. They also seek to simplify functions to make products more user-friendly rather than complex and onerous. For example, WeChat, which is used by more than one billion users worldwide, has always retained a simple interface with minimal buttons (see Chapter 6). Though more demands continually arise, the product team prioritises emphasising the essence of the needs rather than reacting hastily to competitors' actions or implementing every user suggestion.

Tencent is also adept at understanding the preferences of younger generations when innovating its products to maintain the competitiveness of older products (see Chapter 7). As shown during the COVID-19 pandemic, Tencent understands the nature of social interaction and can create popular features that enhance communication among younger people. However, this does not mean that product teams consider all user needs. They set priorities and establish phases of product design by applying their product skills and technical capabilities to develop products that are suitable for the market.

9.1.2 Directed Innovation

Directed innovation concerns innovation endeavours that are focused on specific goals, challenges, or priorities identified by a company or wider society (Fu and Shi, 2022; Moscona and Sastry, 2023). This approach contrasts with spontaneous or serendipitous innovation, where new ideas and advancements arise more randomly. Tencent believes that innovation should be purposefully directed by critical factors, including user needs and societal needs, in line with its guiding principle of 'Value for Users, Tech for Good'. This approach can help to overcome specific challenges, such as global grand challenges to achieve impactful innovations that benefit not only the company but also its users, partners, industries, and broader society.

Tencent has a keen ability to identify and seize emerging market opportunities. By closely monitoring technological advances and consumer trends, Tencent remains at the forefront of innovation. This proactive approach enables the company to quickly adapt and capitalise on new developments in social media, gaming, fintech, and other sectors. For instance, Tencent identified the emergence of the mobile internet era and developed WeChat, which is the foundation of its current social media domination.

Over the past twenty years, Tencent has ensured that its initiatives resonate with national priorities – such as the development of digital infrastructure, smart cities, and greener technology – promoting sustainable innovations for social value (see Chapter 8). By aligning with governmental goals, the company has ensured regulatory compliance and gained support for its projects. This alignment is evident in the 'WeCity' initiative, which integrates digital technologies to enhance urban services and management, supporting China's smart cities agenda. While committed to profitability and market leadership, Tencent is equally focused on creating a positive societal impact. The company's products and services often aim to address broader social issues, including digital inclusion, healthcare, and education (see Chapter 8). For example, WeChat's integration of payment services has significantly advanced financial inclusion in China, making financial services more accessible to a broader population. Tencent's initiatives also aim to promote environmental conservation and social responsibility, with the company committed to achieving carbon neutrality in its operations and investing in green technologies and practices. In addition, Tencent's 'Tech for Good' philosophy emphasises its commitment to using technology to address societal challenges. This includes supporting disaster relief initiatives, promoting public health through AI-driven medical research, and fostering digital literacy.

Tencent's innovation strategy applies a directed approach to some extent, effectively leveraging opportunities and aligning with government policies to advance its business interests and deliver broader social impacts. This comprehensive and multifaceted innovation strategy enables Tencent to balance its business acumen with a profound commitment to societal well-being, helping to maintain the company's sustained growth and competitiveness and cementing its position as a responsible and forward-thinking global technology leader.

9.1.3 Invisible Innovation

Invisible innovation represents innovation that is not immediately visible to the public but has a significant impact on processes, systems, and outcomes (Djellal and Gallouj, 2010; Hastings and Finch, 2007). Tencent has embedded powerful technological innovations in its products and services, often in ways that are invisible to its users. It can be difficult for users to appreciate the technical challenges associated with a single button, a page refresh, or a function during their daily use, but each of these modifications significantly enhances their experience. For example, the stability and security of WeChat and its ability to protect user privacy rely on significant technological capabilities and innovation. As a digital product with over 1.3 billion MAUs and comprising a variety of functions and interfaces, users perceive WeChat to be a simple, intuitive messaging app. However, the platform relies on a robust backend infrastructure capable of managing billions of messages daily. At peak usage, such as during the Chinese New Year holiday, billions of red packets are sent within a few seconds, creating surges in message volumes and data traffic. However, WeChat can maintain stability and fluency owing to its invisible technological capabilities. During the 2023 Chinese New Year, WeChat processed over ten billion red packet interactions within twenty-four hours without a noticeable delay. Users also experience uninterrupted chats and video calls during these high-demand periods. The seamless integration of different functions and services with excellent user experience is supported by advanced distribution systems and optimisation techniques that Tencent has developed over many years to ensure low latency, high reliability, and seamless scalability without users becoming aware (see Chapter 6).

In addition, the WeChat ecosystem includes millions of mini-programs that provide app-like experiences. Tencent's innovations in lightweight application architecture enable these programmes to run efficiently without downloads, providing users with seamless functionality. In the case of QQ's rejuvenation, while users experienced smoother performance and enhanced security, they remained unaware of the immense work taking place to maintain the app. The product team meticulously rewrote the code for tens of thousands of feature points, overcoming significant technical challenges to maintain both data integrity and user trust and to ensure that QQ's daily operations were uninterrupted. The result of these extensive endeavours appeared effortless to users (see Chapter 7).

These examples highlight how Tencent prioritises user experience by embedding cutting-edge technology in ways that are invisible to the end-user. Similarly, Tencent Docs has hosted a significant volume of users without crashing and has enabled a rapid response to emergencies, as was evident during the COVID-19 pandemic and the Henan floods in 2021. Tencent Docs claims the largest user capacity of all online collaborative document tools, supporting over one million users to open and work on a single document simultaneously. In addition to its stability and extensive use, Tencent Docs also operates efficiently, with the speed of online document opening and editing almost as fast as that of an offline document. All of these features rely on invisible innovation supported by robust technology and product capabilities.

9.1.4 Compound Innovation

Compound innovation concerns the integration of multiple innovations within a single platform, with each innovation not only introducing new products or services but also generating additional value through their interactions. These interconnected innovations work synergistically, enhancing and supporting each other and ultimately increasing the overall value of the product or company. We found that Tencent benefits from compound innovation through the integration of multiple innovations – for example, product innovation, process innovation, business model innovation, service innovation – owing to its platform ecosystem and powerful technologies. Rather than individual innovations existing independently, these various aspects interact to enhance the overall value of the product.

Given that Tencent's products experience significant volumes of users, their smooth operation is challenging. To provide reliable and stable products and services that meet user needs, Tencent promotes diversified innovation that integrates product innovation, process innovation, and business model innovation. WeChat represents a good example, not only offering multi-applicability across various scenarios and industries but also ensuring the safety and stability of large-scale use (see Chapter 6). WeChat's technological advances maintain the product's long-term stability, confidentiality, security, and reliability for its large user community under various conditions. WeChat has transcended previous conceptual boundaries, establishing a unique relationship dynamic distinct from other social media platforms. WeChat has also invested significant effort in refining its functionality and adapting it to real-world scenarios. In addition, by leveraging the integration of its functions, WeChat demonstrates productive business model innovation, including social e-commerce based on Official Accounts and Mini Program, social network finance using WeChat Red Packet, community group buying through Mini Program, and the online–offline integrated model using WeCom.

Moreover, Tencent's expansion of its business territory and the development of its ecosystem have been supported by combinations of different forms of innovation that are interrelated, interconnected, and interactive. This comprehensive approach has included both incremental and original innovations, and their interactions have produced incredible reactions while meeting the diverse needs of their users. All of these aspects are connected to the company's continuous learning from external sources, in-house R&D, self-innovation, and strategy of substantial investment in innovation.

In addition, the company's social innovation benefits from the interactions of its technological, product, and business developments (see Chapter 8). Technological innovation underpins its social innovation by enabling the company to generate original technological breakthroughs in response to specific user needs or societal issues, as well as apply existing technologies to new scenarios. Product innovation then provides the pathway for social innovation. Tencent leverages its capabilities to develop and deliver products that meet user needs and provide more efficient solutions. Business model innovation involves exploring novel business models that enable Tencent to create social value through its business operations. While business model innovation builds on technological and product innovations, Tencent's innovative business model has a focus on expanding and sustaining social value and can stimulate further advances in technology and product development. By integrating its technological, product, and business model innovations, the company amplifies its social value through its business operations in a sustainable and long-term manner.

9.2 Tencent Innovation Mechanisms: Market-Type Organisation and OCEAN Ecosystem

What comes to mind when you hear the word 'ocean'? A few images may appear, including its vastness, depth, mysteries, calmness, and diversity. An ocean can be calm one moment and stormy the next, highlighting its dynamic nature and resilience. An ocean's resources and raw power – such as its tides and currents – highlight its vital role in sustaining the planet's health and nurturing life. An ocean also functions as a self-contained and diverse ecosystem, characterised by a complex, balanced, and interconnected internal network, but it simultaneously interacts with external systems, contributing to the formation of a broader, integrated ecological framework.

Our findings reveal that Tencent is a market-type organisation with an OCEAN ecosystem, characterised by its core principles of openness, coopetition, empowerment, autonomy, and addressing the needs of its stakeholders (see Figure 9.2). Through its diverse range of technologies, products, and services, the company fosters an environment that nurtures a wide range of participants within its ecosystem. While Tencent emphasises openness and collaboration, it simultaneously possesses substantial energy and strategic capabilities to influence industries and navigate the complexities of a competitive global market. The robust ecosystem it has cultivated – both internally and in partnership with external entities – has made Tencent a key leader and influential force in the digital era.

9.2.1 Openness ('O')

Tencent has both an internal and an external open environment that enhances its capacity for innovation and value creation. We can draw this conclusion from the many examples described in this book.

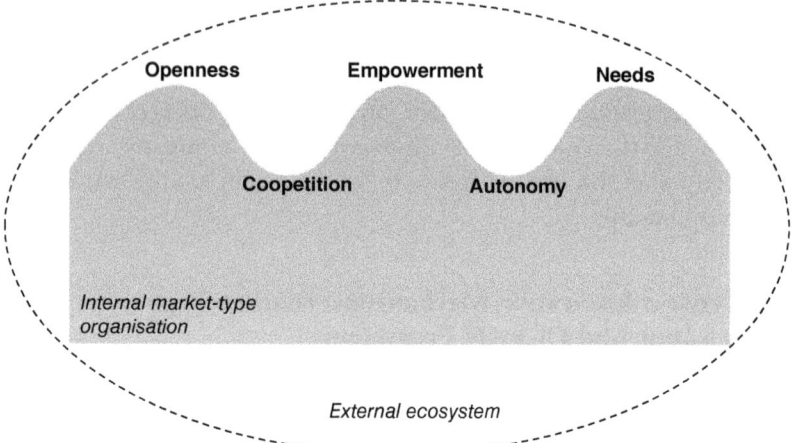

Figure 9.2 Elements of Tencent's OCEAN model of innovation.

Tencent operates an open internal market for most of its activities – including innovation – with business units bidding for resources from the company's principal executives. This open atmosphere provides its business units with significant autonomy, permitting them to operate semi-independently. In addition, Tencent's unique environment of coopetition fuels its dynamic innovation environment. Different business units compete to develop the best solutions or products in similar business fields, promoting a higher standard of excellence and enabling Tencent to find the product most suited to the market. Simultaneously, with this openness, employees can cross departmental borders and collaborate with anyone in the company, sharing resources, technologies, and insights to create the most competitive products for the market (see Chapter 3). The openness is also reflected in the company's tolerance of failure and active pursuit of new business directions, fostering a culture of entrepreneurship and empowering teams to make rapid decisions, experiment with new ideas, and respond quickly to market changes (see Chapter 7).

The Flowing Water programme described in Chapter 5 gives employees access to an open jobs market, enabling them to transfer to other teams and pursue individual career development. The whole company has built an open and distinctive culture and has demonstrated a supportive attitude towards this internal mobility policy.

Thus, resources are mobilised and used within a competitive and open environment that benefits Tencent by promoting dynamism, strengthening employee self-motivation, advancing organisational agility, and driving innovation across the company.

Chapter 6 provides a good example of how this open strategy benefits Tencent's long-term development and competitiveness. Through its open, decentralised, and inclusive ecosystem that provides an innovative and supportive environment for other businesses, WeChat attracts a wide range of partners seeking mutual growth. WeChat does not operate as a manager in the ecosystem; rather, its position is that of a powerful tool that provides a robust set of functions, services, and fundamental infrastructure for third-party service providers, offering ample space to innovate and grow. This open ecosystem not only enhances its internal product capabilities but also empowers parties in this ecosystem – including individual consumers and businesses – to create new services and value based on the principles of fairness and decentralisation. Tencent understands that opening itself to other parties can produce greater mutual benefits and foster win–win outcomes.

9.2.2 Coopetition ('C')

Within the free-market system built by Tencent, teams and units not only compete for resources and market space but also cooperate to achieve mutual success through coopetition. Within Tencent, teams and units are empowered to both independently seek out partners and compete on the same track. Many of Tencent's leading products were developed through this mechanism – including WeChat, *Honor of Kings*, and its HunYuan Model.

Chapter 3 shows how Tencent combines collaboration and competition as a catalyst for innovation and agility. Coopetition has a central role in promoting innovation and fostering growth. This dynamic model, in which internal competition and cooperation coexist, creates a unique environment that can yield significant benefits. Coopetition encourages teams to constantly innovate to maintain their position. In addition to fierce external competition, this environment creates internal competition that pushes teams to develop better solutions, while an atmosphere of cooperation enables the sharing of knowledge and resources. This combination can produce ground-breaking innovations that may not have emerged in a purely competitive or cooperative setting.

During this process, executives invest resources in products with the most market potential. This capacity to establish and then dissolve partnerships as required enables teams to remain agile and responsive to market changes. This flexibility is crucial in the fast-paced technology industry and can provide a significant competitive advantage. While internal competition can waste resources, this redundancy is important in enabling technology companies to seize opportunities, create standout products, and gain competitive advantages in the rapidly changing marketplace. Coopetition also fosters a culture of continual learning and improvement. Employees are motivated to develop new skills and knowledge to remain competitive, while collaboration provides opportunities for mentorship and knowledge exchange. This environment can produce a more skilled and versatile workforce, giving Tencent a competitive advantage regarding talent in the digital era.

9.2.3 Empowerment ('E')

Tencent never seeks to place restrictions on the potential of its employees or control its partners or wider ecosystem parties because it understands that empowering others can benefit the company in many ways. Empowerment within a supportive environment can encourage the self-motivation of employees and the willingness of partners to co-create, enhancing individual and collective growth.

Tencent typically supports and serves its employees, as well as encourages employees to participate in company management. As noted in Chapter 4, the digital HR products produced by Tencent are not managerial control tools; rather, they provide mechanisms that support employees to become more involved in daily operations as a means of self-management. Thus, the digital HRM system provides self-service and self-management channels for Tencent employees, stimulating self-motivation and empowering creativity.

Tencent officially implemented its open strategy in 2011, building an open platform to attract developers, enterprises, and social organisations and creating an enormous ecosystem. Specifically, by developing WeChat, its 'all-in-one' super app, Tencent established an open and inclusive ecosystem that connects people, services, and goods, through which the company collaborates with a wide range of partners – even competitors – to advance its strategic interests (see Chapter 5). This platform empowers its partners to develop new services and create value for its partners based on the principles of fairness and decentralisation. The ecosystem design of the WeChat platform not only promotes the development of WeChat itself but also fosters the growth and prosperity of the wider ecosystem.

Through significant investments and mergers and acquisitions in several areas – including gaming, e-commerce, finance, and entertainment, Tencent has expanded its business scope and market share. For example, the company has invested in numerous start-ups and tech companies worldwide, which reflects its strategy of fostering growth through cooperative ventures – even with potential market rivals. Through active cooperation with partners across various industries to jointly develop new products and services, this collaborative ecosystem supports mutual growth rather than focusing on seizing each other's market share. The continual development and improvement of this ecosystem provide a solid foundation for Tencent's long-term development.

Tencent has also built a specific unit to create social value (see Chapter 8). This team focuses on implementing the company's products and technologies to develop novel solutions to societal problems. By responding to opportunities quickly, the company collaborates with external parties to create value for itself and society. Tencent's digital capabilities (including advanced technologies and innovative products) are an important enabler of social innovation, and the company provides bespoke services and solutions for specific industries (including healthcare, education, and carbon neutrality). For instance, Tencent represents a reliable source of authoritative medical information and provides tools to enable the digitalisation of medical institutions and associations, empowering users with essential healthcare knowledge and enhancing public health management. Tencent encourages external parties to become involved in social value creation and has established principles for stakeholder access and involvement in co-creation. This approach emphasises openness, fairness, and decentralisation, promoting legitimacy and credibility within co-creation. The company also supports stakeholders of all sizes and from all sectors to engage in co-creating sustainable social value.

9.2.4 Autonomy ('A')

Individual employees and teams at Tencent are granted considerable autonomy. With this freedom, employees are highly motivated to take the initiative and pursue their ideas. Tencent's management believes that self-motivation is the best path for the company's development. Once employees are self-motivated, they can exhibit their skills and talents and fulfil their career ambitions while contributing to the company. Therefore, Tencent strives to provide freedom and autonomy to its employees and empower team independence, fostering an atmosphere of accountability and creativity. This has made Tencent a market-type company comprised of many highly autonomous small groups. This freedom has enabled the company to diversify its products and services and innovate across various sectors, including social media, gaming, fintech, and cloud computing.

Chapter 3 describes how Tencent promotes innovation through coopetition. This form of company resilience is not designed and enforced by executives through a top-down approach. Rather, it has developed organically as a result of the high levels of autonomy and tolerance within the company. Employees also thrive in its environment, which values collaboration and sharing. Employees are more willing to contribute their insights and support colleagues, fostering a culture of mutual assistance and collective problem-solving. During critical projects, this spirit of cooperation is even more evident (see Chapter 3). Employees voluntarily offer their expertise and work together to overcome challenges. By investing in employee development and a collaborative environment, Tencent ensures that its talent remains engaged and self-motivated.

In addition, the company provides numerous opportunities for personal and professional development. Its Flowing Water programme (see Chapter 5) gives employees autonomy and creates a supportive and flexible environment, with employees able to take an active role in shaping their professional journey, even amid organisational changes. Other opportunities include training programmes, mentorship, and open pathways for career advancement. This management approach facilitates the efficient development and allocation of company resources, including human talent. This culture of internal mobility has had a positive effect on innovation and creativity. By encouraging its employees to move between roles, projects, and teams, Tencent promotes the sharing of ideas, skills, and experiences, which is crucial for fostering innovation (see Chapter 5). In return, employees gain a broader understanding of the company's diverse operations and bring fresh perspectives to their new roles. This mobility also supports personal and professional development, increasing employee satisfaction and retention in a competitive job market.

The examples of QQ and Tencent Docs provided in Chapter 6 show how Tencent grants significant autonomy to its BUs, enabling them to operate semi-independently, explore technological innovations, tackle challenges, and ultimately develop valued products. Self-starters are encouraged to design and implement innovative solutions, knowing that they have the freedom and support to explore new opportunities. Employees are given autonomy to work on projects that align with their interests and expertise, fostering a sense of ownership and self-motivation, and in return, employees are more likely to meet the needs of users.

9.2.5 Needs ('N')

Tencent strives to meet the needs of its users, employees, and wider society. By focusing on 'user value' as a guiding principle, Tencent aims to incorporate social responsibility into its products and services and support societal development.

Many organisations understand the importance of meeting the needs of their users. However, Tencent is acutely aware of the importance of talent to innovation and competitiveness in a highly dynamic marketplace and has always supported the needs of its talent. With a strong product focus from the outset, the company's HR department regards its employees as users and develops internal products based on employee needs. This user-oriented value forms part of Tencent's DNA and is not only rooted in its business operations but also affects its HRM system.

Chapter 4 describes how the company serves its talent through its HRM system. Viewing its employees as users, the HR department not only fulfils typical HR functions but also delivers HR services through its digital products, encouraging employee self-motivation and creativity. As such, Tencent uses the HRM system to effectively serve, support, and motivate its employees. While the digital tools used by other companies are largely targeted at management, Tencent's digital HR products focus on managerial procedures, organisational policies and strategies, and employee experiences, ensuring that their needs are considered alongside managerial and business needs.

Chapter 5 also describes how the company supports its employees to pursue their individual development through its internal mobility policy. This transfer process is being continuously optimised to enhance its efficiency, fairness, transparency, and ease after the company detected the presence of obstacles to internal mobility – such as obstructions put in place by an employee's existing supervisor. As such, employees sense the company's support and are more willing to engage with its mobility programme, increasing employee retention and enhancing the company's dynamism and creativity.

Chapters 6 and 7 show that meeting user needs is key to ensuring that products remain competitive. Updates and iterations of WeChat features are always based on changes in user needs across various settings. To avoid onerous complexity and redundancy, Tencent's R&D teams follow the first principles approach to product design and examine the intrinsic characteristics of user feedback. Thus, the company strives to make products that are simple yet meet user needs. For example, both QQ and Tencent Docs seek to create user-oriented product value, with user needs captured at various developmental stages. Tencent has consistently emphasised the importance of capturing user needs, viewing this as a cornerstone of product development and iteration. The ongoing vitality of QQ is related to its iterative innovation; this is primarily based on user feedback, which helps to ensure that the end product continues to meet the tastes and needs of younger generations. Tencent Docs was able to grasp new opportunities in the individual consumer market by responding to user needs during social events and a range of other scenarios, including memory recording of high school graduates and sales information updates of e-commerce companies. However, regardless of whether a product is old or new, this approach remains the best way to ensure that it continues to meet user needs and maintain its position in the market.

Chapter 8 describes how Tencent focuses on social needs to create social value and social innovation. Tencent is founded on a mission-driven approach, creating value beyond profit to include societal impact. Tencent balances this focus on social value and economic value creation. Tencent develops solutions to address social issues experienced by different user groups, particularly disadvantaged, socially excluded, or marginalised groups, such as elderly people and people with disabilities. Tencent has invested in digital technologies and tools, tailoring services and solutions to the needs of particular industries to help improve small business efficiency. It also leverages its digital capabilities to support rural revitalisation, disaster and emergency response, digital philanthropy, and carbon neutrality. With social innovation as a pillar of Tencent's overarching strategy, the company actively creates sustainable social value through its operations.

Overall, Tencent's approach of combining the market-type organisation and the OCEAN ecosystem is pivotal to its capacity for innovation and maintaining a competitive edge, ensuring agility when navigating the fast-paced and dynamic global technology landscape.

9.3 Open Corporate Innovation System

Previous literature has proposed the national innovation system (NIS) framework for analysing the innovation performance of a country (Freeman, 1987; Lundvall, 2007; Nelson, 1993). The NIS framework argues that the NIS is the source of national competitiveness and is the result of the collective effect of institutions, organisations, and technological innovations. The framework emphasises the interactive process needed to produce innovation and that this mainly works at the macro level. More recently, scholars have sought to focus this framework at the corporate level and have introduced the concept of the corporate innovation system (CIS) (Lundvall and Rikap, 2022; Rikap, 2024), which is defined as 'global systems in which the overall R&D orientation is set by a leading company that disproportionately captures the bulk of associated profits – intellectual rents – even if innovation is co-produced with many others, such as universities, public (research) organisations and start-ups' (Rikap, 2024). This framework is useful when considering the coevolution of large companies and the NIS; however, within a company, the intrinsic factors and how they interact and work to promote a company's innovation performance need to be analysed further.

We proposed an open CIS based on the case of Tencent (see Figure 9.3). Previous research has suggested that a company's corporate innovation performance (CIP) is determined by its capabilities, the incentives it provides, and the organisations and institutions within the company (Fu, 2015). These three elements are interactive and are correlated with each other; for example, incentives transfer investment into capabilities. Tencent's innovation history reflects an open innovation framework in which the CIS interacts with external parties within the ecosystem it has built using its digital platforms to realise its DDIC innovations. Different aspects of the OCEAN ecosystem have contributed to this system in many ways.

Regarding capabilities, Tencent has made significant and continuous R&D investments, investing in human capital (particularly in R&D) and robust digital infrastructure within emerging technologies (see Chapter 2). In terms of incentives, in addition to the fierce external market competition that pushes employees to evolve, Tencent has used both financial and non-financial incentives to promote innovation and creativity. It is worth noting that non-financial incentives account for a large part of this investment, including providing freedom and autonomy, flexible and open resource allocation through coopetition, internal mobility (see Chapters 3 and 5), and valuing and serving employee needs (see Chapters 4 and 5). Regarding institutions, these consist of at least three parts: namely, building a corporate culture based on inclusiveness, which encourages intrapreneurship and tolerates failure (see Chapter 7); establishing the corporate vision of 'Value for Users, Tech for Good' that not only focuses on employee needs but also aims to meet user and social needs (see Chapters 6 and 8); and external government policies, which are a significant factor influencing the company strategy and future direction, and aim to meet societal needs and pursue sustainable development. The whole innovation process is driven by user needs and its operational value. However, it is not a closed system. Rather, it is an open and collaborative system that enables the co-growth of both Tencent and its partners across different sectors, regions, and even countries; it is an ecosystem that empowers its participants and realises the full potential of its partners (see Chapter 6). Equipped with these aspects, Tencent undertakes successful DDIC innovations.

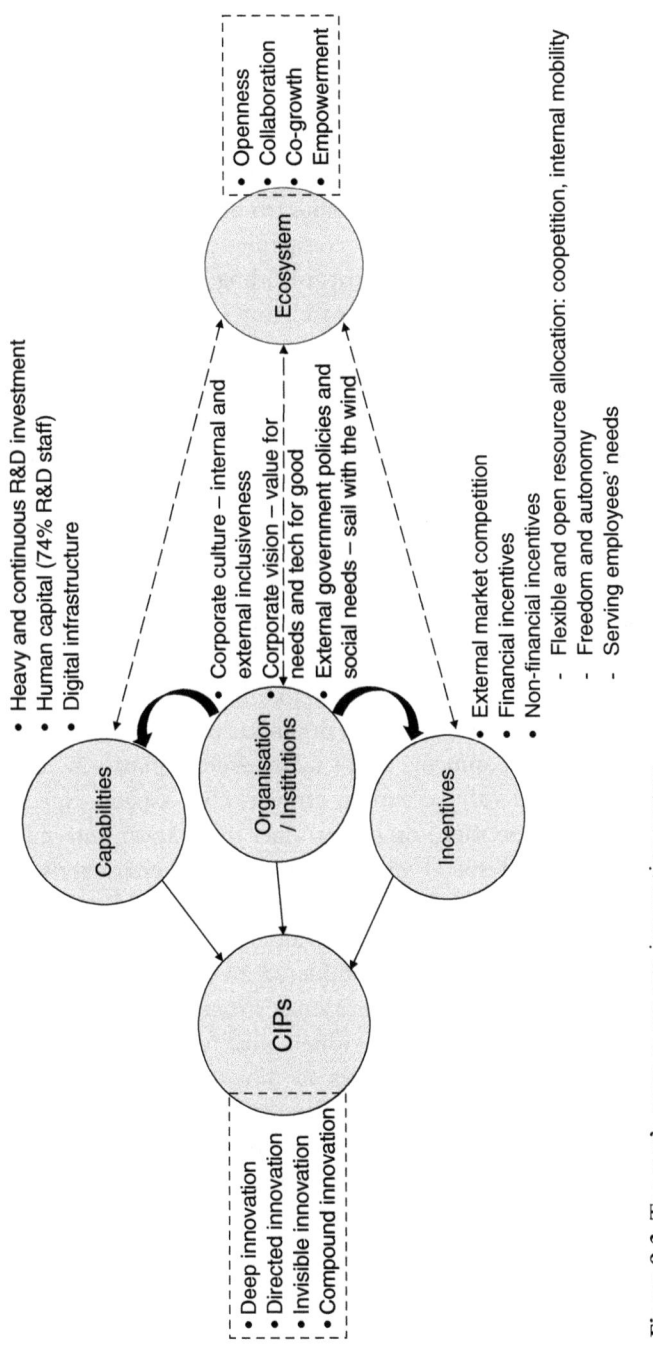

Figure 9.3 Tencent's open corporate innovation system.

9.4 Contribution of This Book

This book contributes to academic literature and business management in several ways. Regarding our case selection, it appears that systematic research into innovation in China's leading internet companies is limited. While there are many books and edited volumes on innovations in Western technology companies, to the best of our knowledge, there are very few on technology companies in China. Several books have introduced emerging and world-leading companies from China to Western readers; however, research on Tencent remains limited. These books mainly cover the leadership or corporate development of these companies without focusing on their innovation management practices. This book provides a systematic analysis of how and why Tencent, a world-leading internet-based platform company from China, has emerged at the global technology frontier through innovation. Tencent's innovation is multi-dimensional and includes technology, product, management, and social innovations. Thus, this analysis enriches our understanding of the mechanisms for innovation in the digital era. Our findings provide valuable insights for both companies and governments in developing and developed countries.

Regarding the research content of this book, it provides valuable insights into the company's culture, organisational structure, incentives policy, product development, talent management, platform ecosystem building, and social value creation, among other aspects. Specifically, we focused on coopetition, digital product innovation, internal talent mobility policy, and social value creation – key characteristics that have been previously overlooked by scholars and underestimated by leaders in other companies – to provide a more complete picture of Tencent's innovation. We also conducted an in-depth analysis of the impact of the company's organisational structure and the incentives supporting the creativity of individuals and found that Tencent has focused on non-financial incentives to motivate employees. In addition, we examined the impact of the digitalisation of management on the innovation performance of the company's employees, complementing the existing literature on how digital HRM systems energise employees in their workplaces. These findings provide further insights into Tencent's innovation mechanisms, breaking existing stereotypes regarding Chinese technology companies.

In terms of research methods and data, existing research on Tencent is largely based on analyses of secondary data from newspapers and other media (Casanova et al., 2018; Chen, 2022; Tang, 2019) or limited first-hand data, constraining the breadth and credibility of the research conclusions. This book is the first academic study to examine Tencent's management of innovation based on a detailed four-year mixed-methods (a combination of qualitative and quantitative methods) case study, using abundant first-hand fieldwork and survey data and contributing to the broader field through the use of micro-level (individual-level) data.

Finally, this book contributes to the concept of the CIS (Granstrand, 2000; Lundvall and Rikap, 2022) through a theoretical and empirical analysis of the development of innovation systems and the linkages between them. Using Tencent as a case study, we propose an open CIS, extending the existing argument that a company's CIP is determined by its capabilities, the incentives it provides, and the organisational policies within the company and its institutions (Fu, 2015). The three factors are interactive and are correlated with one another. Proposing an original and novel OCEAN ecosystem built by a market-type organisation, we argue that the company's openness, coopetition, empowerment, autonomy, and focus on needs support the operations of the CIS. This open ecosystem enables the co-growth of both Tencent and its ecosystem parties across different sectors, regions, and countries and has encouraged the company to undertake a sequoia-like innovation (DDIC) over the past twenty years. In particular, we conclude that Tencent is not merely imitating other organisations but has produced many original innovations. It applies deep innovation that does not blindly follow user needs but rather has a long-term perspective. This includes invisible innovation, which is not obvious to the user or the wider public but has a significant impact on outcomes. Tencent employs directed innovation with a clear vision and strategy rather than innovation conducted in a diffused or disordered way. It also uses compound innovation, which extends beyond business model innovation and involves multiple innovations that work synergistically, enhancing and supporting each other and ultimately enhancing the overall value of both the products and the company.

9.5 Lessons from Tencent

In this section, we extract key lessons from Tencent's innovation practices, examining them through the lenses of organisational strategy, product and technical development, resource allocation, ecosystem building, and organisational culture. We also assess the applicability of these insights to other companies and contexts.

9.5.1 Strategic Patience and 'Longtermism'

One of the most defining – and often underappreciated – factors behind Tencent's enduring success is its deep-rooted commitment to *strategic patience* and *long-term value creation*. In an era where much of the tech industry is driven by short-term metrics, rapid iteration, and pressure to deliver quarterly results, Tencent takes a markedly different path. It is guided by what founder Pony Ma describes as **'patient capital'** – a philosophy that prioritises *sustainable growth* over immediate returns and is willing to wait years, even decades, for investments to bear fruit.

This long-term mindset is not confined to rhetoric; it is embedded across the company's strategic and operational fabric. Whether in its development of traditional products or in newer ventures such as cloud services and social innovation, Tencent consistently demonstrates a willingness to resist short-term gratification in favour of enduring impact. A striking example is WeChat, which was deliberately not designed as a profit engine in its early years. Instead, Tencent focused on perfecting the user experience, building network effects, and earning user trust – eventually resulting in one of the most dominant and irreplaceable social platforms in the digital economy. Similarly, Tencent Cloud endured sustained financial losses for over a decade. While other companies might have pivoted or pulled back under shareholder pressure, Tencent remained steadfast, investing in talent, infrastructure, and product capabilities. Today, that patience has paid off: Tencent Cloud has emerged as China's second-largest cloud services provider, playing a central role in the country's digital transformation. This philosophy also extends to Tencent's approach to social value creation. Unlike short-lived CSR campaigns aimed at brand visibility, Tencent invests in long-horizon initiatives that are aligned with systemic change – whether in education, public health, or environmental sustainability. The company understands that meaningful social value takes time to unfold and often does not conform to the timelines of traditional ROI frameworks.

Central to this approach is Tencent's role as **'gardeners, not hunters'** – a metaphor that encapsulates its long-term view of ecosystem building. Rather than aggressively extracting value or seeking immediate wins, Tencent focuses on cultivating an environment where value can grow organically over time. This involves investing in foundational infrastructure, empowering partners, supporting entrepreneurship, and nurturing emerging industries. In doing so, Tencent fosters a resilient, interdependent ecosystem in which success is distributed and sustainable.

For modern companies, Tencent's example underscores a vital strategic lesson: the importance of **strategic patience.** In a world driven by speed and short-term performance, the ability to remain committed to a long-term vision – while still delivering incremental value along the way – can be a profound source of competitive advantage. Tencent proves that innovation, trust, and influence often require time to mature, and that companies willing to wait and cultivate these assets deliberately are the ones best positioned to shape the future.

9.5.2 Staying Close to Customers/Users but Retaining Independent Thinking

Tencent exemplifies a disciplined yet user-centric approach to product development, striking a careful balance between being deeply attuned to user needs and maintaining independent strategic thinking. At the core of this philosophy is Tencent's internal practice known as the '10/100/1,000 Rule'. This structured framework mandates that product managers engage directly with users for ten hours per month in online communities and forums, dedicate 100 hours per year to analysing user behavioural data, and conduct 1,000 user interviews annually. This immersive, data-informed process ensures that Tencent's product teams remain closely aligned with evolving user behaviours, pain points, and expectations.

However, Tencent does not equate user proximity with uncritical responsiveness. While the company values user feedback, it is intentionally cautious about overreacting to every suggestion or complaint. A critical aspect of this methodology is Tencent's conscious effort to avoid over-indexing on the preferences of any single user group. By preventing any one segment from disproportionately influencing product strategy, Tencent protects the overall integrity and scalability of its offerings. This prevents a common pitfall in user-centric design: building for the vocal minority while neglecting the silent majority.

Rather than treating feedback as a set of directives, Tencent follows the first principles, which helps to identify the basic or core nature of a product or function. This approach ensures that product development remains vision-driven rather than reaction-driven, enabling product teams to pursue long-term innovation without being derailed by short-term demands. Tencent places strong emphasis on mastering the core logic and purpose of each product. Rather than merely reacting to articulated needs, the company seeks to identify latent user desires – those users may not yet be able to express – by understanding the underlying behaviours and aspirations revealed through data and observation. This deep, conceptual grasp allows product teams to innovate with intent, delivering features that anticipate and exceed user expectations, rather than simply following them. In essence, Tencent's product culture demonstrates how proximity to users, when paired with rigorous independent thinking and strategic clarity, can lead to meaningful, deep and forward-looking innovation. It is a model that balances responsiveness with originality and insight with discipline – resulting in products that are both loved by users and strategically sound.

9.5.3 Harmonising Technological Capabilities with Real-world Application Scenarios

A defining feature of Tencent's innovation strategy is its ability to harmonise cutting-edge technological capabilities with practical, real-world application scenarios. Unlike many tech companies that pursue innovation as an end in itself, Tencent adopts a problem-first approach: innovation begins not in the lab, but in the lived experiences of users. The company is acutely aware that technology without relevance risks becoming a 'solution in search of a problem' – an all-too-common trap in the digital age.

Tencent ensures its foundational R&D efforts are tightly aligned with actual market needs, business priorities, and social contexts. This discipline enables the company to convert technological potential into real-world value-delivering products that are not only technically sound but also contextually resonant and widely adopted. The outcome is a powerful blend of technological depth and pragmatic execution, which helps Tencent avoid the profit challenges of pure tech companies, while also transcending the incrementalism that plagues many traditional internet companies.

A striking example of this philosophy is the creation of WeChat Red Packets. Inspired by a longstanding cultural tradition of gifting money during traditional Chinese holidays, Tencent seamlessly integrated this practice into the digital payment ecosystem. By embedding a familiar ritual into the WeChat platform, the company not only enhanced user engagement but also catalysed mass adoption of mobile payments in China. This innovation did not rely on cutting-edge financial technology – it succeeded because it fit seamlessly into users' daily lives, combining cultural relevance, intuitive design, and technical reliability. In this way, Tencent demonstrated that contextual innovation – where the right technology is applied at the right moment in the right setting – often has a more transformative impact than abstract technological breakthroughs.

9.5.4 Art of Leveraging Resources

Another valuable lesson from Tencent lies in its sophisticated approach to resource utilisation – an approach that encompasses not only the efficient deployment of internal resources but also the strategic leveraging of external ones. Internally, Tencent adopts a flexible and pragmatic stance toward resource allocation, deliberately allowing a certain degree of redundancy in order to stimulate innovation. One striking example of this is internal horse racing, the practice of encouraging multiple teams to independently develop and test similar product ideas. While this may appear inefficient on the surface, it fosters a competitive spirit, accelerates iteration, and increases the likelihood of breakthrough innovations and grasping the business opportunities in complex and rapidly moving world by exploring different approaches in parallel.

At the same time, Tencent is equally adept at promoting cross-team collaboration when circumstances demand a more integrated approach. For projects that require diverse expertise or significant investment, Tencent encourages cooperative efforts and resource pooling across departments. This ability to alternate between competition and collaboration within the organisation requires a high level of managerial sophistication. Leaders must carefully assess the nature of each product, project, and team dynamic to determine the most effective mode of engagement – balancing autonomy with alignment, and competition with coordination.

In addition to managing material and technical resources, Tencent demonstrates exceptional capability in human resource mobilisation. Through initiatives such as the Flowing Water program, the company ensures the fluid movement of talent across business units based on shifting strategic priorities and individual strengths. This system provides the agility to redeploy human capital where it is most needed, especially during times of organisational transformation, when venturing into new markets, or during social emergency. Not only does this improve operational responsiveness, but it also enhances employee engagement by offering greater career mobility, skill development, and opportunities to contribute meaningfully to new initiatives.

Externally, Tencent's philosophy diverges from traditional models of resource control. Rather than hoarding resources for competitive advantage, Tencent actively shares its platforms, technologies, and user traffic with partners in its broader ecosystem. This collaborative stance supports the growth of smaller companies and developers, which in turn reinforces the vitality and resilience of the ecosystem as a whole. A prime example is the development of the open WeChat ecosystem – a deliberate strategic move born from the recognition that Tencent alone could not meet the diverse needs of users and developers. By opening up APIs, providing toolkits, and allowing third-party integration, Tencent transformed WeChat into a thriving platform that empowers countless businesses and content creators. This approach to external resource sharing not only broadens Tencent's influence but also aligns long-term interests among ecosystem participants, ensuring mutual benefit and sustainable innovation. Rather than pursuing short-term control or dominance, Tencent cultivates interdependence and trust – a hallmark of strategic ecosystem thinking.

In summary, Tencent's nuanced resource strategies – whether through competitive redundancy, collaborative efficiency, dynamic talent deployment, or open ecosystem building – demonstrate a high level of managerial insight. These practices illustrate that effective resource utilisation is not simply about efficiency or control, but about creating the conditions for innovation, adaptability, and long-term value creation both inside and beyond the organisation.

9.5.5 Promoting Co-growth instead of Controlling the Ecosystem

One of the most important lessons from Tencent's success lies in its ecosystem philosophy – a strategic mindset centred on enabling co-growth rather than enforcing control. Unlike traditional business models that prioritise dominance, ownership, or vertical integration, Tencent empowers a wide network of external stakeholders to grow in tandem with itself. This philosophy reflects a deep understanding of the dynamics of the digital economy, where value creation increasingly depends on interconnectivity, openness, and mutual empowerment.

Rather than building a closed, self-contained system designed to extract maximum value or maintain rigid control, Tencent positions itself as an enabler, orchestrator, and connector. It provides the foundational infrastructure – including technical platforms, traffic flow, development tools, and financial investment – while granting startups, developers, content creators, and even potential competitors the freedom to innovate independently within the broader ecosystem. In brief, Tencent sets the stage, but allows others to perform.

A clear example of this philosophy in action is the WeChat ecosystem. Tencent does not attempt to monopolise all services within WeChat, nor does it build every app or solution internally. Instead, it opens the platform to third-party developers and entrepreneurs through mini-programs, APIs, and monetisation tools. This approach enables a wide range of businesses – from e-commerce to education to public services – to operate within WeChat's infrastructure while maintaining their own autonomy. Tencent benefits from the increased user engagement and ecosystem vitality, while partners are able to scale their businesses more effectively than if they had to build from scratch.

Tencent offers the tools, resources, and access needed to succeed, but it does not impose excessive constraints or attempt to capture all the value. It creates the conditions for innovation rather than trying to dictate its direction. This, in turn, fosters a long-term partnership. Ecosystem participants are more deeply engaged because they are not mere users or vendors – they are co-creators and co-beneficiaries of shared success. It transforms the relationship between platform and partner into a 'win–win' dynamic, replacing the zero-sum logic of control with a logic of mutual empowerment. Therefore, in a digital economy driven by networks and platforms, sustainable success often comes not from controlling others, but from helping them succeed. The scale, diversity, and resilience which co-growth creates are rarely achieved with centralised control.

9.5.6 Building Inclusive and Intrapreneurial Organisational Culture

Tencent's inclusive and intrapreneurial culture has been a foundational pillar of its innovation-driven success. This culture cultivates an environment where employees at all levels are encouraged to take initiative, contribute ideas, and assume ownership of their work, regardless of their rank or role within the organisational hierarchy. By embedding a sense of autonomy, responsibility, and entrepreneurial spirit into its corporate DNA, Tencent empowers its teams not only to improve existing products but also to transform and rejuvenate them in ways that keep pace with – or even anticipate – market shifts and user needs.

Crucially, this culture fosters a mindset of exploration and calculated risk-taking. Employees are given space to experiment, and encouraged to venture beyond their comfort zones, embracing unfamiliar challenges and emerging technologies, even if it might lead to failure. The organisation actively supports such intrapreneurial endeavours, creating mechanisms that allow teams to experiment with new ideas, iterate quickly, and learn from failure without fear of punitive consequences. In addition, by valuing diverse perspectives – across roles, disciplines, and backgrounds – Tencent fosters a more inclusive environment where creative solutions emerge from different viewpoints. This blend of freedom and support enables Tencent to continually generate breakthrough innovations. It fuels the creation of innovative products, services, and business models, while simultaneously sustaining a dynamic, engaging work environment that attracts and retains top talent.

In addition, we explore how lessons from Tencent's practices can be applied in other companies or contexts. Table 9.1 outlines the key elements or dependencies, along with practical notes, to illustrate when and how these insights might be effectively implemented elsewhere.

Tencent's practice of 'strategic patience and long-termism' rests on leadership's commitment to a future-oriented outlook. Rated as

Table 9.1 *Lessons from Tencent*

Tencent Practices	Degree of applicability	Key Dependencies/elements	Practical notes
Strategic patience and 'longtermism'	★★★★	Long-term perspectives in leadership	Allocate a portion of R&D budget to long-term, high-risk bets while maintaining core revenue streams.
Staying close to customers/ users but keeping independent thinking	★★★★★	User-centric culture, Clear awareness of products and market	Innovate for users without being captive to them
Harmonising technological capabilities with real-world application scenarios	★★★	Built on technology, applied through scenarios	For companies in emerging economies, they could prioritise solving real user needs with existing technologies rather than chasing disruptive innovation for its own sake
Promoting co-growth instead of controlling in ecosystem	★★★ (Platform businesses)	Shared value orientation, open platform architecture, long-term relationship building	While short-term profitability may be challenging for platform enterprises, with empowerment and co-growth, the long-term benefits are sustainable. However, maintaining and governing the ecosystem remains difficult, particularly in a volatile, uncertain environment.
Art of leveraging resources	★★★★★	Strategic flexibility in resource allocation, adaptive governance	Companies with abundant resources allow for 'controlled redundancy' to spark innovation. However, for companies with limited resources, it is key to allocate resources for key projects. Think ecosystem-wide, not just company-wide. Companies should consider how the resource decisions affect employees, partners, suppliers, and even competitors.
Building inclusive and intrapreneurial organisational culture	★★★★	Empowerment at all levels, tolerance for failure, cultural norms of trust and openness	Focus less on controlling output, more on creating environments where ideas can emerge and grow. Recognise and reward initiative – not just results. Make it safe to propose, fail, and try again.

Notes: Five stars indicate the highest applicability, followed by a decreasing order accordingly
Source: Authors' elaboration

highly applicable (five stars), this principle is illustrated in its advice to split R&D budgets: allocating some funds to high-risk, break-through projects while maintaining stability through core revenue streams. This approach enables companies to pursue future-shaping initiatives without jeopardising immediate financial health, striking a balance between present success and long-term innovation.

The principle of 'staying close to customers while maintaining independent thinking' thrives on a user-centric culture and sharp product-market awareness. Also highly applicable (five stars), it encourages companies to innovate for users without being con-strained by them. Organisations should deeply understand user needs but use that insight as a guide rather than a limit, ensuring solutions both resonate with customers and push the boundaries of innovation.

'Harmonising technological capabilities with real-world application scenarios' emphasises technology built for practical use. With strong applicability (four stars), this practice suggests – especially for emerg-ing economies – focusing on solving concrete user problems with existing technologies rather than pursuing disruptive innovation for its own sake. The goal is to ensure that technical potential translates into real-world utility.

The principle of 'promoting co-growth instead of control in eco-systems' is tailored for platform businesses. Based on shared value, open architecture, and relationship-building, it is moderately appli-cable (two stars). While this approach may reduce short-term profit-ability, the long-term payoff lies in sustainable ecosystem co-growth. Still, governance in volatile markets is challenging, requiring a shift from control to collaborative nurturing.

'The art of leveraging resources' – driven by flexible allocation and adaptive governance – is another highly applicable practice (five stars). Larger companies can adopt 'controlled redundancy' to stimulate innovation, while smaller ones must concentrate resources more nar-rowly. Importantly, resource decisions should consider the broader ecosystem – including partners, suppliers, and even competitors – fostering a collaborative, system-wide strategy.

Finally, 'building an inclusive and intrapreneurial organisational culture' is enabled by empowerment, tolerance for failure, and trust-based norms. Highly applicable (five stars), this principle empha-sises creating an environment where ideas flow freely, and employees are encouraged to act as intrapreneurs. Companies should reward initiative as much as outcomes, making it safe to experiment, fail, and try again – ultimately fuelling internal innovation and resilience.

As this book neared completion, Tencent released its second-quarter results for 2025, marking another milestone in its innovation journey. The company reported revenues of RMB 184.5 billion (approximately USD 25.7 billion), up 15 per cent year-on-year, with gross profit reaching RMB 105 billion (Roach, 2025). Growth was fuelled by strong gaming performance – driven by new titles such as *Delta Force* alongside evergreen hits like *Honor of Kings* and *Valorant* – as well as AI-powered advances in advertising and enterprise services. Advertising revenue rose 20 per cent, while capital expenditures surged 119 per cent as Tencent accelerated investment in AI across its businesses. Tencent Music also continued to expand, with robust growth in subscriptions, live concerts, and the fan economy, pointing to stronger-than-expected full-year performance.

Looking forward, Tencent is doubling down on AI and cloud as strategic priorities. It is embedding its HunYuan foundation models into Weixin and its AI-native assistant, Yuanbao, while also expanding its cloud presence internationally – targeting Europe's competitive market against global hyperscalers such as Amazon, Microsoft, and Google. Yet this push unfolds amid an unprecedented wave of disruption, as AI companies worldwide race to release breakthrough products at astonishing speed. What lies ahead remains uncertain. One thing, however, is clear: Tencent's ability to cultivate a culture of openness, coopetition, empowerment, autonomy, and deep user insight offers valuable lessons for organisations navigating the digital age. As platform companies evolve into societal infrastructures, the challenge is no longer merely how to innovate, but how to do so wisely, inclusively, and sustainably. In that sense, Tencent's story is still being written – one that may yet inspire the next great wave of global innovation.

References

Abrami, R. M., Kirby, W. C., and McFarlan, F. W. (2014). 'Why China Can't Innovate', *Harvard Business Review, Harvard Business School Publishing*, 92(3), pp. 107–111.

Agrawal, A., Cockburn, I., and McHale, J. (2006). 'Gone but Not Forgotten: Knowledge Flows, Labor Mobility, and Enduring Social Relationships', *Journal of Economic Geography*, 6(5), pp. 571–591.

Agarwal, R., Echambadi, R., Franco, A. M., and Sarkar, M. B. (2004). 'Knowledge Transfer through Inheritance: Spin-Out Generation, Development, and Survival', *Academy of Management Journal*, 47(4), pp. 501–522.

Anning-Dorson, T. (2018). 'Innovation and Competitive Advantage Creation', *International Marketing Review*, 35(4), pp. 580–600.

Bai, G. and Liu, G. (2023). 'The WeChat Ecosystem: Unleashing the Potential of the Long Tail to Stay Innovative', *Harvard Business Review*. Available at: https://store.hbr.org/product/the-wechat-ecosystem-unleashing-the-potential-of-the-long-tail-to-stay-innovative/CB0275#:~:text=Product%20.

BCG Global (2021). 'Overcoming the Innovation Readiness Gap.' Available at: www.bcg.com/publications/2021/most-innovative-companies-overview.

Benson, A. and Rissing, B. A. (2020). 'Strength from Within: Internal Mobility and the Retention of High Performers', *Organization Science*, 31(6), pp. 1313–1620.

Birkinshaw, J., de Diego, E., and Ke, D. L.-H. (2019). *Innovation and Agility at Tencent's WeChat*. London: London Business School Case Collection, pp. 1–26.

Birkinshaw, J., Ke, D., and de Diego, E. (2019). 'The Kind of Creative Thinking that Fueled WeChat's Success', *Harvard Business Review*. Available at: https://hbr.org/2019/10/the-kind-of-creative-thinking-that-fueled-wechats-success.

Birkinshaw, J. and Lingblad, M. (2005). 'Intrafirm Competition and Charter Evolution in the Multibusiness Firm', *Organization Science*, 16, pp. 674–686.

Bleach, T. (2023). 'From Twitter to the "Everything App": Can X Transition into a Financial Super App?'. Available at: https://thefintechtimes.com/twitter-turns-x-financial-super-app/.

Bondarouk, T., Parry, E., and Furtmueller, E. (2017). 'Electronic HRM: Four Decades of Research on Adoption and Consequences', *International Journal of Human Resource Management*, 28(1), pp. 98–131.

Bonina, C., Koskinen, K., Eaton, B., Gawer, A. (2021). 'Digital Platforms for Development: Foundations and Research Agenda', *Information Systems Journal*, 31(6), pp. 869–902.

Bouncken, R. B. and Kraus, S. (2013). 'Innovation in Knowledge-Intensive Industries: The Double-Edged Sword of Coopetition', *Journal of Business Research*, 66, pp. 2060–2070.

Bowen, D. E. and Ostroff, C. (2004). 'Understanding HRM-firm Performance Linkages: The Role of the "Strength" of the HRM System', *Academy of Management Review*, 29(2), pp. 203–221.

Brandenburger, A. M. and Nalebuff, B. J. (1996). *Co-opetition*. New York: Bantam Doubleday Dell.

Caridà, A., Colurcio, M., and Melia, M. (2022). 'Digital Platform for Social Innovation: Insights from Volunteering', *Creativity and Innovation Management*, 31(4), pp. 755–771.

Casanova, L., Cornelius, P. K., and Dutta, S. (2018). 'Tencent: A Giant Asserting Dominance', in *Financing Entrepreneurship and Innovation in Emerging Markets*. Amsterdam: Elsevier, pp. 81–115. https://doi.org/10.1016/B978-0-12-804025-6.00004-6.

Chamakiotis, P., Petrakaki, D., and Panteli, N. (2021). 'Social Value Creation through Digital Activism in an Online Health Community', *Information Systems Journal*, 31(1), pp. 94–119.

Chen, L. Y. (2022). *Influence Empire: Inside the Story of Tencent and China's Tech Ambition: Shortlisted for the FT Business Book of 2022*. London: Hachette UK.

China Academy of Labour and Social Security (2022). 'Digital Ecosystem Employment and Entrepreneurship Report'. Available at: www.tisi.org/24430.

China Internet Network Information Center (CNNIC) (2022). 'The 49th Statistical Report on China's Internet Development'. Available at: www.cnnic.com.cn/index.htm.

Choudhury, P. (2020). 'Intra-Firm Geographic Mobility: Value Creation Mechanisms and Future Research Directions', in *Employee Inter- and Intra-Firm Mobility 41*. Advances in Strategic Management. Bingley, UK: Emerald, pp. 179–195.

Christensen, C. M. (1997). *The Innovator's Dilemma: When New Technologies Cause Great Firms to Fail*. Boston, MA: Harvard Business Review Press.

Cirillo, B., Brusoni, S., and Valentini, G. (2014). 'The Rejuvenation of Inventors through Corporate Spinouts', *Organization Science*, 25(6), pp. 1764–1784.

Clark, D. (2016). *Alibaba: The House that Jack Ma Built*. New York: HarperCollins.

CompaniesMarketCap (2024a). 'Market Capitalization of Tencent (TCEHY)'. Available at: https://companiesmarketcap.com/tencent/marketcap/.

CompaniesMarketCap (2024b). 'Largest Companies by Marketcap'. Available at: https://companiesmarketcap.com/.

Constantinides, P., Henfridsson, O., and Parker, G. G. (2018). 'Introduction-Platforms and Infrastructures in the Digital Age', *Information Systems Research*, 29(2), pp. 381–400.

Cooper, R. G. (2019). 'The Drivers of Success in New-Product Development', *Industrial Marketing Management*, 76, pp. 36–47.

Cowgill, B. and Koning, R. (2018). 'Matching Markets for Googlers'. Harvard Business School Case, pp. 718–487, March.

Damanpour, F., Walker, R. M., and Avellaneda, C. N. (2009). 'Combinative Effects of Innovation Types and Organizational Performance: A Longitudinal Study of Service Organizations', *Journal of Management Studies*, 46(4), pp. 650–675.

Djellal, F. and Gallouj, F. (2010). 'Invisible Innovation and Hidden Performance in Services: A Challenge for Public Policy', *Intereconomics*, 45(5), pp. 278–283.

Du, J. and Chen, Z. (2018). 'Applying Organizational Ambidexterity in Strategic Management under a "VUCA" Environment: Evidence from High Tech Companies in China', *International Journal of Innovation Studies*, 2, pp. 42–52.

Edwards, M. R., Zubielevitch, E., Okimoto, T., Parker, S., and Anseel, F. (2024). 'Managerial Control or Feedback Provision: How Perceptions of Algorithmic HR Systems Shape Employee Motivation, Behavior, and Well-being', *Human Resource Management*, pp. 1–20. https://doi.org/10.1002/hrm.22218.

Elad, B. (2023). 'Tencent Statistics by Apps, Revenue, Technology, Active Users, Business Insights, WeChat Users, Games Revenue, OTT Video Services, Platforms, Online Music'. Enterprise Apps Today. www.enterpriseappstoday.com/stats/tencent-statistics.html.

Fast Company (2018). 'The World's 50 Most Innovative Companies 2018'. Available at: www.fastcompany.com/most-innovative-companies/2018.

Fischer, B., Lago, U., and Liu, F. (2013). *Reinventing Giants: How Chinese Global Competitor Haier Has Changed the Way Big Companies Transform*. Hoboken: John Wiley & Sons.

Flamholtz, E. (1995). 'Managing Organizational Transitions: Implications for Corporate and Human Resource Management', *European Management Journal*, 13(1), pp. 39–51.

Forbes (2019). 'Greater China Ranks No. 2 on New Forbes Digital 100 List'. Available at: www.forbes.com/sites/forbeschina/2019/10/10/greater-china-ranks-no-2-on-new-forbes-digital-100-list/?sh=76b39e1d6fae.

Forbes (2022). 'The World's Largest Tech Companies in 2022: Apple Still Dominates as Brutal Market Selloff Wipes Trillions in Market Value'. Available at: www.forbes.com/sites/jonathanponciano/2022/05/12/the-worlds-largest-technology-companies-in-2022-apple-still-dominates-as-brutal-market-selloff-wipes-trillions-in-market-value/?sh=1712a5223448.

Freeman, C. (1987). *Technology, Policy, and Economic Performance: Lessons from Japan*. London: Pinter.

Fu, X. (2015). *China's Path to Innovation*. Cambridge: Cambridge University Press.

Fu, X., Avenyo, E., and Ghauri, P. (2021). 'Digital Platforms and Development: A Survey of the Literature', *Innovation and Development*, 11(2–3), pp. 303–321.

Fu, X. and Ding, X. (2022). 'Intrafirm Coopetition and Innovation Performance – Employee Level Evidence', paper presented at R&D Management Conference, 9–12 July, Trento, Italy; and BAM Conference, 3 August–2 September, Manchester, UK.

Fu, X., McKern, B., and Chen, J. (eds) (2021). *The Oxford Handbook of China Innovation*. Oxford: Oxford University Press.

Fu, X. and Shi, L. (2022). 'Direction of Innovation in Developing Countries and its Driving Forces', Social Science Research Network, 1 April.

Fu, X. and Wei, W. (2023). 'Digital Productisation of HRM and Delivery of Human Resource Services: A Case of Tencent', *Academy of Management Proceedings*. https://doi.org/10.5465/AMPROC.2023.13475abstract.

Galunic, D. C. and Eisenhardt, K. M. (1996). 'The Evolution of Intracorporate Domains: Divisional Charter Losses in High-Technology, Multidivisional Corporations', *Organization Science*, 7, pp. 255–282.

Granstrand, O. (2000). *Corporate Innovation Systems: A Comparative Study of Multi-Technology Corporations in Japan, Sweden and the USA*. Gothenburg: Chalmers University.

Greeven, M. J., Xin, K., and Yip, G. S. (2021). 'How Chinese Retailers Are Reinventing the Customer Journey', *Harvard Business Review*, September–October, pp. 84–93.

Greeven, M. J., Xin, K., and Yip, G. S. (2023). 'How Chinese Companies Are Reinventing Management', *Harvard Business Review*, 3–4.

Greeven, M. J., Yip, G. S., and Wei, W. (2019). *Pioneers, Hidden Champions, Changemakers, and Underdogs: Lessons from China's Innovators*. Cambridge, MA: MIT Press.

Harkonen, J., Haapasalo, H., and Hanninen, K. (2015). 'Productisation: A Review and Research Agenda', *International Journal of Production Economics*, 164, pp. 65–82.

Hastings, A. F. S. J. and Finch, J. H. (2007). *Hidden Innovation: How Innovation Happens in Six 'Low Innovation' Sectors*. NESTA Report to DTI, London, p. 72. Available at: https://media.nesta.org.uk/documents/hidden_innovation.pdf.

Hein, A., Schreieck, M., Riasanow, T. *et al.* (2020). 'Digital Platform Ecosystems', *Electron Markets*, 30(1), pp. 87–98.

Hill, C. and Rothaermel, F. (2003). 'The Performance of Incumbent Firms in the Face of Radical Technological Innovation', *Academy of Management Review*, 28(2), pp. 257–274.

HR Excellence Center (2020). *China Corporate Internal Hiring Practices Survey Report*. Available at: www.hrecchina.org/UpLoadFile/20200305/%E4%B8%AD%E5%9B%BD%E4%BC%81%E4%B8%9A%E5%86%85%E9%83%A8%E6%8B%9B%E8%81%98%E5%AE%9E%E8%B7%B5%E8%B0%83%E7%A0%94%E6%8A%A5%E5%91%8A.pdf.

Hu, L. (2017). *Ma Huateng and Tencent: A Business and Life Biography*. London: LID.

Isaacson, W. (2014). *The Innovators: How a Group of Hackers, Geniuses, and Geeks Created the Digital Revolution*. New York: Simon & Schuster.

Jiménez-Jiménez, D. and Sanz-Valle, R. (2005). 'Innovation and Human Resource Management Fit: An Empirical Study', *International Journal of Manpower*, 26(4), pp. 364–381.

Juro, O. (2017). *Tencent Finally Makes a Big Bet on Artificial Intelligence*. Available at: www.theinformation.com/articles/tencent-finally-makes-a-big-bet-on-artificial-intelligence.

Kahn, K. B., Barczak, G., Nicholas, J., Ledwith, A., and Perks, H. (2012). 'An Examination of New Product Development Best Practice', *Journal of Product Innovation Management*, 29, pp. 180–192.

Kalnins, A. (2004). 'Divisional Multimarket Contact within and between Multiunit Organizations', *Academy of Management Journal*, 47, pp. 117–128.

Kharpal, A. (2025). *Chinese Tech Giant Tencent Posts 13% Revenue Jump as Growth at Key Gaming Unit Surges*. Available at: www.cnbc.com/2025/05/14/tencent-q1-2025-earnings-report.html.

Kirkpatrick, D. (2011). *The Facebook Effect: The Inside Story of the Company that Is Connecting the World*. New York: Simon and Schuster.

Krapivin, P. (2018). *How Google Is Using AI to Power Internal Talent Deployment*. Available at: www.forbes.com/sites/pavelkrapivin/2018/10/01/how-google-is-using-ai-to-power-internal-talent-deployment/.

Leonard-Barton, D. (1992). 'Core Capabilities and Core Rigidities: A Paradox in Managing New Product Development', *Strategic Management Journal*, 13, pp. 111–125.

Lepak, D. P., Marrone, J. A., and Takeuchi, R. (2004). 'The Relativity of HR Systems: Conceptualising the Impact of Desired Employee Contributions and HR Philosophy', *International Journal of Technology Management*, 27(6–7), pp. 639–655.

Lepak, D. P., Taylor, M. S., Tekleab, A., Marrone, J., and Cohen, D. (2007). 'An Examination of the Use of High-investment Human Resource Systems for Core and Support Employees', *Human Resource Management*, 46(2), pp. 223–246.

Livingston, T. (2014). 'The Race to Become the WeChat of the West'. Available at: https://medium.com/@tedlivingston/the-race-to-become-the-wechat-of-the-west-3fe52c8db946#.b1r0xiyt3 (accessed 1 December, 2024).

Lundvall, B. (2007). 'National Innovation Systems-Analytical Concept and Development Tool', *Industry and Innovation*, 14(1), pp. 95–119.

Lundvall, B.-Å. and Rikap, C. (2022). 'China's Catching-up in Artificial Intelligence Seen as a Co-evolution of Corporate and National Innovation Systems', *Research Policy*, 51(1), p. 104395. https://doi.org/10.1016/j.respol.2021.104395.

Luo, Z., Jiao, H., and Xu, Y. (2015). 'Tencent WeChat's Micro-Innovation of Integration and Iteration under Technical Paradigm Transformation', *China Economist*, 5, pp. 106–122. Available at: www.chinaeconomist.com/index.php/2016/06/12/tencent-wechats-micro-innovation-of-integration-and-iteration-under-technical-paradigm-transformation/ (accessed 10 May 2021).

Ma, H. (2022). *HR Digitalization Mode: The HR Transformation and System Innovation in Chinese Enterprises (in Chinese)*. Beijing: Renmin University Press.

Madsen, T. L., Mosakowski, E., and Zaheer, S. (2003). 'Knowledge Retention and Personnel Mobility: The Nondisruptive Effects of Inflows of Experience', *Organization Science*, 14(2), pp. 173–191.

Mannix, E. and Neale, M. A. (2005). 'What Differences Make a Difference? The Promise and Reality of Diverse Teams in Organizations', *Psychological Science in the Public Interest*, 6(2), pp. 31–55.

McKern, B., Yip, G. S., and Jolly, D. (2022). 'Innovation Strategies of Multinational Corporations in China and Their Contribution to the National Ecosystem', in Fu, X., McKern, B., and Chen, J. (eds), *The Oxford Handbook of China Innovation*. Oxford: Oxford University Press, pp. 397–414.

Meijer, A. and Boon, W. (2021). 'Digital Platforms for the Co-Creation of Public Value', *Policy & Politics*, 49(2), pp. 231–248.

Microsoft (2017). *Digital Workplace for HR: Supercharging HR with Data, Insight*. Available at: https://info.microsoft.com/rs/157-GQE-382/images/ Digital%20Workplace%20for%20HR_Supercharging%20HR%20 with%20Data.pdf.

Ministry of Ecology and Environment of the PRC (2025). 'The Number of High-Value Invention Patents per 10,000 People in China Has Reached 14'. Available at: www.mee.gov.cn/zcwj/zclcfh/202503/t20250329_1105003 .shtml.

Monaghan, S., Tippmann, E., and Coviello, N. (2020). 'Born Digitals: Thoughts on Their Internationalization and a Research Agenda', *Journal of International Business Studies*, 51, pp. 11–22.

Monks, K., Kelly, G., Conway, E., Flood, P., Truss, K., and Hannon, E. (2013). 'Understanding How HR Systems Work: The Role of HR Philosophy and HR Processes', *Human Resource Management Journal*, 23(4), pp. 379–395.

Morrison, R. (2022). 'WhatsApp Business to Drive Meta Growth, Says Zuckerberg'. Available at: www.techmonitor.ai/digital-economy/big-tech/whatsapp-business-meta-mark-zuckerberg.

Moscona, J. and Sastry, K. A. (2023). 'Does Directed Innovation Mitigate Climate Damage? Evidence from U.S. Agriculture', *Quarterly Journal of Economics*, 138(2), pp. 637–701.

Mou, X. and Sia, S. K. (2018). *WeChat Work: Bringing Social Networking into Enterprise Workplace*. Singapore: Asian Business Case Centre.

Mueller, M. L. (2011). 'China and Global Internet Governance: A Tiger by the Tail', in *Access Contested: Security, Identity, and Resistance in Asian Cyberspace*. Cambridge, MA: MIT Press.

Murmann, J. P. and Zhu, Z. (2021). 'What Enables a Chinese Firm to Create New-to-the-World Innovations? A Historical Case Study of Intrafirm Coopetition in the Instant Messaging Service Sector', *Strategy Science*, 6(4), pp. 305–330.

Nelson, R. R. (1993). *National Innovation Systems: A Comparative Analysis*. Oxford: Oxford University Press.

Park, O., Bae, J., and Hong, W. (2019). 'High-commitment HRM System, HR Capability, and Ambidextrous Technological Innovation', *International Journal of Human Resource Management*, 30(9), pp. 1526–1548.

People's Daily (2021). 'Over 70% of Users Use Mobile Payment Every Day'. Available at: http://paper.people.com.cn/rmrbhwb/html/2021-01/19/ content_2029778.htm.

Peters, T. J. and Waterman, R. H. (1982). *In Search of Excellence: Lessons from America's Best-Run Companies*. New York: Harper & Row.

Pew Research Center (2022). 'Teens, Social Media and Technology 2022'. Available at: www.pewresearch.org/internet/2022/08/10/teens-social-media-and-technology-2022/.

Ponciano, J. (2022). 'The World's Largest Tech Companies In 2022: Apple Still Dominates as Brutal Market Selloff Wipes Trillions in Market Value'. Available at: www.forbes.com/sites/jonathanponciano/2022/05/12/the-worlds-largest-technology-companies-in-2022-apple-still-dominates-as-brutal-market-selloff-wipes-trillions-in-market-value/.

Prud'homme, D., Chen, G., and Tong, T. (2023). 'Are Super-Apps Coming to the U.S. Market?', *Harvard Business Review*, April. Available at: https://ssrn.com/abstract=4434451.

Questmobile (2023). *Insights into the 'Post-00s Generation'*. Available at: https://stock.hexun.com/2024-03-12/212142838.html.

Qureshi, I., Pan, S. L., and Zheng, Y. (2021). 'Digital Social Innovation: An Overview and Research Framework', *Information Systems Journal*, 31(5), pp. 647–671.

Ray, C. (2023). 'Internal Mobility: A Review and Agenda for Future Research', *Journal of Management*, 50(1), pp. 264–306. https://doi.org/10.1177/01492063231180826.

Reinganum, J. F. (1983). 'Uncertain Innovation and the Persistence of Monopoly', *American Economic Review*, 73(4), pp. 741–748.

Rikap, C. (2024). 'Varieties of Corporate Innovation Systems and Their Interplay with Global and National Systems: Amazon, Facebook, Google and Microsoft's Strategies to Produce and Appropriate Artificial Intelligence', *Review of International Political Economy*, 31(6), pp. 1735–1763.

Ritala, P. (2012). 'Coopetition Strategy – When Is It Successful? Empirical Evidence on Innovation and Market Performance: Coopetition Strategy', *British Journal of Management*, 23, pp. 307–324. https://doi.org/10.1111/j.1467-8551.2011.00741.x.

Roach, A. (2025). 'Chinese Tech Giant Tencent's Quarterly Revenue Jumps 15% on AI Investments, Gaming Unit Boost', CNBC News, 13 August. Available at: www.cnbc.com/2025/08/13/tencent-q2-earnings-report.html.

Rodan, S. and Galunic, C. (2004). 'More than Network Structure: How Knowledge Heterogeneity Influences Managerial Performance and Innovativeness', *Strategic Management Journal*, 25(6), pp. 541–562.

Schmidt, E. and Rosenberg, J. (2014). *How Google Works*. New York: Grand Central.

Schuler, R. (1992). 'Strategic Human Resources Management: Linking the People with the Strategic Needs of the Business', *Organizational Dynamics*, 21(1), pp. 18–32.

Seeck, H. and Diehl, M. (2017). 'A Literature Review on HRM and Innovation – Taking Stock and Future Directions', *International Journal of Human Resource Management*, 28(6), pp. 913–944.

Shih, W., Yu, H., and Liu, F. (2015). 'WeChat: A Global Platform?'. Harvard Business School Case 615-049.

Shipilov, A., Godart, F. C., and Clement, J. (2017). 'Which Boundaries? How Mobility Networks Across Countries and Status Groups Affect the Creative Performance of Organizations', *Strategic Management Journal*, 38, pp. 1232–1252.

Singh, J. (2005). 'Collaborative Networks as Determinants of Knowledge Diffusion Patterns', *Management Science*, 51(5), pp. 756–770.

Stone, B. (2013). *The Everything Store: Jeff Bezos and the Age of Amazon*. New York: Atlantic/Little, Brown.

Strese, S., Meuer, M. W., Flatten, T. C., and Brettel, M. (2016). 'Examining Cross-functional Coopetition as a Driver of Organizational Ambidexterity', *Industrial Marketing Management*, 57, pp. 40–52.

Stross, R. E. (1996). *The Microsoft Way: The Real Story of How the Company Outsmarts Its Competition*. Boston: Addison Wesley Longman.

Sullivan, J., (2013). 'How Google Is Using People Analytics to Completely Reinvent HR'. Available at: www.tlnt.com/how-google-is-using-people-analytics-to-completely-reinvent-hr/.

Sutherland, W. and Jarrahi, M. H. (2018). 'The Sharing Economy and Digital Platforms: A Review and Research Agenda', *International Journal of Information Management*, 43, pp. 328–341.

Tang, M. (2019). *Tencent: The Political Economy of China's Surging Internet Giant*. New York: Routledge. https://doi.org/10.4324/9780429202896.

Tian, T., David, D. C., and Wu, C. (2018). *Huawei: Leadership, Culture, and Connectivity* (1st ed.). Thousand Oaks, CA: SAGE Publications.

Tian, T. and Wu, C. (2015). *The Huawei Story*. New Delhi: SAGE Publications.

Teece, D. J. (1998). 'Capturing Value from Knowledge Assets: The New Economy, Markets for Know-How, and Intangible Assets', *California Management Review*, 40, pp. 55–79.

Tencent (2018). 'Tencent, the First Company Winner of the UNESCO Emir Jaber Al Ahmad Al Jaber Al Sabah Prize for Digital Empowerment of Persons with Disabilities'. Available at: www.tencent.com/en-us/articles/2200007.html.

Tencent (2019). 'A Brief Innovation History of QQ 20th Anniversary'. Available at: http://ip.people.com.cn/n1/2019/0428/c426211-31055150.html.

Tencent (2020). Tencent Annual Report 2020.

Tencent (2021). 'People Turn to Technology to Help Victims of Devastating Flood'. Available at: www.tencent.com/en-us/articles/2201182.html.

Tencent (2022a). Tencent Annual Report 2022.

Tencent (2022b). 'At Tencent, There is a Program that Over 60,000 People Have Applied For'. Available at: https://mp.weixin.qq.com/s/cDMncgBIJoW0ghA5C-5ofQ.

Tencent (2023). *Tencent Sustainable Social Value Report 2022*. Tencent Holdings Limited.

Tencent (2024). *Tencent Sustainable Social Value Report 2023*. Tencent Holdings Limited.

Tencent Docs (2022). 'The Growth of a "Document"'. Available at: https://mp.weixin.qq.com/s/Tl_lWMKuI_HE6h---aWr4w.

The Economist (2024). 'China is the West's Corporate R&D Lab. Can It Remain So?', 14 July, pp. 49–50.

Theeke, M. (2016). 'The Effects of Internal and External Competition on Innovation Breadth', *Journal of Business Research*, 69, pp. 3324–3331.

Tsai, W. (2002). 'Social Structure of "Coopetition" within a Multiunit Organization: Coordination, Competition, and Intraorganizational Knowledge Sharing', *Organization Science*, 13, pp. 179–190.

Ulrich, D. (1997). *Human Resource Champions: The Next Agenda for Adding Value and Delivering Results*. Cambridge, MA: Harvard Business Press.

United Nations (UN) (2024). 'China-Based Inventors Lead on Global GenAI Patents'. Available at: https://news.un.org/en/story/2024/07/1151761.

Van Der Have, R. P. and Rubalcaba, L. (2016). 'Social Innovation Research: An Emerging Area of Innovation Studies?', *Research Policy*, 45(9), pp. 1923–1935.

van Wijk, J., Zietsma, C., Dorado, S., de Bakker, F. G. A., and Martí, I. (2019). 'Social Innovation: Integrating Micro, Meso, and Macro Level Insights from Institutional Theory', *Business & Society*, 58(5), pp. 887–918.

Vise, D. A. and Malseed, M. (2008). *The Google Story: Inside the Hottest Business, Media, and Technology Success of Our Time* (updated ed.). New York: Bantam.

World Intellectual Property Organization (WIPO) (2022). 'Worldwide IP Filings Reached New All-Time Highs in 2021, Asia Drives Growth'. Available at: www.wipo.int/pressroom/en/articles/2022/article_0013.html.

World Intellectual Property Organization (WIPO) (2023). 'PCT Yearly Review 2023'. Available at: www.wipo.int/ipstats.

World Intellectual Property Organization (WIPO) (2024). 'Global Innovation Index 2024: Unlocking the Promise of Social Entrepreneurship'. Available at:. https://doi.org/10.34667/tind.50062.

Wu, X. (2016). *Tencent Biography over 1998–2016: The Evolution of Chinese Internet Firms*. Hangzhou: Zhejiang University Press.

Wu, X. (2017). *Tencent Biography over 1998–2016: The Evolution of Chinese Internet Firms*. Zhejiang University Press.

Wu, X., Murmann, J. P., Huang, C., and Guo, B. (2020). *The Transformation of Huawei: From Humble Beginnings to Global Leadership*. Cambridge: Cambridge University Press.

Xiaoxi (2024). 'Dialogue with Tencent Docs's Yan Xianqing'. Available at: https://36kr.com/p/2740337900742919.

Xinhua (2014). '20 Years of the Internet in China'. www.china.org.cn/business/2014- Available at: 04/20/content_32150035.htm.

Yang, X., Sun, L. S. and Lee, R. P. (2016). 'Micro-Innovation Strategy: The Case of WeChat', *Asian Case Research Journal*, 20(2), pp. 401–427.

Yi, J. J. and Ye, S. X. (2003). *The Haier Way: The Making of a Chinese Business Leader and a Global Brand*. Paramus: Homa & Sekey Books.

Yip, G. S. and McKern, B. (2016). *China's Next Strategic Advantage: From Imitation to Innovation*. Cambridge, MA: MIT Press.

Zhang, X. (2021). 'Interview with Liang Zhu, Head of Tencent QQ: A Generation Will Eventually Grow Old, but QQ Will Stay Forever Young'. Available at: https://36kr.com/p/980234775039110.

Index

For EU product safety concerns, contact us at Calle de José Abascal, 56–1°, 28003 Madrid, Spain or eugpsr@cambridge.org.

www.ingramcontent.com/pod-product-compliance
Ingram Content Group UK Ltd.
Pitfield, Milton Keynes, MK11 3LW, UK
UKHW022136120526
471007UK00012B/1081